YOU'RE HIRED!

Putting Your Sociology Major to Work

YOU'RE HIRED!

Putting Your Sociology Major to Work

BY

CHERYL JOSEPH
Notre Dame de Namur University, Belmont, CA, USA

United Kingdom — North America — Japan — India — Malaysia — China

Emerald Publishing Limited
Howard House, Wagon Lane, Bingley BD16 1WA, UK

First edition 2017

Reprints and permissions service
Contact: permissions@emeraldinsight.com

British Library Cataloguing in Publication Data
A catalogue record for this book is available from the British Library

ISBN: 978-1-78714-490-3 (Print)
ISBN: 978-1-78714-489-7 (Online)
ISBN: 978-1-78714-945-8 (Epub)

ISOQAR certified
Management System,
awarded to Emerald
for adherence to
Environmental
standard
ISO 14001:2004.

Certificate Number 1985
ISO 14001

INVESTOR IN PEOPLE

You don't have to see the whole staircase, just take the first step.

— Martin Luther King, Jr.

This book is dedicated to my students — past, present, and future — as well as the teachers, mentors, and supporters who have provided me with direction and motivation throughout my own journey.

CONTENTS

PART II

PART III

RESOURCES

PREFACE

You're Hired! Putting Your Sociology Major to Work has its origins in the questions, concerns, and misconceptions that have
emanated from my students, their parents, other faculty, counselors, advisors, and employers over the nearly 40 years that I have
been teaching. I have also been deeply touched by the numbers of
former students who continue to correspond with me long after
graduation, excitedly extolling new jobs, job transitions, new-
found career goals, and especially, the life changes brought
through marriage, family life, travel, and relocation. I've been
impressed by the variety of career opportunities these graduates
have found and how often they speak of loving their job. I am
equally amazed by those who have been plying their trade for
years and yet still demonstrate the excitement of fledgling sociologists as they speak of new research, responsibilities, and interests
at the professional meetings I attend.

Yet, I recognize that the nature and value of sociology still
remains largely misunderstood. So, through the stories of practicing sociologists, I intend for this book to clarify and demystify the
confusion often associated with this discipline. Further, I hope this
book will nurture growing interest in sociology by providing
insights about its use in our contemporary world and rapidly
changing labor market. Moreover, I am hopeful that the information, particularly in Part III, will benefit not just sociology majors
but anyone pursuing a new career or transitioning to another.
Additionally, I anticipate this book will spark enthusiasm about
the vast array of exciting and fulfilling career opportunities avail-

able to sociology majors in particular, but those with degrees in the liberal arts or other social sciences as well. Finally, I wish that you readers will find the stories of the people contained in this book enjoyable and that they will inspire each of you to pursue your dreams, however tentatively formed they might be at this time.

ACKNOWLEDGMENTS

Nearly every work ever published begins with a lengthy roll call of those to whom the author is grateful. This book is no exception.

I am most ingratiated to the individuals who shared their experiences and insights with me then patiently persevered as I edited their stories to most accurately reflect them. These contributors include: Laura Barulich, Gary Battane, Diane Binson, Carolina Cervantes, Mel Coit, Lakeshia Freedman, Bee Friedlander, Lincoln Grahlfs, and Janet Hankin. I am equally indebted to Danica Wise Hill, Lynnett Hernandez Kinnard, Stephen La Plante, Maria Lara, William (Bill) McNeece, Carolina Cervantes, Eileen Monti, Rebecca Morrison and Sr. Roseanne Murphy, as well as Christine Oh, Adam Ortberg, Mylene Pangilinen-Cord, Casey Porter, Mario Rendon, Megan Scott, and Christina Risley-Curtiss. My appreciation also extends to Karen Schaumann, T.D. (Tom) Schuby, Kathleen Soto, Don Stannard-Friel, Amber Brazier Voorhees, and Jana Whitlock.

In addition, my thanks to those who briefly disclosed snippets about the multitude means by which they are using their bachelor's degrees as sociologists in fulfilling occupations. I am thankful as well to the employers who shared their thoughts about the unique skills that sociologists bring to the labor market. Moreover, I extend my appreciation to the American Sociological Association (ASA) for materials from which I drew for the section titled, "Sociologists in the Public Eye." I am also grateful to

Michelle Beese who provided the content that made Part III possible.

For my reviewers, I am immensely appreciative. From them, I received perhaps the most valuable feedback as they read the manuscript from the vantage point of my potential audience. The most noteworthy of these reviewers are Joshua Aguirre, Andrew Durham, Rebecca Flores, Jan Perinoni, and Victoria Strelnikova.

I also thank my colleague and friend, Margo DeMello at New Mexico State Community College, as well as Gina Horwitz from Wayne State University both of whom painstakingly reviewed my drafts and offered valuable suggestions. Of course, I am most appreciative of my publisher, Kim Chadwick, who took a chance on me. I thoroughly enjoyed her British wit and benefited immensely from her publishing expertise.

To Notre Dame de Namur University (NDNU) goes my sincere gratitude for the release time and sabbatical leave they granted me so that I could bring this book to fruition.

I am especially indebted to Tom Schuby, not only for the constructive criticism and direction he gave to this book, but for prodding me to begin my own journey into sociology so many years ago.

On a personal note and possibly most important of all, I am grateful to Russ, as well as Beethoven and Penny, my canine kids, for the infinite patience and emotional support they gave me during this endeavor.

Without all of these individuals, this book would have remained a mere manuscript. Most of all, however, I am indebted to you, the reader. Whether you are a student or someone interested in a student's future, embarking on that first job, or transitioning from one career to another, I wish you the inspiration to put wings to your dreams.

1

INTRODUCTION

SOCIOLOGY: A SCIENCE FOR TROUBLED TIMES AND UNDERSTANDING INTERACTIVE INDIVIDUALS

By the time you read this book, you may have already taken enough classes to know that sociology is a broad-based study of the ways humans behave in groups as well as the ways in which our behavior is influenced by the groups to which we belong. Conversely, sociology also studies the impact that people have on their groups through, for example, collective behavior and social movements. You've likely learned that sociology is not synonymous with psychology, social work, social reform, or socialism although there are many sociologists in each of these arenas. No doubt you've also discovered there is a connection between technology and personal interaction, income security and degree of bigotry, length of incarceration and likelihood of recidivism. Perhaps you've started to observe the behavior of people in crowds, on elevators, and at parties. Even more, you might have found some explanations for your own behavior based on your family, friends, social class, or the other subcultures to which you belong. Best of all, you probably know that sociology is a particularly useful science for life in troubled times as well as interactions between individuals.

Pretty cool stuff, you think. So cool, in fact, that you are considering a major in sociology. The *big* questions, however, loom large: how can I earn a living with a sociology major and what sorts of work do sociologists do? In fact, if you don't ask yourself these questions, chances are your family and friends will.

I am particularly fond of the response a colleague of mine gives to these worried queries. "What can a person do with a sociology major?" he usually repeats for emphasis. Then, with a shrug, the bombshell follows: "Anything. Anything they want." While it is true that most job listings do not specifically ask for a sociologist in the same manner as they might request a bookkeeper, sales manager, or nurse's aid, sociologists are nonetheless found in any number of positions that range from advertising to zoology.

You're Hired! Putting Your Sociology Major to Work will expose you to some of the many and varied opportunities available to people who major in sociology from the perspectives of those who actually work in these professions. Each vignette follows the contributor through their career starting with the forces that influenced their choice of major to their present position and future plans. Some, like Carolina Cervantes, were motivated by the dynamics of their family background. Others, like Gary Battane, were driven by the social events taking place during their college years. Adam Ortberg and Lakeshia Freedman stumbled onto a sociology major quite by happenstance while those like Rebecca Morrison and Diane Binson purposefully selected their major.

Each of the contributors discusses the rewards and realities of their work as well as the challenges and frustrations. Many walk you through their typical workday or work week. They share the sociological concepts and theories, learned in the classroom, that assist them in their work. Several of those interviewed reveal the tactics they used to obtain their positions and all offer sound advice to the fledgling sociologist.

The contributors run the generational gamut. Some, like Laura Barulich, are on the starting block of their careers while others such as Lincoln Grahlfs look back from retirement on their fulfill-ing and meaningful professional lives. All, as the expression goes, have a story to tell. While the experiences and stories are distinctly diverse in both breadth and depth, everyone in this book shares a commonality not always found in the world of work. As theorist Peter Berger so eloquently penned more than years ago, "... for them, sociology is a passion."

READING THIS BOOK FOR BEST RESULTS

This book is meant to be read word-for-word, cover-to-cover, and then placed on your shelf alongside your other reference books. While it would be easy to skip to the career areas that currently attract you or to simply scan this text in preparation for a class discussion, you would do yourself a grave injustice. Most respon-dents share not just one but many careers that led them to their present position. Any one of the professions they discuss might pique your interest and beckon you down your own personal career path.

As you read further, you will see that this book has been written for you, the student, and for those concerned about you. It is not written for the profession; for other sociologists or academics though they may read it. Therefore, it does not contain information you have to memorize for an exam but rather, insights which will guide you to career decisions that are distinctly your own. At the end of the vignettes, current contact information is provided for each of the people about whom you read. I encour-age you to take advantage of this opportunity to communicate directly with the individuals whose vignettes you find most interesting. Ask them the questions that do not appear in their statements but intrigue you nonetheless. While I purposely deleted any references to salaries, for example, you can feel free to query the contributors about this in your interactions with them. All are

willing, indeed eager, to share more of their stories with any
of you who inquire.

Though Part I is divided into 12 sections, each devoted to
a specific area in which sociologists work, there are dozens,
perhaps hundreds more spheres where sociologists are found.
To some extent, "Snippets from the Field" as well as "Sociologists
in the Public Eye" in Part II bring these to light. "Employers
Respond: Why Hire Sociology Majors" materialized serendipi-
tously from administrators and managers who regularly ask me
to recommend majors in my department for positions in their
organizations. These individuals offer observations about the
unique skills and perspectives that sociologists possess.

My hope is that you, the reader, will use *You're Hired!* to
launch your own investigation into the myriad opportunities that
await a sociology major; that you will imagine yourself shadowing
the individuals who share their lives with you; absorb as much
as possible from each vignette; then refer to Part III often as you
begin and foster your career. Above all, I encourage you to learn,
experiment, and enjoy the paths that you travel as you create your
own stories and successes.

2

MEET YOUR AUTHOR

While this section normally appears near the conclusion of a book and is generally limited to a few sentences if indeed it appears at all, I confess to being immodest enough to think you might find my journey as interesting, beneficial, and inspiring as the others about whom you will read in this text. I come to this conclusion based largely on comments from my students. When I ask them to evaluate the strengths of my teaching style (I also ask about the weaknesses!) they typically respond that they enjoy the personal experiences I share with them the most. Queried about the lessons they are most likely to remember in the future, they call up stories from my life that I relate to the course content. As such, you can no doubt see how my students have flattered me into this flight of fancy!

There is yet another reason I've consciously chosen to disclose my narrative and to place it near the beginning. I believe that a written document such as *You're Hired!* provides both the reader and the writer the opportunity to communicate with the other. As you open the cover of this book, I envision you metaphorically reaching out your hand to shake mine. I, in turn, warmly return your greeting. As we would if we met face-to-face, we exchange information about ourselves. I tell you something about me; you decide if you can relate to my disclosure and then respond accordingly. Ideally, you will then reverse this process so that I might learn about you. In doing so, we begin a relationship of sorts.

As such, I hope my own revelations will encourage you to communicate your journey with me in the same way I've shared mine with you. Write to me; email me; phone; or text me. Ask me questions and reveal your concerns. Tell me about your career successes and your challenges. Most of all, know that I wish you well in the fulfillment of all your goals.

CHERYL JOSEPH

Growing up in a working class neighborhood of Detroit as the daughter of a factory worker and labor union organizer, I was probably destined to be a sociologist. Nonetheless, I started my college career as an English major having already foregone my dreams of being a journalist or a translator for the United Nations. This disillusionment followed a high-school education that was mediocre at best. Creative writing came easily to me; I enjoyed reading the classics; and I fantasized that I would one day successfully teach Victorian poetry to high-school students in inner-city Detroit. Secretly, I assumed I would simply meet some nice young man whom I would marry before graduation approached. (In those times, many young women went to college in the sole pursuit of a Mrs. degree!) With my grades below average and difficult classes looming, however, I left college after my freshman year. Following a brief stint working the midnight shift on the assembly line at a Ford Motor company facility and as a keypunch operator for a floral delivery firm, I realized there had to be life beyond tedium. For me, that life resided in the classrooms at Wayne State University (WSU). From that point on, I took my education seriously. Having no idea what "sociology" was though it sounded interesting from the catalogue description, I signed up for the introductory class. There, we talked about social class and socialization, diverse cultures and deviancy, race relations and revolution, power, and privilege — all topics that were in some way relevant to my own life. I was enthralled.

At the same time, the social issues of the sixties surrounded me and begged for explanation. On any given day, I'd leave my neighborhood of factory-workers and homemakers to drive along the Detroit River through one of the wealthiest areas in the nation. I'd see yachts docked behind mansions and mansions that resembled museums. Exiting this elegance, I'd find myself entering a world riddled with blocks upon blocks of abandoned buildings and people whose despair oozed from their pores. Coupled with these disparities, I noted that the complexions of the people changed dramatically on my drive from light-skinned individuals in the wealthy neighborhoods to mostly dark-skinned people in the poor communities. Just as quickly as I'd entered the moonscape of poverty, I'd find myself in an oasis of academia with its modern streamlined buildings blended harmoniously with stately old architecture on pristinely manicured grounds. I wondered why the conditions I was reading about in the classics for my English courses half a world away and a century before still existed in my own contemporary life.

Concurrently, social protests coincided with the war in Vietnam and permeated my personal existence. The boys with whom I'd attended high school were being drafted in record numbers while many of those with whom I shared my college classes were getting military deferments. Almost weekly, I'd hear of a high-school friend who had been wounded or killed in Vietnam while my college classmates, often sons of doctors, lawyers, or pastors, were escaping the war unscathed. It became clear to me that the occupation of one's father could buy privilege.

As the momentum of the anti-war protests swelled, I joined the marches for peace. Right before my eyes, I saw the significance of group solidarity in social movements. I realized that while the activists in a social movement might only comprise a small number, they often reflect the opinions of many more. For me, this was a turning point; it kindled the fires of a fledgling social activist.

Even though I was beginning to glean sociological insights that helped to explain my social environment, it wasn't until I took a class in social stratification that my world was changed radically. Suddenly, the writings of C. Wright Mills and especially, Karl Marx's *The Communist Manifesto* put global events, history, and my own personal life into perspective. By the end of that semester, I'd switched my English major to sociology. Parenthetically, it was also in that class that I met the "nice, young man" whom I *did* eventually marry. Through his patient mentoring, I experienced his fascination with sociology and his love for learning in general that remains a cornerstone in my life today.

At the same time I returned to college, I took a job with a major airline, making reservations for a public relatively new to air travel. I enjoyed using the sociological perspective to comprehend the worlds of passengers whose fears I calmed and whose excitement I stoked. Classes such as the sociology of power helped me navigate the corporate corridors by understanding the parts that social role, groupthink, and bureaucracy played in every aspect of the operation from high-level decision making to individual interactions. In addition, this job afforded me nearly unlimited travel and opportunities to explore other cultures often very different from my own. Sociology made me a traveler rather than a tourist and helped me truly understand the nature of culture and reasons for differences. Moreover, I used my sociological imagination to connect the seemingly disparate events in one country to those of another.

In my senior year, I enrolled in a year-long internship where I worked with a nonprofit organization in a poverty-stricken area of Detroit. There, I helped a group of mothers determine the causes of their community's exorbitant infant mortality rate. Through these women, I learned tactics for organizing communities, both as an insider and an outsider. They showed me the necessity of garnering support from sympathetic politicians and media as well as that of building coalitions. I teach these same techniques in my classes to this very day.

Simultaneously, I took a class in social research that required me to design and conduct my own study. Since I was living in an inner-city neighborhood, I focused on the prostitutes and pimps who regularly conducted business there. Using the case study technique, I interviewed several dozen streetwalkers to learn about their personal histories and their everyday lives. I learned how to gain the trust of marginalized individuals and explore the subjective meanings these women gave to their activities.

This study soon resulted in another, one that allowed me to examine the inner world of convicted rapists. I wanted to know *why* men rape. As such, I conducted focus groups at a state prison where I posed questions to small clusters of men and then listened as they discussed their responses among themselves. The results of this study became part of the political platform used by a candidate who ran successfully for a judgeship in Detroit.

These endeavors allowed me to hone my methodological skills and build my resume along with my reputation. This led to a study investigating the extent, causes of, and solutions to spousal abuse. The findings ultimately aided in the establishment of shelters and some of the legal protections that battered women in Michigan can depend on today.

After completing my undergraduate degree, I continued to work for the airlines. Because there was little opportunity for advancement through the traditional channels, I created a niche for myself that concentrated on motivational training for the existing sales force. In that capacity, I addressed the high burn-out rate that plagued the staff, designing workshops focused on the ability to be creative even within the confines of a constraining job. My social psychology and sociology of occupations classes helped immensely.

During that time, Detroit was experiencing yet another economic recession and still shaking off the ravages of the 1967 riots. Crime was pervasive and fear was rampant. The influx of different cultures made people reluctant to acknowledge let alone associate with their neighbors. Recognizing that food is a commonality as well as a necessity, I joined a group of friends to establish a food cooperative in a destitute neighborhood comprising blacks, Arabs (both Christians and Muslims), and poor whites who had migrated to Detroit from the Appalachian Mountains. We opened our doors to just 30 households but eventually the attraction of inexpensive, nutritious food attracted some of the more intrepid residents of the community.

Affiliation required a commitment from a household member to work four hours a month at the co-op for which they received three large bags of groceries each week. Word of these benefits spread quickly and soon neighbors were working side-by-side, sharing common interests and concerns. In about three years time, the membership had expanded 10-fold. Best of all, we experienced the germination of a community where none had existed before.

Once our co-op became an accepted part of the community, we used it as a base for education and empowerment. I already knew how poverty can steal pride, self-esteem, and confidence leaving hopelessness and ruin in its wake. To counter this impact, the co-op organized numerous practical classes that were taught by people living in the neighborhood. Women shared their cooking, canning, and sewing skills, for example, while men demonstrated minor car repairs. Sharing knowledge with their neighbors engendered, for many, a newfound sense of dignity and self-worth.

During that same period, large numbers of women from all social classes were joining the workforce. With that social shift came new problems that begged to be addressed. Educated, professional, and largely middle class women found answers and sustenance in formations like the National Organization for Women (NOW). For women who worked in factories, phone banks, secretarial pools, restaurants, and the like, there were no such support systems. Joining my friends once again, we created a city-wide, cross-cultural counterpart to NOW specifically for working class and poor women. At monthly meetings, speakers addressed topics related to our members' concerns: single parenting, women's health, changing marital relations, domestic violence, and legal issues like eviction, sexual harassment, and the formation of labor unions.

Further, we established a telephone hotline whereby callers were referred to an array of resources that provided free and low-cost services to our members. These resources included doctors, lawyers, child care workers, therapists, pregnancy counselors, and social workers. I found it exhilarating to build an organization like this from its inception. I enjoyed creating the monthly events and then organizing the details that made them successful. I was far less excited, however, about the committee meetings at eleven o'clock at night and at five in the morning. I also became frustrated by the personal politics that increasingly hampered productive outcomes.

By then, too, the social climate had shifted. The War in Vietnam had ended, the Civil Rights Movement was institutionalized, and the Women's Liberation Movement was on solid footing. If I had learned anything at all, it was that I had more to learn. Graduate school beckoned and I answered the call.

For the next 10 years, I continued my full-time employment with the airline while I immersed myself in school. From time to time, I also dabbled in other career possibilities. In one case, I hosted a local television talk show that required me to research social issues then locate experts willing to discuss the subject with me in a conversational format that would air live at 5:30 every Sunday morning. At another point, I led groups of tourists through the New England states. These supplementary jobs were all pleasant diversions that allowed me to intentionally expand my growing network of contacts. This proved invaluable to my professional life.

Admittedly, those 10 years were overwhelming. To maintain focus on my ultimate goal of obtaining a doctorate while still sustaining myself financially, I had to forego countless social and cultural events. On reflection, however, I can say with certainty that my sacrifices were far outweighed by the rewards. Upon completion of my doctorate, I transferred to San Francisco with the airlines and, within three years, began teaching full-time at the university where I remain today.

I purposely chose a small university with an emphasis on experiential learning and engagement with communities of vulnerable
populations. In addition, this university afforded me opportunities
to help mold and nurture a newly-founded sociology department.
All of these elements were important to me.

By early 2000, I detected a new area of focus developing in the
discipline; one that would allow me to combine another of my
passions with sociology: the relationships people share with
other animals. This interest sent me on a year-long sabbatical to
research the topic on a variety of levels ranging from personal and
cultural to environmental and institutional. Armed with my findings, I returned to the university to create a new concentration
within the sociology major titled "Animals in Human Society."

There is little that I do not like about teaching at a university
level especially now that I've been able to incorporate the study
of animals into my curriculum. I most treasure the moments when
I see my students succeed, often knowing the formidable obstacles
they've overcome. However, I am always disappointed by those
students who do not appreciate education; who view it as a piece
of paper that indicates they've graduated from a four-year institution rather than the chance to learn for its own sake. (And there
is a difference!) Even with this, I still smile on my drive to school,
as I enter my classrooms, and interact with my students.

A typical week will include teaching a full load of four or
five classes with the attendant research and preparation. This is
usually complemented by meetings with individual students. Then
there are the faculty meetings and those with community leaders
who make the students' community education projects possible.
Finally, the ubiquitous phone messages and emails round out my
work week which invariably exceeds the stereotypic 40 hours.

If I were to begin my career anew, I'd probably make more
careful choices about the people I let into my life as I've come to
realize how the personal and the professional impact each other.
Making better choices, I think, would have given me the confidence

I needed to pursue academic leadership positions that otherwise intimidated me.

I try to impress on all of my students the importance of keeping doors open and, in fact, opening doors with respect to personal and career opportunities. This means getting business cards or contact information from speakers they find interesting, starting a file of people who might assist them in the future, and writing thank you notes to individuals who help them. I encourage my students to get acquainted with their professors as they will be a likely source of recommendations for graduate school and future jobs.

I also urge students to view their professors as their employers instead of parents or friends. In a competitive market, gestures like these can set a job-seeker apart from numerous others who might be pursuing the same position. Finally, I recommend that students start to implement these suggestions early in their college lives. Freshman year is not too soon.

You may contact me, Dr. Cheryl Joseph, by email at cjoseph@ ndnu.edu or by phone at 650-355-0969.

PART I

Neither the life of an individual nor the history of a society can be understood without understanding both.

— C. Wright Mills

The philosophers have only interpreted the world in various ways; the point is to change it.

— Karl Marx

3

SOCIOLOGISTS IN BUSINESS AND POLITICS

This section introduces four sociologists: *Mylene Pangilinan-Cord, Casey Porter, Mario Rendon*, and *Maria Lara*, each of whom has chosen to use his or her major in the business world or the political arena. These two institutions, the economic and the political, are viewed by most sociologists as the cornerstones around which all other social institutions, or social structures, are built. Therefore, the economic and political systems are the most significant of all the institutions.

Mylene Pangilinan-Cord describes how sociology has helped her operate in a multinational corporation. Not only does she use the sociological imagination to explain her company's role in a global economy but to assist the corporation's employees in her human resources and diversity inclusion functions.

Casey Porter discusses how he applied a sociological analysis to the presidency of his university's student body to understand the "whole picture" while he was still an undergraduate and how he does so now as a regional talent acquisition manager for an international car rental company. While Porter initially planned to teach high school, he recognizes that he still educates though his students are employees in the business environment.

Mario Rendon began his career in politics with an internship in the office of a state representative during his senior year of college. Then through his network of associates, he proceeded to work with a national politician and later, at the county level. After five years with a for-profit major utility company, Rendon came full circle and is back to the political world that he loves.

Maria Lara chose city politics as the avenue by which to address disparities and injustices. Following short periods in academia, corporate America, and family support services, Lara now focuses on her local community with an eye on permanent improvements in its social systems. With several successful years as an Assistant City Manager to her credit, she aspires to a run for City Manager in the future.

MYLENE PANGILINAN-CORD

For *Mylene Pangilinan-Cord,* the path to her major was paved by the first two sociology classes she took as a freshman at a small liberal arts college in Northern California. Even as she fulfilled her general education requirements in other subjects, she realized she had a passion for learning about interactions between people. She was intrigued by the ways that individuals behave in groups, from the simplest to the most complex, and she wanted to unearth the reasons behind their actions. She yearned to know, for example, how an individual's definition of themselves as an introvert or extrovert shapes their conduct and how culture influences the formation of a Type A or Type B personality. She asked about the influences of ethnicity, gender, and social class on personal behavior as well as the effects of geographic environments on human actions. She found that sociology provided her with answers to many of her questions even as it raised more. With Mylene's eyes opened to the value of sociology in her own life as well as the contemporary world, she decided that sociology would be a perfect complement to the business management major she was already pursuing.

When Mylene started college, she was already working for The Gap Inc., an international clothing enterprise, and planned to continue doing so to pay her tuition. While she balanced her studies with her retail job, Mylene's managers recognized her potential and helped her create a career development plan. By Mylene's junior year, she entered the company's work-study program, an intensive plan designed to build a pipeline between talented professionals and leadership positions in their stores. During this time, she progressed quickly from retail sales associate to store manager. Clearly, Mylene was on the fast-track, learning business acumen, merchandising, operations, and human resources while she was still completing her undergraduate degree. Following graduation, she moved into the corporate offices where she concentrated on the human resource function in such areas as learning and development as well as staffing and recruiting.

From there, Pangilinan-Cord proceeded to The Gap's Diversity and Inclusion Division where she remains till today. In this role, she oversees the strategy and implementation for the diversity, learning, and development initiatives. Mylene states, "I am fortunate to work for a company that was willing to invest in me. As a result, I could take lessons I learned in the classroom to work with me and at the same time, bring my experiences from work back to the classroom for analysis. By allowing me to showcase the skills I learned both in college and in the stores, everyone benefited — me, my classmates, and The Gap."

Mylene's studies in sociology built the framework for her focus on human resources. Concepts like social exchange theory and humanism allowed her to see that the most important investment any successful company makes goes beyond store products, operations, or finances. Above all, a good organization invests in its people and, since it is The Gap's policy to develop and retain the personnel they hire, Mylene found her own values consistent with those of her employer. This compatibility was critical to Mylene.

In the retail environment, Ms. Pangilinan-Cord also relies heavily on her sociology background to understand the dynamics of the everyday operations as well as The Gap's position and future in a global economy. She uses symbolic interactionism; Weber's concept of *verstehen*; and Goffman's presentation of self, for instance, to glean the meanings that people attach to clothes, fashion, and self-image. Moreover, the concept of self-actualization helps her grasp some of the reasons designers are inspired to create products for consumers. Since a significant part of Mylene's job involves motivating managers to be effective leaders, she finds her knowledge of leadership styles, socialization, and conflict resolution skills invaluable. Her position also requires Mylene to find compatibility between an employee's strengths and the company's needs in ways that add value to both. Team-building is yet another essential component of her job. For this, she relies on her insights about personality, corporate culture, and organizational behavior.

Finally, Mylene devotes much of her energy to the creation of a company culture that respects diverse styles, talents, subcultures, and individuality. Mylene observes, "Sociology is an integral part of my life and my job. It is important that I am attuned to what is going on in my company, community, and the world because it is all interconnected. In a sense, my job embodies the heart of sociology."

To perform her job effectively, Mylene built a strategy that focuses on The Gap's employees, customers, and workplaces with respect to three sociological concepts: culture, demographics, and socioeconomics. One of her projects, for instance, entailed a look at the changing demographics of the future workforce wherein she determined that the fastest growing category of workers is age 55 and older. She also found that, in less than a decade, 70% of new workers in the United States will be women and people of color. Information like this allows Mylene to then design and implement hiring, training, and retention programs that concentrate on these groups.

With respect to the customer base, Mylene and her team found that the demographics of purchasing power have also shifted. To wit, the aging baby boomer population in the United States alone now spends over two trillion dollars a year and the lesbian/gay/bisexual/transgender segment spends more than 600 billion during that same time. As Gap Inc. is expanding globally at an extremely rapid pace, this is another crucial consideration. Data like these signal Mylene that her programs must reflect and serve a variety of cultural needs if her company is to maintain its place as the best world class specialty retailer.

The creation of workplace environments that are friendly and welcoming to everyone is also part of Mylene's responsibilities. "Whether it is in our stores or our offices," Mylene emphasizes, "it is mandatory that we not just tolerate but that we embrace an array of experiences, ethnicities, races, religions, ages, social classes, and cultures. In such an atmosphere, employees feel valued and can contribute to the company as well as their communities in meaningful ways."

To help meet these goals, she currently manages the company's Heritage & Awareness Months whereby she coordinates events to include keynote speakers, performances, workshops, and trips to cultural museums. This provides Gap employees with venues to exhibit their own cultures and subcultures as well as learn about those of their colleagues. Mylene hopes that ultimately knowledge and acceptance of other cultures will assure a competitive advantage for Gap Inc.

The same elements that Mylene likes most about her job also contribute to her frustration. She particularly notes the criticism Gap receives for the conditions under which its workers labor in developing countries. Under these situations, Pangilinan-Cord can find it difficult to remain tolerant especially when the critics don't have all the facts. "I remind myself that I can't please everyone because we all have different value systems. What I can do, however, give everyone respect."

Regardless of the project she undertakes, Mylene is generally responsible for managing its development and implementation from beginning to end. To do so effectively, she needs to be a resource for her team and to ensure that any obstacles challenging her team's success are minimized. In addition, she is accountable for bringing her team's efforts to the attention of the senior executives so they are aware of its contribution to profitability. Oftentimes, Mylene is the final decision-maker on a project and must confidently and knowledgeably act alone in the best interests of her team and even the company at large. "Performing these endeavors requires an appreciation of complex social situations and the corporate-political climate," she acknowledges. "I use my sociological perspective to step inside the other person's shoes and understand their viewpoint. This, in turn, lets me to be flexible and to compromise when necessary."

Mylene also finds her understanding of research methods, analysis, and statistical techniques crucial to her performance. A recent project, for example, required her to review U.S. Census Tract data then compare those findings to similar statistical categories for The Gap. From that, she designed a template that makes quarterly reports easily available for review by the Board of Directors. In addition, Mylene frequently researches case studies to clarify the policies of the Equal Employment Opportunity Commission (EEOC).

In a typical month, Mylene estimates that she spends about 40% of her time at work in project management. Another 20% of her time is spent in meetings to ensure that the projects she oversees are progressing satisfactorily. Approximately 10% of her month is taken up by administrative responsibilities like responding to emails, returning voicemail messages, and scheduling meetings for herself and her boss. An additional 20% of her month is devoted to networking; then Mylene dedicates the remaining 10% of her work life to her own career development. She concedes that networking often takes her out of her comfort zone but, in doing so, she meets people from whom she learns. In return, she reciprocates by sharing her talents.

With such a busy schedule, Mylene admits that effective work–life balance can be difficult. Therefore, she maintains a firm policy about meetings with her staff: none before 9 AM or after 4 PM. She recognizes that balance is vital not only to her own well-being but that of her employees and hopes she is a role model for her team in this respect.

Ms. Pangilinan-Cord is currently next in line for Chief of Staff to The Gap's brand president and she may elect to focus on that move. In the meantime, however, Mylene is exploring opportunities with The Gap's philanthropy and social responsibility departments which concentrate on community investment and ethical business practices. This move will allow her to accentuate her own thoughts about the interconnectedness of the world's people and the impact of each individual on the future of humanity. Mylene believes that transitioning from diversity to social responsibility work within Gap Inc. is a natural step that will allow her to stretch her own capabilities and continue to build her career in a supportive environment reflective of her own values. Furthermore, Pangilinan-Cord believes that The Gap will provide her with the best opportunities to promote change in developing communities worldwide and help people better their lives.

As to what Mylene might do differently if she were to start her career over again, she replies thoughtfully, "I started working for Gap when I was 16 years old and it is the only place I've ever worked. Much as I love my work here, I wish I had worked for a couple of different companies in my early years so that I could have gained some experience outside the retail business."

Mylene maintains that there are a multitude of opportunities for sociology majors since it provides a general background useful in a large number of professions. However, she suggests a double major or a minor in another area such as business management, criminal justice, or social services. "That way," she explains, "you can open up your options in the corporate world, law enforcement, city planning, community advocacy, the arts, and a great many other avenues."

In addition, Pangilinan-Cord encourages students in any major to start networking early. She contends that networking was crucial to her advancement with Gap Inc. "Even in my first job, I networked with the corporate employees who came to my location. While I assisted them with their shopping, I told them about my career goals. As a result, many of the shoppers from headquarters invited me to call them when I graduated. Creating this familiarity allowed me to establish comfortable relationships with some of the managers and executives by the time I was ready for my first career move."

Mylene also advises students to build relationships with their professors as they will be likely sources of recommendation at least at the beginning of their career. She also urges students to create a presence on social media in order meet new people who can assist with one's career development. Finally, Mylene suggests finding a mentor willing to help navigate the sometimes rocky road inherent in starting and building a career.

For more information about Mylene Pangilinan-Cord and her work, please contact her by email at mylene_cord@gap.com

CASEY PORTER

Imagine a toddler joyfully amusing his grandparents; a young boy gleefully entertaining his little friends; and a high school senior directing student government. There you have *Casey Porter*, a self-described born people person.

Given this, Porter entered college as a business major, reasoning that his social skills would accelerate his success in the corporate world. After all, he had worked at a local movie theater since his junior year in high school and quickly found his way to house manager by the time he was eighteen.

As his freshman year at Notre Dame de Namur University (NDNU) proceeded, however, he found himself drawn to a major in political science. He reasoned that politics exists in every business. As expected, he soon found these classes in his new major not only informative, but also engrossing. They broadened his knowledge of the political scene nationally and globally; historically and currently. "But something was still missing," Porter admits.

Casey's long-term goal had been to educate high school students. "I've always admired teachers," he reflects. He recalls volunteering in the main office of his high school with such frequency that by his senior year his career interests had expanded to school administration. He realized it was probably not the classroom instruction that he sought so much as a learning environment in which he could utilize his leadership abilities and people skills.

Yet another turning point came during his sophomore year at NDNU when a friend suggested Casey take a sociology course. "I was instantly hooked," he remembers. "Sociology gave me insight into the world around me that other fields had not. It complemented my political science major and together they gave me a more complete world view. Since sociology is, by definition, the study of the social institutions which humans create and that alternately shape our actions, and politics is one of the institutions that drives our behavior, I figured that sociology provided the framework of the puzzle while political science was one of its most important pieces."

Casey's first opportunity to fuse the two majors pragmatically came with his election as president to the university's Associated Students' Organization (ASNDNU). Since he had served as student body president of his high school, he assumed he was familiar with the responsibilities that would befall him. To his surprise, he discovered this new endeavor would be far more extensive and complicated than he could have imagined.

Porter took the position during a university presidency that was both unpopular and divisive. Moreover, a new university structure had just been implemented. As such, his first task was to coordinate several different student groups to rewrite the organization's constitution. Then, based on a needs assessment, Porter had to incorporate items of concern to specific populations like commuter students and the various ethnic clubs into the overall culture of the student body and then, the entire university. Casey relied heavily on his knowledge of the sociological perspective and the sociological imagination to accomplish this task. Sociological concepts such as statuses, organizational culture, traditions, and scarce resources gave Casey an appreciation for the complex social web that defined the university's structure.

By his junior year, he had left his job with the local theater and began working part time with the Enterprise Rent-a-Car. The company actively recruited college students through an internship program designed to provide them with experience and insight into running a business. At the same time, they prepared possible future employees for a career with Enterprise. "Although my sites were still set on educational administration, I needed a job so working for Enterprise was a win-win situation," Casey concedes. "I figured this internship with Enterprise would supply me with the piece of the business education I missed by switching majors."

Working for Enterprise turned into far more than just a part-time job for Porter, however. He quickly learned to manage a multimillion dollar venture, working with a wide spectrum of managers, coworkers, customers, and business leaders in the process. As a new hire, Porter was immersed in an intensive training course, given projects to complete, required to make a variety of presentations, and groomed to run every aspect of a branch's operation.

While the company's training program was extremely comprehensive, Casey still found sociological concepts such as formal organization, types of authority and leadership styles, impression management, and internalization of norms helpful in comprehending functions of the business. Moreover, when he compared Enterprise's practices to concepts like Theory X, Fordism, and McDonaldization that he had studied in his sociological theory class, the unique advantages that Enterprise could provide him became evident.

With his bachelor's degree completed, a double major in political science and sociology, and the potential of a promising career in business before him, Casey struggled with his choice of paths: education or business, business or education. Part of him still wanted to work in the educational environment. Yet, he was already working successfully with a company that built on his strengths and allowed him to incorporate much of what he learned in his undergraduate studies. He recognized that his leadership style and skills could be translated into a multitude of possibilities yet he wrestled with his decision for over a year after he graduated. Would he feel like he had abandoned his dream if he pursued the business career? Would he find the same excitement and satisfaction in education that he experienced in the business world?

During that year, Casey worked full time at Enterprise while he took classes in an education credential program and continued to weigh his options. "In the end," he admits, "it wasn't an easy choice to make. I just asked myself what I was good at, what I enjoyed, and what I imagined myself doing in five years. Truthfully, at that point in my life I could have gone either way but there were other factors to consider. On the one hand, there were lots of opportunities for growth with Enterprise while conversely, the governor of my state was firing teachers and the market for educators was tightening. I could imagine myself as a leader with Enterprise; I had already made a name for myself in the short time I was with them and had been asked to continue my career with them. With the prospects of full employment at a strong, reputable organization tipping the scale, I pursued the career with Enterprise."

Once Porter made that decision, he was promoted to assistant manager. In this role, he serviced customers, tracked down missing vehicles, and ensured proper execution of policies and procedures. Although he already had an extroverted personality in his favor, his application of sociological concepts like mirroring, attending, and empathy allowed him to connect with his customers and coworkers in more effective, meaningful ways. By doing so, Casey found himself better able to assess situations and make appropriate judgment calls. "A situation that occurs all-too-frequently," he recounts, "is the customer who arrives at our office with too little money for the rental. Company policy requires either a credit card hold or a cash deposit to secure the car though there is room for variance on the rules. However, if the car is stolen or damaged or the bill is not paid by the customer, the employee who made the final decision will come under scrutiny." It is often up to Porter to determine the proper course of action in these circumstances. He will evaluate the facts — why is this person renting a vehicle, do they provide valid contact information, and do they live locally. Then he will chat with the customer for a while to observe their verbiage and nonverbal behavior during the interaction.

Casey contends that his background in sociology is an advantage, helping him to differentiate someone who is down on their luck but honest from an individual who is unscrupulous. Moreover, by implementing concepts such as confirming messages, compliance-gaining strategies, and perception checking as well as understanding the power of language, Casey has strengthened his ability to be objective yet compassionate. "This in turn," he maintains, "has made me a better manager."

Porter argues that while he may not be instructing pupils on the mechanics of the American political structure or the sociology of our institutions he does, nonetheless, find himself shaping the attitudes and strengthening the job knowledge of his staff. When he was promoted to branch manager, employee development and retention became his primary focus. Casey was expected to foster the growth of every employee he managed as a leader, team player, and viable worker invested in the company. By doing this job well, he made his branch one of the most successful in his region.

Reaching out to the variety of personality types and building upon the social psychological foundations individuals provide has proven to be Casey's most weighty challenge and one with which his sociology background has been infinitely useful. In this regard, he recalls one employee in particular. Nadine came to his branch, cast off by other managers who considered her a lost cause. Porter could see that she had the characteristics to become an excellent employee since she was personable, bright, and eager to excel. Moreover, she seized upon additional technical training and readily incorporated the lessons she learned into her job performance. The problem, however, soon surfaced: her personal life regularly overshadowed her professional functions. A bad day at home could create a tidal wave of emotions that spilled into her interactions with coworkers and customers. To combat this behavior Casey made extra efforts to have heart-to-heart talks with her that typically comprised tears and promises. However, concepts like free will, boundaries, social roles, and stand-point theory along with his use of non-ambiguous language helped Casey address Nadine's issues. Eventually, her self-confidence improved considerably, at least for a while. (This could have been the outcome of the Hawthorne Effect, Porter acknowledges.) With a move to another branch, however, Nadine's performance faltered once again and, sadly, she was eventually fired.

"This failure taught me the limits of my ability to make someone else fit into our corporate culture," Casey admits. Yet, that lesson resulted in a triumph with another of Porter's employees. This time Casey, as an area manager, needed to address a branch manager who, like Nadine, struggled to leave his personal problems behind when he came to work. Trevor's position as manager overseeing a handful of employees demanded immediate attention. He, too, was an intelligent, dedicated employee anxious to find his career with Enterprise. Casey provided Trevor with the emotional support he needed to grow professionally but in this case, used sociological concepts such as conformity orientation, divergence, and facilitative emotions which helped Trevor take responsibility for his behavior. Today, having quashed much of his irresponsible personal behavior, Trevor is one of the best-performing managers in his region.

In the 15 years he has worked for Enterprise, Casey has been promoted seven times and is currently a regional talent acquisitions manager. In this capacity, he recruits college graduates for the management training program. As such, much of his time these days is spent on college campuses providing professional development for student clubs while working closely with campus career centers. To assist him with his recruiting choices, Porter uses behavioral interviewing techniques to create the best balanced teams possible. "Goffman's theory of dramaturgy helps me view the development of a team as a theatrical production in which each person's strengths and weaknesses complement or compensate for those of another team member," Casey explains.

Looking forward, Porter might be interested in pursuing a master's degree in business administration (MBA) to enhance his knowledge, improve his skills, and expand his options for future promotion. He cannot imagine working in an environment that doesn't involve regular social interaction. As such, he suspects he will always work in a sales-oriented atmosphere. Casey plans to continue climbing the ranks of leadership with Enterprise, moving next into a human resource position.

"It is ironic," he remarks, "how many sociological concepts are used in everyday life without a person even knowing it. For instance, we make a fundamental attribution error by assuming that a politician is a brilliant speaker when, in fact, they are probably reading the words off a monitor that the audience cannot see." Casey maintains that once students learn about sociological concepts and theories, they will be able to see a multitude of examples in their daily lives. Suddenly, sociology will not seem so mysterious after all. "In fact, it will help them better understand their own lives and gain insights into the lives of others around them."

If you would like to know more about Casey Porter and his work, please contact him by email at casey.k.porter@erac.com

MARIO RENDON

Mario Rendon's family immigrated to the United States from El Salvador when he was three years old. Although his first language was Spanish, he quickly absorbed enough English from watching *Sesame Street*, a television program for children, that by kindergarten age he was promoted to the first grade. The youngest of three, he grew up with a foot in two cultures — a traditional Hispanic household with socially conservative parents and a middle class suburb in the progressive San Francisco Bay area. In high school, Mario fell into a college track because that was where his friends were and chose Notre Dame de Namur University (NDNU) in Belmont, California, after a recruiter to his high school gave him a personal tour of the college campus. Four years later, Mario became the first in his family to graduate from college.

Eventually deciding on a double major in sociology and Latin American studies with a minor in English, Mario was exposed to sociology through the required introductory class. There, he learned to observe people as part of their groups instead of individual, self-contained entities. "What a fascinating approach," Mario remembers thinking. The truth is Rendon had always been interested in human behavior, recognizing that "our lives are intertwined with people and institutions. There is no escaping." Given this, Mario felt that learning why people behave the way they do and the factors that influence them would serve as a solid foundation for whatever profession he chose.

Though Mario initially targeted international law with a focus on Latin America for his future career, his path can best be described as happenstance at its best.

Since his sociology major required that every senior engage in a two-semester internship in the field they wanted to pursue after graduation, Mario sought out law firms but found them reluctant to take on a college undergrad as an intern. The course instructor brought to Mario's attention a posting at the university's career center for an unpaid position with a local State Assemblywoman's Office. Though Mario was unsure about working for a political representative, he interviewed and accepted the position when it was offered. He could not have made a more fateful and propitious decision.

There, Mario was exposed to a whole new world of ideas and opportunities. Even as an intern, he saw the inner workings of government, the policy formation process, and the political machinations that made it possible. He learned that in the hands of a dedicated and savvy legislator, government could be the solution to everyday problems faced by a local community. The Assemblywoman for whom Mr. Rendon interned primarily addressed consumer protection, governmental efficiency, education, and health issues. As such, her local office dedicated much of its time to helping her constituents connect with the appropriate resources. The experience was far more satisfying than Mario had ever expected and it sparked a new interest.

When a paid staff position became available, Mario applied and was immediately hired with the caveat that he would work in the Assemblywoman's office for just one year and then start law school. As a staff member, Mario assisted with outreach, event planning, project management, and the coordination of interns and volunteers. Essentially, he represented the Assemblywoman to her local community. Further, Rendon stayed abreast of the legislation she sponsored even though it was handled in the state capitol. Sociological concepts such as groupthink, organizational reform, and reactivity versus proactivity had prepared him for these functions.

Rendon quickly found that no workday in the office of an elected official is typical. So much is driven by external factors — people calling for assistance, invitations to events, and requests made by the elected official. A day in the life of a staff member might start with a breakfast fundraiser for a nonprofit organization and then be followed by meetings with city officials seeking the elected official's support for a new policy. Then there might be some time to return calls or to work on a constituent's case. If an issue is generating controversy, the phones will ring nonstop as people weigh in. Sometimes the issue is not even one the elected official can influence. Under those circumstances, the staffer will educate the individual about the appropriate place to take their concern. As a staffer, Mr. Rendon may have had lunch at another event or he might have stayed at his desk still answering incoming calls and emails. Later in the afternoon, there may be more meetings, followed by more desk time. The day might wrap up with yet another community event or a dinner to which a staff member would be sent as a representative of the elected official.

Mario found that as a staff member he was a reflection of that official and therefore, attention to what he said and how he did so was crucial to success at his job. "Being disparaged and criticized by those who don't agree with my boss' position was an occupational hazard," Mario acknowledges. "Nonetheless, patience and active listening helped immeasurably."

In this role, Mr. Rendon frequently participated in any number of external committees, internal groups, and task forces. For these, he found his sociological understanding of group dynamics and perceptions useful. "People would sometimes attribute ulterior motives to me or my boss. The ability to create trust and build relationships helped me move my boss' agenda forward in a productive way," Mario submits.

After a year with the Assemblywoman, Mario started law school though he remained in her office on a part-time basis. Unfortunately, law school wasn't what Mario expected. After the first semester, in fact, he knew he would probably never practice. The focus was geared toward an adversarial method of conflict resolution and Mario's approach was more collaborative. But because he had started, he felt he had to finish. By the time Rendon concluded his second year in law school, however, he was anxious to do something meaningful again. Since the

Assemblywoman would soon vacate her office, Mario was recommended for a position with a local Congresswoman. In this new position Rendon had to navigate the bureaucracy of the federal government as the issues with which he dealt were more policy focused and complex. The office was also much more political than the previous one, with decisions made along partisan lines. Mario soon found the concepts of rationality, conformity, and associational groups extremely useful.

Though Rendon began a job search in the private sector after two and a half years with the Congresswoman, he was lured back to the political world when a County Supervisor hired him as his Chief of Staff. In this capacity, Mario developed the office's policy agenda. He found satisfaction in working on issues that would have wide-ranging impact in a relatively short time. Unlike the State and Federal governments, County government moved fast. An idea could go from development to deployment in just a few months.

County government allowed Mario to work closely with staff from different departments that addressed a range of issues including health care, transportation, education, and civic management. He quickly noticed how each department had its own culture. An approach that might work well with one department failed miserably with another. Mario had to navigate the politics in each department's culture to get his own job done. He found his knowledge of values, norms, traditions, and social control beneficial.

While working with the County Supervisor, Mario and his new wife bought a home in the foothills of Yosemite National Park, some 180 miles from the life they knew. His wife is a teacher but even on a dual income, they could not afford a home in the San Francisco Bay Area. She found another teaching position in their new community and Mario's boss allowed him to work four ten-hour days each week. Nonetheless, when the opportunity to work close to home arose, Mario had a difficult decision to make.

A longtime acquaintance who worked for Pacific Gas and Electric Company (PG&E), a major utility company in Northern California, informed Mario about an opening and encouraged him to apply. The work would be similar to that with an elected public official, he reasoned, except that he would represent a private company. And best of all, he could be home for dinner at night. Ultimately, Mario left government for the private sector and spent a year engaged in government relations work for PG&E in California's Central Valley before another opportunity presented itself.

Like all of his previous positions, the transition to Human Resources at PG&E was unexpected. Another acquaintance was creating a new workforce development program and recruited Mario to help her expand the program. An innovative idea designed to train people for employment; it was reminiscent of his days with county government. Mario was immediately attracted to the position. Although his title was that of a Human Resources Program Manager, he worked as a generalist, focusing on communications, public and governmental relations, marketing, policy development, and building collaborative relationships.

He enjoyed being part of a small team again and learning the culture of the company as well as the Human Resources Department. PowerPathway, the workforce development program his team had launched, was gaining national attention. Conceived and implemented as the Great Recession was deepening, the fact that a utility was training and hiring diverse candidates, especially military veterans, set it apart from the rest of the industry. However, the Human Resource leadership was not quite sure what to do with the program's success. Rather, as Mario later found out, the program was perceived by many in leadership as a "pet project" of the then CEO.

To further complicate matters, in September 2010, a PG&E gas transmission pipeline exploded in the city of San Bruno, California, killing eight people and destroying 38 homes. The company took immediate responsibility but the employees were traumatized. Though the story dominated media coverage for years, the impact on the employees was never fully explored. The sorrow they suffered from the constant criticism of PG&E surprised Mario. This emotional distress felt especially by the field personnel contrasted sharply with the media's portrayal of those in corporate headquarters.

The company invoked a media blackout, not publishing anything positive for fear it would be perceived as a public relations ploy. However, in recognition of PowerPathway's success, PG&E's CEO was invited to a roundtable on workforce development with President Barak Obama. In essence, Mario's small team was responsible for breaking the company's silence. This was a source of pride for Mario's team, but a source of concern for Human Resources and the other departments that couldn't comprehend the program's value.

The program continued to thrive externally, while Rendon's boss fought the internal battles related to PowerPathway. Mario functioned as chief of staff for his boss, though without the title. When his boss abruptly announced her resignation for a prestigious appointment in the State government, she named Rendon to her position as Director of the Workforce Development Department on an interim basis.

In this role, Mario managed the team, learned the norms and expectations of the executives in Human Resources and other company departments, and served as the public face of the PowerPathway program. In addition, Rendon dealt with an internal struggle over the direction and future of the program. "This really opened my eyes." he contends. "I could see clearly that some in the corporate world are more concerned about their own personal gain and glory than the good of the organization. While I was able to keep the team and program intact despite a constant barrage of threats, decisions made by a particular vice president thoroughly disillusioned me." Consequently, Rendon declined to make his interim position permanent sensing that doing so would legitimize the stances taken by the vice president and other leaders. Instead, he returned to his previous role as a Principal Program Manager, functioning as second in command to the new Senior Manager who was hired to lead the PowerPathway team. "Based on decisions this new boss made, along with acquiescence from the vice president, I no longer felt any loyalty to PG&E. I knew it was time to move on," Rendon concludes.

At that point, serendipity once again stepped in. A colleague from Mario's early days in government — in his first job working for the Assemblywoman — had just won a seat in the State Assembly and asked if Mario would work for him. "It was an easy decision for me and thankfully, my wife agreed. So back we moved to the San Francisco Bay Area."

Twenty years after he started in state government, Mario has come full circle. Today, he serves as the Assembly member's District Director, developing the communications, public relations, and constituent service strategy for the office. He also supervises a small team that represents his boss in his district. Further, Rendon acts as his chief advisor on local policy and politics. "This gives me tremendous freedom and trust. I feel like I'm making a difference again and contributing to the greater good," he enthuses.

Mario's career was consistent for 15 years after graduating from college. His progression from state to federal to county government is typical of staff to elected officials. His transition to the private sector brought a new level of understanding and insight that he previously did not possess. His career was, for a while, pushed to the back burner by other priorities but he was always confident that opportunities would present themselves — and they did! Mario acknowledges, however, that these breaks would not have materialized had he not built a network that he started in his undergraduate days.

Working in the private sector provided Mario with insight into a profit-driven organization. Time to reflect has enabled him to ascertain the values important to him and importance of living those values. "For the past few years, PG&E has been running a PowerPathway television ad around Veterans' Day," he notes. "This validates for me that I made the right decisions as the PowerPathway leader. The company didn't get it at the time but they do now."

While Mario has no intention of ever practicing law, he admits that the law school training provided him with a useful way of thinking. Though hindsight is 20/20, Mr. Rendon would probably choose another graduate degree to pursue if he could start his career over again. A master's degree in English leading to a doctorate may have taken Mario into academics. An advanced degree in public policy or political science would have probably provided a better fit for his interest in government. Clearly, though, they have not been required for his career success.

Rendon believes that "sociology as well as the other social sciences equips a person with excellent preparation for any career. Sociology will not limit you to a traditional career. Instead it will broaden your horizons and give you more choices."

To learn more about Mario Rendon and his work, please contact him by email at mario.rendon@asm.ca.gov

MARA LARA

As the eldest daughter in a family that immigrated to the United States from Mexico, *Mara Lara* has always functioned comfortably in both cultures. In fact, she has found her heritage a distinct asset throughout her professional life. As a university freshman, Maria planned to teach elementary school. She soon became disinterested in her education classes and gravitated instead toward Latin American studies. She reasoned that this major would be useful for any aspect of work in the San Francisco Bay area. Besides, she was intrigued by the Latin culture, history, and language.

Then, she took a required course in sociology and found herself able to connect the dots between the behaviors of people, cultures, and even history. "It was as if I was awake for the very first time," Lara remembers. "Being the pragmatic person that I am, however, I immediately thought about the kind of career I could pursue with a degree in sociology. Social work came to mind but didn't appeal to me. Nevertheless, I decided to double major in sociology and Latin American studies." The wisdom of her choice was affirmed during a service learning project where she worked in Guadalajara, Mexico with special needs children and their families. There she observed the first-hand the impact that absent social systems can have in a developing country. She committed then and there to become a public servant.

Following the completion of her bachelor's degree, Maria was hired as a recruiter for a small, liberal arts college. She soon realized that even though her title indicated that she would simply enlist students to attend that institution, the job entailed far more. "It was all about fit, connections, and relationships," she explains. "For students and their parents, college represents a critical chapter in a young person's life and a possible stepping stone to success." Given this, Maria found herself listening to the experiences of potential students and their family members as well as sharing her own. In doing so, she established personal ties. Further, she smoothed the path for her recruits by helping them obtain the appropriate applications, introducing them to the campus, registering them for classes, and generally assuaging their concerns. These responsibilities required familiarity with a plethora of concepts that Maria had learned in her sociology classes; concepts like empathy, perception, and self-fulfilling prophecy.

After a time, Maria was persuaded by a family member to apply for a position with the County District Attorney's Office in the Family Support Division. There, Maria observed in practice the impact of poverty, parental absence, prejudice, and discrimination on individual socialization and ultimately, the community ruin that results. She turned to such concepts as cultural transmission, typicality effect, and social dilemma to understand the conditions she observed. As a caseload manager, Lara secured legal assistance, health care, housing, food subsidies, child support, and whatever other services her clients needed to survive.

While she enjoyed working with her clients, she felt constrained by the required paperwork and government dictates with which she had to comply. She was frustrated by the incessant delays she encountered as she tried to find resources for people living on the brink of poverty and homelessness. She was often overwhelmed by the sheer number of cases she had to manage and the magnitude of the problems with which her clients had to cope. "At the end of each day," Maria admits, "I knew I was responsible for a few more families getting the assistance they needed temporarily. However, the fact that I was helping to maintain a system where I was essentially powerless to improve my clients' lives long-term was agonizing." Lara reminded herself this was not the reason she had majored in sociology. Instead, she wanted to be part of an effort that could implement positive and permanent change. At the urging of a former colleague, therefore, she applied for a position as an Administrative Analyst of Community Development in her hometown. What better place to work, Maria reasoned, than that where the schools, parks, and people contributed to the person she had become.

In her new capacity, she translated for non-English speaking members of the community who requested the city's services, conducted research regarding citizen complaints, and recruited personnel for a variety of divisions within the city government. After just a few months, Ms. Lara was promoted to Manager of the Community Preservation Section. Along with the seven employees she managed, she worked with community groups and businesses to ensure that the existing buildings were maintained in compliance with state and local codes. Additionally, she and her staff addressed blight and physical deterioration of residential and commercial properties. To perform her job successfully, Maria turned to such diverse concepts as cognitive response, cooperative interdependence, built environment, and the impact of building design on human behavior.

Her new responsibilities provided Lara with opportunities to interact with the City Manager and the city council members on a regular basis. "Suddenly, I was introduced to amazing new challenges," she enthuses. "It was like the awakening I felt when I first discovered sociology! I wanted more. I knew this work was meaningful and could make the difference I was looking for."

At the urging of her City Manager, Maria decided to pursue a degree in Masters of Public Administration (MPA) and cast a far-reaching net. When she was accepted at both University of Southern California as well as University of Kansas, though, she had some difficult decisions to make. On the one hand, it had been five years since she was a full-time student and she felt rusty. Further, she would sacrifice medical benefits and an excellent salary if she left her job. Most of all, she would have to move away from home. Conversely, Maria was curious and yearned to meet people who had life experiences different from her own. Besides, she reasoned, the degree would open new professional possibilities for her and she could always go home again. Given this, she packed her bags and enrolled at University of Kansas.

Their MPA program paired extensive coursework with internships offered to metropolitan communities. Ms. Lara worked in the City of Lenexa (Kansas) during her first year but took an internship with the City of Phoenix (Arizona) in the second. These internships allowed her to evaluate various management styles and learn from professionals in local government. "After five years of working in various organizations with only limited mentoring," Maria comments, "I felt extremely fortunate to have these experts willing to share their specialized knowledge with me. They provided me with some of the most valuable advice, professionally and personally, that I've ever received."

Lara found it insightful to work in cities as diverse as Lenexa with its population of 70,000 and Phoenix with 1.3 million residents. "These two experiences reinforced for me that one size does not fit all," she points out. "I quickly observed that differences in the size of the population, the kind and extent of the people's needs, and the availability of economic opportunities all require different operational models." Furthermore, Maria realized the efficacy of local government depends largely on the interconnectedness of the departments and the relationships shared by the employees within them. Her understanding of concepts like nurturing culture, norm of reciprocity, openness—closedness dialectic, and even power distance were among those that helped her to function constructively in these environments.

Upon completion of her MPA, Maria returned home. Away from California for more than two years, she found an economy still recovering from the earlier financial fiasco of the dot.com bust industry. With local government jobs scarce, Lara felt fortunate to obtain a temporary position as a budget assistant. Though this job was short-lived, it provided her with the stepping stone she needed for her next career move.

Soon, as the Principle Analyst to the smallest city for which she had ever worked, she was supervising an office staff; managing the front office, overseeing the budget, managing contracts, and serving as the public information liaison to a fire department in a nearby city. Lara realized this city, like all the others, would have a culture unique to itself and she would have to learn its particular method of conducting business. As such, she set about studying its operations, hierarchy, and its formal as well as informal lines of authority. Maria especially liked the relaxed atmosphere she found in this new environment. Moreover, the City regularly offered workshops that were staff-friendly and encouraged dialogue, both attributes that Maria values. In addition, the Fire Department commonly introduced opportunities for employees to implement new ideas and take on new projects. While Lara appreciated these parts of the job, she eventually recognized that her interests and skills would be better served in a larger department that offered her more opportunities for career growth.

With the support of another city manager, she was hired as the Management Analyst for the jointly operated fire department of two jurisdictions. In this capacity, once again, she had to practice the flexibility she had learned in past jobs. She found that working for a department where two cities shared its costs and benefits required a particularly distinctive way of conducting business. "Although I relished the learning opportunities this position provided me, I often found it challenging to balance the interests of all the players," Lara concedes. "I was frequently caught in the middle of different management styles. As I tried my best to meet the needs of the two cities equitably, I felt pulled in a variety of directions. My position could isolate me as well. At times, I felt like I was responsible to everyone and yet didn't belong to anyone."

Recognizing that the sense of isolation and alienation could potentially lead to burnout, Maria responded by attending joint meetings and participating in the committee projects of both cities even though they were outside of her required scope. In addition, she developed a social network that not only benefited her personally but profited the fire department as well. She soon found her investment of time and effort ensured that she represented both cities fairly. Further, it fostered a strong working relationship between the two cities and kept the fire department at the forefront of both cities' attention. Moreover, she obtained the collaboration of the fire fighters themselves.

To establish these social networks, Maria once again relied on the interpersonal communication skills she learned in her undergraduate sociology classes. She regularly visited the fire station to converse casually with the people there about families, hobbies, career histories and the like. She would listen to their concerns or help them with projects related to large purchases, memoranda that changed processes, grant writing, and software issues. Lara admits, "I sometimes take a tunnel-vision approach to my responsibilities. I would wonder why I was asking about someone's recent vacation or new baby when I had work to do. The time I spent socializing, however, paid off enormously when I needed information or assistance to do my job. Because of the relationships I had created, I knew I could pick up the phone at any time and get help with a project of my own. Although I no longer work for the fire department, that situation is true to this very day."

Lara's progressive career successes and the consequent reputation she developed ultimately led to a position as the Assistant to the City Manager. In this role, Maria brought art to the downtown area in an attempt to deter graffiti. In addition, she supervised the update of a joint master plan for the city's youth, managed the city's legislative agenda, and directed its lobbying efforts. She is especially proud to have successfully completed the city's emission analysis whereby she, along with a local organization, raised awareness and documented the city's greenhouse gas emissions. "This was the first step to developing a climate action plan to reduce greenhouse gases," she points out. In addition, Maria trained potential leaders in the community to facilitate focus group discussions on issues that concern the city and its citizens. After eight years in this position, Ms. Lara accepted a promotion to Finance Director of a small town in Northern California's wine country where she and her family currently reside.

Maria emphasizes that she has loved all of her jobs because they gave her the chance to serve the people and the communities in which she lived. She notes that all of her positions have included some level of complexity but this current job is the most interesting and fulfilling of all. She enjoys the learning experiences her projects provide but contends it is the opportunities to interact with people; to understand their values, perspectives, and lifestyles then to find common ground between them that is the key to her success. "The completion of a project itself is always satisfying," Lara acknowledges, "but even more so is the collaboration that makes it possible. That and knowing we've made a difference."

Over the years, Ms. Lara's career has grown from task orientation to that of visionary. Her last two jobs in particular, Assistant to the City Manager and Finance Director, have obliged her to focus on long-term goals, strategies, and connections to the big picture. Increasingly, Maria has developed her capacity to manage a staff that will carry the projects she designs to fruition. Each of her positions has been a conscientious springboard to the next. As such, she has nurtured her communication and analytical skills. She has absorbed whatever learning opportunities she was offered, cultivated the widest professional network possible, and worked hard to develop a favorable reputation that both precedes and follows her. On that latter point, Lara has learned to choose her words carefully to avoid misunderstandings and the very real possibilities of being misquoted since as she observes, "The world really is a very small place." Asked about her future career plans,

Lara replies that she would one day like to be a city manager herself.

Maria recommends to sociology majors that they balance the people skills they learn in this discipline with technical expertise germane to their field as both will be critical to career success. "That said," she stresses, "the ability to work well with others, to develop positive relationships and sustain them will continue to be crucial in this fast-paced, technologically evolving, and ever-changing world of ours. Sociology will help you appreciate other perspectives and adapt, when necessary, to new and changing social environments." "That," Ms. Lara concludes, "will make the difference between failure and success."

To learn more about Maria Lara and her work, please contact her by email at: m.glara@yahoo.com

4

SOCIOLOGISTS IN CULTURE AND DIVERSITY

Culture and diversity as sociological concepts take an array of forms, influencing literally every aspect of human life as the careers of *Christine Oh* and *Rebecca Morrison* demonstrate.

Motivated by her experiences as a Korean woman in the mainstream culture of the United States, Christine Oh found solace and explanation in her sociology classes on race, social class, youth, and gender. Her interest in these areas led her to a career wherein she evaluates educational programs that serve disadvantaged and underrepresented youth.

Rebecca Morrison selected a hands-on approach to her career immersing herself in the Chinese culture upon her acceptance in the Peace Corp. Morrison expects that ultimately, she will utilize her sociology major and her experiences in the field as a recruiter for the Peace Corps then later, in some facet of international relations.

CHRISTINE OH

Growing up as a second-generation Korean female, *Christine Oh* constantly felt the burden of living in two conflicting cultures. On one hand was the conservative, traditional, and collective Korean culture while on the other, its complete antithesis: mainstream American culture with its focus on individuality and progress. As a result, she often felt trapped between the two worlds without a sense of ever belonging completely to either.

When Christine took her first sociology class in her freshman year at University of California-Irvine (UCI), she was thoroughly repelled. She could make no sense of the theories to which she was being introduced. Marx' premise that society is grounded in conflict and Durkheim's deduction that functionality is the basis for social structures could not explain Christine's own experiences. It seemed to her that old, white men were arguing nonsense about politics, economics, and ideology. Only when she took a class on race and ethnicity was her interest in sociology piqued. She still remembers her professor: loud, assertive, but nonetheless charismatic. In his first few words to the class, he described the manner in which he believed the American government exploited communities of color around the world. Christine was shocked yet she simultaneously resonated with his courageous accusations.

So with each lecture that followed, the words of Marx and Durkheim, Weber and Mills became more meaningful. Sociological theory finally took on relevance and Christine came to understand how sociology could help her make sense of her own world. Using a sociological lens, she began to see how all the inequities her family faced as immigrants and those she continued to encounter as a Korean-American and as a woman were actually manifestations of the larger social structure in which she lived.

As Christine's fascination with sociology grew and became apparent to her professors, she was invited to join an honors thesis class where she was one of a select few able to get a taste of graduate school while still an undergraduate. This promising opportunity allowed her to research a topic significant to her personally under the guidance of several faculty members in her department. Christine leapt at this chance, opting to explore the mental health of second-generation Korean youth living in the United States. She examined the ways in which various demographic factors like socioeconomic status, race, and gender affected the assimilation processes of Korean students attending a local community college. By extrapolating the data she derived from the larger population, Christine became better able to understand her individual experiences. From this, Oh recognized she could turn her personal interests into academic research questions that would ultimately produce greater knowledge about human activity.

Oh found this process not only educationally satisfying, but also self-reflective. As she conducted more research in the areas of race, ethnicity, and immigration, her passion for sociology grew even more pronounced. All the questions she had about the self-identity of immigrants trying to fit into American culture were slowly revealed and answered through the research she was conducting as an academic rookie.

At that point, pursuit of a master's degree and then a doctorate in sociology seemed like the obvious next steps. Taking graduate classes such as Race and Ethnic Opportunities, Second-Generation Youth, and Mexican Migration further opened her eyes to the role of race in the continuation of social inequality. As her grasp on sociological theory became more refined, therefore, she built her master's thesis around the honors topic she had explored as an undergraduate. Hence, she researched the patterns of mental health common to Korean-American students attending UCI and compared them to Mexican American students on the same campus. This provided Oh with the prelude to her PhD dissertation which looked at the manner in which group positioning affected achievement and self-esteem among members of these groups.

Christine concluded that for students of color, navigation through college is contingent on the resources and tools with which they are provided (or lack) from their own ethnic communities as well as the social position of that ethnicity in the society-at-large.

With the dissertation complete and graduation looming, reality sank in. Christine realized her career opportunities in academia would be constrained by the faltering economy that earmarked the early twenty-first century. Moreover, her duty as a second-generation eldest daughter of Korean descent demanded she remain close to her parent's home. Initially, this reality check crushed her idealized dreams of ever working as a sociological theorist. Although she looked online for job after job and pursued the contacts she had acquired through networking, she found few academic openings for a sociologist in the entire state of California. Of those she did find, it seemed to Christine that at least a million other people were applying for those same positions. In addition, many of the jobs were a stretch from her graduate school specialization.

Given these factors, Dr. Oh was forced to re-invent and market herself for a more practical, applied job where she could still utilize her degree. After much thought, she promoted herself as a race and education specialist, a highly sought-after proficiency especially in a place like California. With that, Christine turned to education departments for work in sociological research. Doing so turned up a position as an Educational Researcher at the University of California-Los Angeles (UCLA) where she remains today.

By the end of the first year following her graduation, Dr. Oh was managing a large, statewide project that evaluates after school programs for both elementary and high school students. In a typical day, she goes on-site to observe and interview teachers as well as staff members who serve a disadvantaged community of Latino students. She helps the staff work as a team to provide mentorship and teach leadership skills to youth who might otherwise be overlooked. In addition to the on-site visits, a representative work day usually finds Christine working on some aspect of a research project. Depending on the needs of her project, she might analyze data, write excerpts for a report, conduct a literature review, or hold meetings with her research team. When time permits, she also works on her own publications and searches for grants that might potentially bring funding to race and education programs.

These responsibilities demand that Dr. Oh manage a team of researchers effectively, work as a team player in a collective environment, and maintain her professional network of contacts. She must also multitask effectively and complete several running project deadlines at the same time. Christine contends that she uses her sociological background in every aspect of her job. "It allows me, first of all, to examine racial/ethnic disparity as well as promote educational equity and access for all students regardless of color. Moreover, I have to respect and balance the different interactions and work styles among the people on my own team. Finally, I have to use a variety of organizational techniques that I developed as a sociology student to productively coordinate and complete our projects." Therefore, she consistently relies on her knowledge of sociological concepts such as prejudice, institutionalized discrimination, self-fulfilling prophecy, cultural relativism, socialization, standpoint theory, and social mobility along with those like perception, collectivism, defensive listening, facework, high- and low-context language, and conflict styles that are relevant to interpersonal/intercultural communication.

As a manager, Dr. Oh finds her understanding of such concepts as "we" language, win-win problem solving, authority, problem orientation, and the openness—closedness dialectic critical to her performance. In addition to these concepts, Dr. Oh must also employ her skills in educational needs assessment, design, development, and evaluation.

Working as an educational researcher, Oh quickly found that the research process can be messy and frustrating especially when she is attempting to obtain data from obstinate school administrators who do not respect her expertise. Nonetheless, she enjoys her work because the social issues that she addresses are personally salient to her. Increasingly, Christine finds that the research she undertakes focuses on educational policy and implications for funding. For this reason, she has created and implemented quality-based programs at the university level to proactively help first-generation and otherwise disadvantaged students successfully integrate into university environments.

To gain insights that would help her, Oh volunteered as a mentor with Upward Bound, a precollege program that prepares underperforming students transition successfully to a four-year university. Dr. Oh chose this program as a model because it teaches critical thinking and assertive learning techniques. "Competencies such as these are culturally-based and don't come naturally," Oh claims, "They have to be taught but once they are learned, they can be used over a life-time."

In the future, Dr. Oh plans to build on her experiences as a researcher/evaluator to pursue a directorship at the university level. In that capacity, she wants to implement long-term programs specifically designed to assist students of color and first-generation students so that they can successfully navigate through the complexities of college. She hopes to establish programs that aid students in more seamless transitions to college and to design multicultural programs that foster mentorships and leadership training. In addition, Christine would like to create programs that are tailored to the needs of specific populations like academic skills development for Latinos and African Americans as well as positive self-identification for Asian Americans.

Beyond these goals, Christine has her sights set on a deanship in academic affairs or student development at a small liberal arts college in California. She feels that fusing theoretical foundations with practical applications will both balance and expand her endeavors.

If Dr. Oh could revisit her career choices, she would have achieved more balance between scholarship and a practical, applied environment earlier than graduate school. She wishes she had been more involved in the student affairs department at her undergraduate institution and interned there while completing her formal education.

Based on her own experiences, Christine would advise a potential sociology major to identify an issue about which they are passionate and then engage in real-life practice through internships while they are still in school. "This is extremely important," Oh cautions, "because it will be your degree PLUS your work experience that will make you an asset to an employer. Furthermore, while you are setting goals and planning your future, remember to maintain some flexibility. Happenstance can lead you down roads to destinations even more fulfilling than you initially envisioned."

To learn more about Dr. Christine Oh and her work, please contact her by email at: cjoh@uci.edu

REBECCA (BECKY) MORRISON

Even as a child, **Rebecca (Becky) Morrison** was captivated by people who were somehow different from her whether ethnically, racially, or culturally. "When I couldn't meet these individuals face-to-face," she recalls, "I was reading about the Masai-Mara, the Inupiat, the Tongans, and anyone else who caught my attention at the moment." *National Geographic* magazines lined the bookshelves in my bedroom and I longed to travel the world. Given these beginnings, Morrison submits that sociology was the ideal major for her as it enabled her to pursue her passions and leverage them into career opportunities

After graduating from high school in a small Pennsylvania town, her daring spirit inspired her to move across the United States to the San Francisco area. It was bound to be amazing, she reasoned, but the adrenaline rush of the move soon faded as culture shock crept in. Suddenly, she was exposed to a cultural spectrum different from anything she had imagined. Everything from the food to the clothes to the political views seemed strange. The differences forced Becky to acknowledge that while she had always enjoyed learning about diversity, it was from a distance. Actually experiencing the variations first-hand made her feel surprisingly vulnerable. After sulking for a few weeks, Morrison reminded herself that she had come to California because she craved change and adventure. "Fortunately, I've always been pretty extroverted," she claims, "so I just opened up and started connecting with people. This alone made a difference. From that point forward, I let myself be completely engulfed by my new and eclectic home."

Becky soon enrolled at a small, liberal arts college where she majored in sociology and focused on cultural studies. As she learned more about the world's multiple cultures, she yearned as always to experience them directly. So in her junior year, Morrison embarked on a journey around the world with Semester at Sea. She saw for herself how ecological and functionalist theories explain cultural variations and influence individual behaviors. While engaged in a rigorous class load that revolved around the places she visited, she immersed herself in the ways of life celebrated in 11 very different countries stretching from many of the Caribbean and South American nations to others in Africa and Asia. "Suddenly, the concepts I had studied in my classes became real and I relished every minute of the experience" Becky reveals.

These encounters, among others in her life, motivated Morrison to apply for the Peace Corps upon graduation. Fortunately, she had been forewarned about the length of the application process with its extensive paperwork, essays, interviews, and medical exams as well as the legal, competitive, and suitability reviews. Therefore, Becky returned home to Pennsylvania while she waited and sought employment as a substitute teacher. In this context, she found ideas such as social integration, hidden agenda, middle-class bias, teacher expectation effect, and correspondence principle helpful to understand the educational system and its impact on students. Within a few months, however, Becky found this work frustrating and a bit thankless so she pursued a job in public relations. "In that capacity," she relates, "I observed the behaviors of the subcultures to which I was appealing. Then I would alter my approach accordingly implementing concepts like impression management, presentation of self, norm of reciprocity, and mirroring."

A little more than a year after Becky filled out her first online application for the Peace Corps, she began serving as a US–China Friendship Volunteer in Chengdu, Sichuan, China. "The three months of professional, cultural, and language training was exhaustive but absolutely necessary," she remembers. Morrison's typical day consisted of two to four hours learning about personal health, safety, and security issues. This would be followed by another six to eight hours during which she studied the language of her region and proper etiquette for living in that environment.

She insists, however, that the most beneficial part of the training was living with a Chinese host family. "Despite our language barrier, my family and I learned much from each other and formed a deeply emotional bond."

Following the completion of her training, Rebecca was assigned to the province of Guizhou where she taught English at Xing Yi University for two years. "To have been placed in a country with a 5,000-year-old civilization and a province that is home to 18 of China's 56 ethnic minorities was indeed an honor," she reflects humbly. Every day, she learned something new from her students, the multicultural faculty, and the people in her community. She saw concepts like cultural unity and cultural integration come alive and she better understood the reasons for variations in economic structures, political ideologies, taboos, and symbols. She faced the power of language on a daily basis and better comprehended the Sapir–Whorf Hypothesis.

Recalling that associations are primary agents of socialization, Becky soon began to form clubs that involved her students in learning through diversionary entertainment. The activities, she explains, were largely mechanisms for instilling knowledge about the United States. Therefore, she showed her students dance styles such as hip-hop and line dancing; introduced them to jazz and blues; shared her own favorite recipes; and engaged them in hiking and camping. In addition, Morrison had the students observe their birthdays with American-style parties; organize a senior prom that was attended by over 700 people; and celebrate American holidays like Thanksgiving, Halloween, and Christmas. In doing so, Morrison called to mind Mead's theories about the significance of play in the socialization process.

For Becky, the Chinese people and the other Peace Corps volunteers whom she befriended became the best part of her journey. In fact, in the absence of her own family, many of her new acquaintances became the primary group upon whom she depended for social and emotional sustenance. "A close second, though, was the scrumptious food followed by the rich culture and the sheer geographic beauty of my province," she adds quickly. She firmly believes that the Peace Corps provided her with an opportunity beyond comparison, allowing her to transcend cultural barriers in mutual cooperation with another part of the global community. "My experience exemplifies the sociological imagination as well," Morrison muses. "As I learned about another world and its people, I discovered innumerable things about myself."

"Not that the experience was *always* positive and stimulating," she concedes. "In fact, some days just crawled by. Being so far away from the familiar, missing weddings, holidays and especially, the death of my grandfather and the birth of my first niece was difficult." Lots of common practices also unsettled Morrison. The fact that dog meat was common cuisine in her province, the litter in the streets, and the ubiquitous puddles of spit on the sidewalks were unnerving, she admits. It took some time to adapt to the "squatty potties" as well. Chinese babies in her province, Becky explains, are not diapered. They simply have slits in their pants and crouch down wherever they are; whenever they have to relieve themselves. This could be on the side of the road, in a trash can, or even in the middle of the street.

Initially, there was the issue of personal space as well though Becky soon acclimated to the constant staring and those who nervously approached her to practice their English. "After all," she admits, "there were only two of us Americans in the entire city and the vast majority of the Chinese here had never spoken with a foreigner." Additionally, Morrison found the limits imposed on critical thinking; the public denial of homosexuality in China; the intense exam-based teaching methods; and the blind love that still exists for Mao Tse-Tung decidedly uncomfortable. On the other hand, the profound sense of community, family values, and the incredible kindness of the people far outweighed any negative perceptions she experienced. "I was humbled by the immense hospitality I encountered in my village," she emphasizes.

"It is difficult for me to imagine the average American welcoming a foreigner in the same way." Above all, she learned that humans are relational beings and that ultimately everyone yearns to connect with and appreciate each other.

When Becky returned to the United States, she was anxious to see her family and to consume lots of cheese, bread, chocolate, and coffee, items not readily available in China. She also correctly anticipated that she would undergo some serious readjustments to her home country — the final stage of culture shock. As such, she wisely took a few months to acclimate before starting her new job with the Peace Corps in Volunteer Recruitment and Selection. After four years, she enrolled in a master's degree program for applied sociology at the University of Maryland. While she is currently a full-time student, Morrison is also working there as the Coordinator for Service and Volunteerism. Though she is uncertain at this point where her future might lead her, she does know that international travel will always be part of her life.

Morrison earnestly recommends the Peace Corps to anyone but especially to sociology majors since "sociological studies impart an elevated level of intercultural awareness and an invaluable global perspective that is priceless." She also urges any volunteer to make the most of the experience while in-country. "Doing so," she promises, "will make it a life-giving opportunity."

To learn more about Rebecca Morrison and her work, please contact her by email at: mo31@umbc.edu or becky10morrison@hotmail.com

5

SOCIOLOGISTS IN CRIMINAL AND COMMUNITY JUSTICE

While deviant behavior is frequently viewed as an individual digression, sociologists try to understand its social structural and cultural origins. Focused sociological interest in this topic began with the explorations of the Chicago School and was expanded by modern theorists such as Robert Merton, Edwin Sutherland, and Edwin Lemert. Most sociologists agree that crime is the most common form of deviance and the most dysfunctional to society-at-large. As such, numerous sociology majors pursue careers in criminal and community justice, choosing from a wide range of opportunities.

Mel Coit, for instance, spent his entire career as a probation officer working with adult males while *Amber Brazier Voorhees* is now a deputy sheriff at a jail in Southern California. Though both fields are beset with frustrations, Coit and Voorhees agree that the rewards of their work are far greater.

Influenced by his mentors, many of whom were sociologists, and an undergraduate internship in juvenile justice, *Gary Battane* continues to work in these environments developing programs and training staff throughout the United States and the Caribbean.

Among myriad positions that he has occupied, *Stephen La Plante* served as the Prison Compliance Coordinator for the State of Arkansas when former U.S. president Bill Clinton was its governor and later, as the Homeless Coordinator for the City of San Francisco, California. At the height of San Francisco's crack cocaine epidemic, La Plante directed the city's juvenile hall; then as Chief of Public Safety in the Department of Health, he oversaw police and security services at San Francisco's main hospital. Today, Steve manages a team of specialists in emergency and disaster medical services.

MEL COIT

Sociology's founding fathers and mothers would be proud to see the development of the discipline by the late 1960s, contends **Mel Coit**. San Francisco State College (now a four-year university) was a buzz of activity led by protesters against the war in Vietnam, advocates of women's liberation, and black power activists. The dubious impact of technology on human relationships was being questioned and capitalism was under the proverbial gun as well. "We were the generation that believed we could (and would) change the world for the better," Coit remembers. "We would end the war; exact racial and gender equality; form a strong middle class to which everyone would belong. My generation was going to change the world but somehow, life changed us instead." Mel starts at the beginning.

Born in the midst of World War II, he spent his childhood on a sugarcane plantation in a remote village on the island of Hawaii; the Islands were just a territory of the United States at that time. In the mid-1950s, Mel moved with his family to San Francisco where they lived in an infamous housing project surrounded by conditions normally associated with ghetto life. On the basis of his grades, however, Mel's geography teacher soon recommended that he attend an elite high school on the opposite side of the city. As a result, he commuted by bus for more than an hour in each direction for the next three years of his youth.

In this new environment, he was exposed to a culture that was completely foreign to him: the upper-middle class. Not only did the students dress better than Coit but they seemed to have a certain inexplicable confidence about education and life in general that completely evaded Coit. Nonetheless, he persevered even as he sensed there was little possibility he would ever be part of that privileged social group. His high school years sensitized Mel to some distinct contrasts in behavior between his own social class and that of "the other" in which he was immersed. He learned, for example, the value of niceties like saying "please" and "thank you" as well as the liabilities of refusing to admit wrongdoing.

Given these experiences, sociology might have seemed like a natural course of study for Mel yet he initially pursued classes that would lead to a career in engineering. As such, he started college intent on finding secure employment in a profession that paid well. After two tedious years of drafting classes accompanied by tiresome hours of advanced algebra, trigonometry, and calculus at a local community college, though, Coit yearned for a major that allowed him interaction with others. He tried education but was quickly disinterested in his courses. A career in sales came to mind but only for a fleeting moment. Finally, his desire to engage with people and understand human behavior led him to explore psychology and sociology. Once again, Coit changed his major hoping at that point to become a marriage and family counselor. By then, he had transferred to a four-year state university in San Francisco and pursued courses in child development, deviant behavior, and social theory all of which he enjoyed immensely.

At this same time, protesters appeared on campus daily, vilifying the military and objecting to U.S. involvement in the Vietnam War. "The calls of the day were 'on strike' and 'shut it down,'" Coit recalls, referring to demands to close the school until the war was ended. In addition, the Black Panther Party advocated revolution against racial oppression and promised equity for people of color by "any means necessary." The Women's Liberation Movement insisted on gender parity in the workplace, the legal system, and the family. Though Mel agreed with the dissenters' desires, the likelihood of significant changes in the social structure seemed untenable; certainly beyond the reach of a few college students. He rationalized that, at least for him, making microlevel changes in his own environment was more sensible. "And to be honest," he confesses, "I was tired of school. I was finally ready to grab my bachelor's degree and get into the workforce!"

Coit concluded his education with a focus on Social Welfare and, since his older brother was already employed by the probation department, Mel submitted an application to the county's juvenile hall. He was hired three months later and spent the next four years as a group supervisor for delinquent juveniles. At that point, Coit was promoted to the adult division as a probation officer where he remained for 30 years until his retirement.

"One would think that my background in sociology would be crucial to a position as a counselor in a juvenile detention facility," Mel muses, "and to an extent it did have some bearing in the hiring process." However, at that time, the department encouraged candidates from a wide variety of disciplines, including psychology, political science, history, and education in order to widen the range of expertise among the staff. Then they relied on in-house, ongoing classes to complete the training process, he explains. Though his degree in sociology may not have been tantamount in obtaining his job, Mel argues that his knowledge of sociological concepts such as antisocial behavior; social control, internalization, and social norms were invaluable to his ongoing success. "My studies in social theory were especially advantageous as they helped me comprehend the models we used to understand and change deviant behavior," he clarifies. "In addition, they provided a common language for reporting and for implementing treatment modalities." Coit was soon exposed to other models like harm-reduction, radical and reality therapies, behavior modification, resocialization, and nondirective therapy, all methods the officers were expected to use in their interviews and remediation of criminal clients. In addition, Mel found sociological paradigms such as structural strain, differential association, and social conflict theory helpful.

"As with any probation officer, I wore many hats so my responsibilities varied greatly," he explains. In his position as a probation officer he was, first and foremost, a California Peace Officer and therefore, expected to implement orders mandated by the criminal court. As such, he was entrusted with the powers to arrest and incarcerate and provided with the tools to do so. Once clients had served their sentence, however, they would usually be released to the care of the probation department with specific conditions they were required to follow. These conditions might range from compliance with a restraining order to a directive for weekly drug testing, for instance. Mel would be assigned to a caseload of clients, both male and female adults, with the expectation that he would help them rehabilitate successfully.

To do so, he would begin by interviewing each defendant and orienting them to the dictates of the court. Then he would explain the conditions which were specific to the case and finally, he would inform the client of the general probation conditions that would be enforced. After Coit read the material on the case, he would assess the defendant and set goals that the client was supposed to achieve during the probation. The probation period was generally three-years long. During that time, sociological tools such as reactance theory, normative influence, self-perception theory, and self-handicapping helped Coit identify antisocial tendencies; document behaviors; observe the abilities of clients; and curtail undesirable behaviors

Coit submits that knowledge of sociology becomes crucial when dealing with the rehabilitation of criminals. "Each probationer is unique in their ability to learn and change," he observes. "Therefore, it is necessary to understand the impact of social environments on individual behavior. Furthermore, a probation officer has to tailor his or her demeanor to each individual client so an understanding of symbolic interactionism, connotative language, and nonverbal communication allows an officer the needed flexibility to converse successfully." Mel has personally found a wide range of therapeutic models, from Carl Rogers' nondirective therapy through transactional analysis to Pavlovian repetition, useful as well. "For example, an older, more educated client usually reacts more favorably if they are allowed to reach their own conclusions with only a little guidance while a nineteen-year-old methamphetamine user typically responds better to consequences with ever-increasing penalties for infractions," Coit elaborates.

Given the wide berth of authority entrusted to probation officers, Coit is constantly awed by the respect with which the vast majority approach their positions; the integrity and concerns with which they treat their clients; and the ability of the system to weed out incompetent officers within a short period of time. "Probation," he believes, "is an extremely satisfying profession and most officers stay in the field until they retire. Moreover, they tend to develop camaraderie among themselves that helps them address difficult situations and avoid burn-out." Mel acknowledges that the bonds he formed with his colleagues are especially strong. In fact, even though he retired recently, he stills meets with a group of long-time friends from the probation department on a monthly basis.

Asked about the most stressful and challenging parts of probation work, Mel replies without hesitation: "It is the number of failures we see in spite of our best efforts." Although approximately 70−80% complete their probation successfully, the probation officer sees only those clients who recidivate unless we happen to run into a success on the street. Coit is sometimes asked if his job is dangerous given that he is working with felons and has the power to return them to prison. "The short answer," he responds, "is 'no'." Although Mel admits he has been verbally threatened numerous times, he has never been injured in his line of work. In fact, he knows of only one probation officer in his county who was ever injured during an arrest. He attributes this record, in part, to the practice of working as part of a team under questionable circumstances and to wearing protective gear in dangerous situations.

"A typical work day for the probation officer is atypical at best," Mel laughs, though a 40-hour week is standard. Each officer generally spends a minimum of one day and one evening in the field during which they make calls at the homes and work-places of their clients, both announced and unannounced. As such, they find themselves responding to situations that require anything from family therapy to on-the-spot drug or alcohol testing. Most of their work, however, is conducted in an office setting where officers interview their clients at least once a month though they see many on a weekly basis. Still others are chemically tested two or three times a week. The level of supervision accorded to each client is determined by the officer's assessment of the case.

How has probation work changed since Coit entered the profession as a bright-eyed young man fresh out of college and ready to engage the world? He responds, "When I started, marijuana possession was a felony offense just like that of heroin and cocaine. The majority of criminals were male and most probation officers were men. As the years brought changes in technology and in our social structure, probation has adapted. Today, for example, the use of medical marijuana has been legalized and in many states, its recreational use is also legal. Heroin has given way to methamphetamines and illegal use of prescription drugs has skyrocketed. Drugs, in general, are more easily available to the average person today and yet, curiously," Mel observes, there hasn't been a substantial up-tick in addition. Perhaps, he speculates, it is because people have been made more aware of the substantial consequences of addiction by the media.

While crimes like murder, rape, arson, kidnaping, and aggravated assault have remained relatively constant throughout Coit's career, he reports that other felonies and misdemeanors declined dramatically in the early 1990s and have stayed relatively constant since that time. The reasons are still subject to debate but Mel theorizes that technology has played a role. Television, surveillance equipment, laptop computers, video cameras, the internet, security systems with alarms, immediate reporting devices, and even new methods of chemical testing have contributed to the slow-down in crime.

Though Coit is extremely satisfied with the career choice he made in the early 1960s, he suspects now he would take a different approach if he could start over again. He gravitated toward the technical and treatment areas of probation because he felt most comfortable there and because he enjoyed the camaraderie he found. "In hindsight," Mel reflects, "I might have made a bigger imprint on my profession had I directed myself toward administration by continuing my education and taking the classes that were available." Furthermore, Mel wishes he had recognized earlier that politics are integral to influencing policies in any profession. If he had, he could have used them more advantageously.

Considering the advice he would give to a sociology major (or any other student for that matter) Coit encourages a commitment to learning: "Academics will make more sense when you interact with real world dynamics. On the other hand, you will better understand real life if you have a strong academic foundation."

To learn more about Mel Coit and his work, please contact him by phone at: 650-307-3756.

AMBER BRAZIER VOORHEES

Even as a child, **Amber Brazier Voorhees** was intrigued by human behavior. "Why did they do that? Why do they live like that? Why do they look so different from us?" she would badger her parents. In time, she began to wonder why people broke the law. By high school, Amber was observing the influence of social and physical environment on myriad people and how they conducted themselves. There, she discovered criminology and her interest in the topic as well. Some of her friends had already been in trouble with the law by that time and Amber tried to determine the reasons. She compared their family backgrounds to her own for answers and questioned the impact of long-term goals. She admits she was also fascinated by all the cop and detective shows on television. "They made me wonder what roles poverty and affluence play in criminality; why men rape; and why certain crimes like child molestation are more prevalent among a certain category of individual. I was also curious about why the media focused so heavily on street crime instead of white collar felonies and what the social consequences might be."

At the community college where Voorhees earned her Associate in Arts (AA) degree, she enrolled whenever possible in courses that most captured her interest. Coincidentally, those classes were usually in sociology and criminology. As such, when the softball coach at Notre Dame de Namur University (NDNU) attempted to recruit her on a scholarship, Amber immediately asked if she could simultaneously major in sociology and criminal justice. Upon discovering it was possible through the university's Sociology: Community & Criminal Justice major, she promptly enrolled.

Though she benefited immensely from her classes, Amber contends that the two-semester internship required by her sociology major was by far the most valuable aspect of her undergraduate years. This experience provided her the opportunity to work with a suburban police department in Northern California. There, she helped officers design and implement a program that alerts high school students to the dangers of driving while being drunk. Voorhees also got to ride along with various officers as they engaged in their normal routines. She was surprised at the degree to which suburban departments participate in neighborhood activities — everything from speaking to elderly citizens about personal safety to supporting a teenage softball league. These encounters plus the variety of administrative tasks Amber performed allowed her to observe the nature of police work as well as the operations of a department in a small, middle-class community.

"I learned that police work has both peaks and valleys, often in the same day," Amber remarks. "One afternoon I walked into a local Starbucks with an officer and saw the faces of the children light up with excitement. The officer engaged the kids in conversation then gave them police stickers that they proudly added to their attire. Later that day, the same officer found drug paraphernalia during a routine parole search and was forced to have Child Protective Services remove the children from that home." Even on the most dispiriting days, however, Voorhees found her time with the department flew by. The internship solidified her desire for a career in law enforcement.

Determined to obtain as much direct experience as possible in preparation for her career, Voorhees took on yet another internship with the local juvenile hall. There, she mentored young men preparing for their General Education Degree (GED). "One of the kids I worked with was only 14 years old, covered with gang tattoos, and eager to tell me about his family," Amber remembers. "This boy had been born into a gang and lived his life surrounded by it. Being arrested, shot at, and seeing loved ones killed was as natural to him as playing softball was to me." Voorhees saw concepts such as associational groups, cultural transmission, differential association, labeling theory along with Merton's Typology of Deviance come off the pages of her textbooks as they brought meaning to the circumstances in which her internship placed her. "When my mentee passed his GED, I was ecstatic," Amber declares. "Yet I also found this work depressing when I realized how few of these kids ever get their GEDs and rise above their environments."

Though Voorhees' classes provided her with the foundation necessary for work in law enforcement, nothing could have prepared her for the lengthy wait that preceded her acceptance at the police academy. She explains that the process started with her application. That was followed by an extensive background check during which her family, friends, and neighbors were interviewed about her character. Next there was the written exam, the physical exam, the psychological evaluation, and finally the polygraph test.

After the seemingly endless wait, Voorhees began the 21-week training program at the sheriff's academy in her county. She quickly realized her sociology courses had already prepared her to scrutinize her physical surroundings; read body language and identify drug users. "These skills are crucial to effective police work," she notes. In addition, her experiences with diverse lifestyles, deviancy, and familiarity with sociological concepts such as anomie, structural strain theory, and control theory helped her maintain an "A" average throughout the academy. Moreover, her internship with the police department gave her an enormous advantage. In fact, Voorhees had already experienced first-hand some of the scenarios on which she was tested.

Upon her graduation, Amber was assigned to a county jail in Southern California as a deputy sheriff. In this capacity, she ensures the safety and security of the inmates; conducts searches for illegally smuggled goods; investigates crimes committed in the jail; and supervises the inmates in work programs. Additionally, her job requires her to document all incidents of suicide, suicide attempts, medical issues, possession of drug supplies, narcotic finds, and any infractions that compromise the well-being of the jail. Moreover, Voorhees books new arrestees first searching them for weapons, drugs, and other contraband. She then fingerprints the individual, obtains their personal data, and either houses or releases them depending on their charges. She also releases inmates from custody by checking for the correct paperwork, returning their personal property, and then discharging them from the county's authority. When the opportunities arise, Amber trains newly-graduated deputies wherein she acclimates them to the operation of the facility, apprises them of their duties and responsibilities, and introduces them to the other staff.

While Amber finds drug use among pregnant females especially frustrating, the satisfaction she derives from seeing inmates overcome their addictions and not recidivate far supersedes the challenges of the job. She also enjoys the variety law enforcement work provides along with the chances she gets to help people. Working with an incarcerated population, Amber finds sociological concepts such as resocialization, internalization of norms, total institution, corrections, recidivism, and free will useful for understanding the impact of prison on personality.

In addition to her regular activities, Voorhees has taken on two collateral activities as a deputy sheriff. As a member of the recruitment team, she attends various community events where she speaks to young people about career opportunities in law enforcement. She finds her knowledge of cultural relativity useful in these situations. Her work with the fugitive detail unit requires her to accompany inmates back to their county of origin when they have escaped to another part of the country. While the travel itself is never glamorous, Amber does enjoy the chance to observe disparate lifestyles in different regions of the country and to compare jail operations in different locales. "It must be the sociologist in me," she smiles.

Since becoming a deputy, Amber has attended numerous training classes on topics like drug trends, narcotics identification, gangs, self-defense tactics, report writing, wiretapping, legal updates, and survival techniques if injured. In the jail patrol program, she was partnered with another officer trained in patrolling the streets. She found this detail informative and is excited to observe more criminal situations outside the jail. When she works in court services, Voorhees furnishes security for murder trials, domestic violence cases, and an array of misdemeanor charges.

As for the future, Voorhees plans to continue learning as much as possible so she can avail herself to the plethora of options available in law enforcement. "That shouldn't be too difficult considering how much I love my job," she admits. "I wake up every day eager to go to work!" She looks forward to working street patrol in the near future and eventually, as a detective in the child sex crimes unit.

Asked what sociology majors can lend to law enforcement, Amber replies thoughtfully. "I think as a society we have been taught to take a psychologistic view of the world. That is to say, we think behaviors are motivated by individual characteristics while we neglect the social and systemic influences. Sociology focuses instead on structural-level explanations." She supplies an example to support her contention. After watching a media report about a gruesome killing, Amber's husband remarked, "I wonder what would make a person do such a thing." Amber responded, "As a sociologist, I have to ask why more people *don't* do these things given their social environments." Clearly, Voorhees maintains, we need sociologists in law enforcement!

To learn more about Amber Brazier Voorhees and her work, please contact her by email at Amb77@sbcglobal.net

GARY BATTANE

On college campuses throughout the United States, the early 1970s were rife with civil unrest, social upheaval, protest movements, and rapid social change. Amidst this climate, *Gary Battane* enrolled at Wayne County Community College (WCCC) in Detroit where he took a variety of social science classes focusing on issues that defined the era. Topics such as militarism, economic inequality, racism, and sexism dominated often-heated discussions both in the classroom and outside.

"During that time," Battane remembers, "I was influenced by some of the most idealistic and altruistic people I have ever met, most of whom were sociologists. They encouraged critical thinking; stressed service to others; and emphasized their belief in human potential. These particular people believed in me when I, myself, was riddled with self-doubt." This was the start of Gary's life-long interest in sociology.

After transferring to Wayne State University (WSU), also in Detroit, to complete his bachelor's degree, Battane signed up for a juvenile justice internship wherein he was assigned an at-risk youth who already had some offenses like truancy on his record. The State Attorney had agreed to drop the latest charge if the boy completed a diversionary program created in collaboration with the sociology department at WSU. At the time, research on juvenile recidivism indicated that such a program would be more effective than placing the boy with probation officers in the juvenile justice system. Several of the sociological concepts he was learning in his classes aided his understanding of this youth. Among them were stigma, cultural transmission, and control theory. In addition, he found his growing understanding of the criminal justice system and the role social environment plays in the creation of criminality useful. "Because of this program and the introduction to the helping professions it provided,"

Battane explains, "I became a staunch supporter of diversionary strategies."

For a short time following his graduation, Gary worked as a counselor at a group home for at-risk teens. There, he applied several principles he had learned in his internship which, along with extensive training, helped him successfully mentor his often-difficult clients. More important, he developed the attitude he needed to function in that environment. Gary notes that he, like most individuals who enter the helping professions, wanted to "make a difference" so it was initially a blow to find that much of the behavioral change he observed in the program was temporary. "For changes to be meaningful and lasting," he shares, "the offender's cognitive processes and the value of change must be continually addressed. This requires vigilant monitoring and follow-up. Otherwise, recidivism will result."

Battane further notes that helpers often find it difficult to establish appropriate psychological distance and an emotional strong-arm with clients. "Yet, it is absolutely critical for the well-being of both the professional and the client to do so," he enforces. These lessons as well as the knowledge he gained about the dynamics of group behavior and the impact of peer pressure helped Gary immeasurably when he later ventured into the arenas of mental health and substance abuse.

After working directly with clients for several years, Battane was invited to pursue a position in staff training and development. "The best part of this job was the opportunity to cultivate positive morale, organizational synergy, and leadership skills."

Presented with a fully-paid scholarship to Mississippi State University in 1978, Gary jumped at the opportunity, moving himself and his new wife south. As much as he wanted a doctorate, however, the institutional racism he found both at the university itself and in the town where they lived proved too distasteful to tolerate. After just two semesters, the couple moved back to Detroit; Gary without a PhD.

Nonetheless, he had learned enough about research design and implementation during his master's program at University of Detroit that he was soon offered a position as the Director of Research and Evaluation in the field of mental health. In this capacity, Gary analyzed the effectiveness of therapeutic techniques, policies, and procedures. Further, he assessed various management styles with regard to their effects on the workplace environment. Battane argues that the challenges of this job rested largely with the toxic relations between staff members. This dynamic alone made it difficult to build an intentional therapeutic community. "More specifically," he clarifies, "big egos and personal agendas counteracted the creation of organizational goals and a common vision. The coercive style favored by so much of management resulted in excessive burn-out among the staff and significant recidivism among the clients. Sadly, despite my best efforts at diversity training, the institutionalized racism and sexism remained insurmountable as well." Almost daily, Gary found himself referencing sociological concepts such as communication climate, authoritarian personality, and power distance for an understanding of his social environment.

When the University of South Florida (USF) undertook the development of a curriculum in juvenile justice and delinquency, they recruited Battane to join their training staff. His employment history as well as his knowledge of family systems helped him enormously. "My entrée into this position was most certainly the result of the networking and relationship-building I had done since my days as an undergraduate," Gary remarks. "Conversely, these same connections also helped me function successfully once in the job because I was able to use those contacts as resources."

Battane's work at USF enhanced his already well-established renown in juvenile justice, mental health, and substance abuse bringing him invitations to train staff throughout Florida, most of the other southern states in the United States, and even the Cayman Islands and Belize. While Gary emphasizes that every training session is unique and therefore, each workday distinctive, he does use a standard model to carry out the training process no matter what his geographic location. First, he familiarizes himself with the culture (or subculture) of his audience. This helps him understand the ways in which the participants might already define concepts that he invariably addresses. He gathers this data from a variety of sources, learning about the history of the region along with its cultural norms and taboos. Next, Gary conducts a needs assessment through which he determines the expectations of his audience and the information the participants will require to function successfully in their jobs. "This is probably the most essential step in the entire training process as it informs the remainder of the curriculum," Battane warns. "Without it, you can find yourself delivering information that, while useful to one group, is useless to another."

With the needs and expectations determined, Gary proceeds to the creation, development, and implementation of the training. Here, too, he is mindful of the audience's characteristics. Are they technologically savvy or paper-and-pencil learners? Socially conservative or progressive? Highly-educated or minimally-schooled? Are they likely to resist or welcome change? Battane insists that each of these factors will require a different instructional approach. "For example," he continues, "individuals with minimal education have typically had negative experiences with traditional classroom methods. So they may be intimidated, fearful, or even hostile if I use the lecture technique. Instead, I want to get a group like this moving around; engaged in activities; and watching relevant films to which they can relate."

Finally, there is the evaluation stage. Not only does Gary devise a final appraisal of the training to which the trainees respond, but he also interweaves mini-assessments throughout the course. These usually take the form of short quizzes, anonymous suggestions, and even casual conversations. This is another critical step, according to Battane. "Knowing immediately how the material is affecting my audience allows me to revise the curriculum mid-course and improve the outcome."

Battane especially enjoys training because of the variety, flexibility, and travel opportunities it provides. Moreover, he is exposed to diverse regional, social class, and cultural perceptions that ultimately influence his personal outlook. On the other hand, some of the same aspects he enjoys about this job are also his bane: the constant travel; long hours in airports; and time away from family and friends. There is also the sometimes bull-headed resistance to new ideas that stem from the local administration.

If Gary had the chance to approach his career differently, he suspects he would have spent more time in youth services and less in the adult sector. "I feel that the youth population is more receptive to transformation. On the other hand," he speculates, "I probably wouldn't have had the patience and resilience necessary to work with juveniles had I not been exposed to the manipulative games I experienced with the adults."

For Battane, the beauty of sociology resides in its dependence on critical thinking so vital to a civil world. To make his point, he relates a situation in which a Chicago man who had been stabbed several times was literally crawling toward the entrance of a hospital emergency room with blood gushing from his wounds. The hospital had recently imposed a policy prohibiting their personnel from assisting anyone until they were inside. Just a few feet from the door, the man died while the hospital staff looked on stoically. "This tragedy reminded me of the Milgram Experiment and how subject humans are to following orders instead of thinking critically," Battane observes. He believes this sort of dilemma occurs in all professions and in many aspects of our lives. "Think about the disaster of inaction in New Orleans during Hurricane Katrina; the worldwide economic meltdowns caused by unscrupulous banking practices; the sanctioned use of torture at Abu Graib; and even the disenfranchisement of certain American voters." All of these examples, according to Gary, demonstrate that our current social structure cannot be counted on to protect its citizens from brutality and injustice. Fortunately, sociology gives us the knowledge, perspective, and skills needed to question wrongdoing and create humane social structures. "To me," Gary acknowledges, "sociology represents hope where there might otherwise be a demise of morality."

Given this framework, Battane is frustrated when students take a sociology class just to fulfill a requirement. He recalls a student who had been absent from his class for several days. Upon her return, she inquired nonchalantly, "Did I miss anything?" He responded, "Every class is a microcosm of human experience that I put together for you to query and ponder. This isn't the only place this can happen but it is one place, and you weren't here." In other words, GO TO CLASS! Take your education seriously; treat it as your job. Learn as much as you possibly can. Appreciate your opportunity to get an education. There are so many people in the world who do not have this advantage.

To learn more about Gary Battane and his work, please contact him by email at grbattane@aol.com or by telephone at 727-385-9452.

STEPHEN LA PLANTE

It was the most blood curdling shriek imaginable. **Stephen La Plante** was interviewing a prisoner on Death Row when he heard the ominous discord. He raced full-sprint to the cell and found two prisoners; one lay unconscious with both eyes gouged out. The other was positioned on his bunk in a fetal position, rocking back and forth, humming loudly. It was immediately clear to Steve that the latter prisoner was in the throes of a psychotic break. La Plante shouted for the officers in charge who, in turn, called the infirmary. Two more prisoners arrived with a stretcher and proceeded to lay "Clarence" on his back. Recognizing the gravity of this move, Steve screamed that Clarence couldn't breathe because he was drowning in his own body fluids and instructed the prisoners to turn the man on his side. With the injured prisoner finally transported Steve turned, exhausted, to the lieutenant and asked in disbelief, "Aren't these guys trained to handle situations like this?" Steve shakes his head incredulously, "I'll never forget his response. He just looked at me like I was crazy."

Such was a typical day in the life of Stephen La Plante as the Prison Compliance Coordinator for the Arkansas Department of Correction and the Arkansas Attorney General's Office. There, La Plante was responsible for enforcing Federal Court orders on prison conditions and the treatment of prisoners. As such, he investigated complaints about discipline, excessive force, working conditions in the prison's fields, and the quality of medical care. As a life-long Californian with both a bachelor's and a master's degree in sociology as well as completed doctoral coursework in the discipline, Steve explains how he got to that point in his career.

He was initially attracted to sociology and criminology as an undergraduate at University of San Francisco (USF) during the heady era of the 1960s. For one of his classes, he interviewed and wrote a paper on the work of a San Francisco police officer who was later elected county sheriff. Later, at The University of Chicago where Steve obtained his master's degree, he was further drawn to the disciplines by a class on discretionary justice. The class was taught by the nation's leading advocate for the use of ombudspersons to redress grievances in the government arena.

Upon his completion of graduate school until he moved to Arkansas, La Plante worked as the first professional jail ombudsman in the United States under the auspices of the San Francisco Sheriff's Department. As a jail ombudsman, La Plante worked closely with the city's health department on medical and dietary issues and investigated complaints filed by the prisoners and jail staff. Steve found his graduate school training in basic fieldwork methods (taught by renowned sociologist, Howard S. Becker) immeasurably useful for conducting the investigations. "The same fundamentals necessary to a successful investigation are the techniques utilized by sociologists carrying out fieldwork research," La Plante explains. "It is how I developed a sociological eye."

During this time, Steve also created and led the first crisis negotiation team ever conducted by the San Francisco Sheriff's Department. In the jails, the team handled work stoppages, hunger strikes, hostage-taking, and unusually tense disputes among prisoners. Additionally, they attended evictions of citizens with histories of mental illness to avert possible violence.

With his background in sociology, La Plante was frequently called upon to develop new policies, procedures, and personnel practices when the previous programs proved ineffective. In every case, Steve found such concepts as deviant motivation, counterculture, criminalization, and prescriptive/proscriptive laws as well as theories like functionalism, differential association, and social learning crucial to the survival of those who worked in the jail environment.

When asked how he obtained these positions, he replies, "Through my contacts for the most part. They knew my work

and would recommend me." As for the prison compliance coordinator, however, La Plante applied to a nationwide search conducted by Bill Clinton, then the Attorney General of Arkansas.

La Plante continued his work in Arkansas' prison system
through Bill Clinton's tenure as governor but when Clinton was
defeated in his first bid for re-election, funding for the prison
compliance coordinator was eliminated. Steve returned to San
Francisco whereupon he was asked by the city's mayor to join her
staff as a criminal justice program manager. In that capacity,
Steve was a liaison between the mayor and the community on
issues of public safety. He assessed conditions and launched
numerous investigations of juvenile hall, the foster care system,
jail overcrowding, and police operations.

Based on his performance as the prison compliance coordinator, La Plante was again approached by the mayor's office and
offered the position of Homeless Coordinator to San Francisco. In
this role, he synchronized the city's services in conjunction with
public and private agencies to effect more organized delivery to
the homeless. In addition, he monitored the hotels where homeless
people stayed, prepared a five-year master plan that managed the
homeless population, and negotiated with the leaders of encampments so they would disband peacefully when requested.

Steve reflects on an average day as San Francisco's Homeless
Coordinator. Following inspections of the hotels or Single Room
Occupancy units (SROs), Steve might meet with any combination
of service providers, advocates for the homeless, and representatives from public agencies. "This was by far the most frustrating
part of the job," La Plante maintains, "since there were many
egos and few people were willing to compromise." His evenings
invariably involved visits to the city's numerous emergency
shelters. Since inadequate funding prevented these shelters from
operating around the clock, the residents were forced to wander
the streets during the day, patronize soup kitchens for their meals,
and queue up late every afternoon in hope of securing a cot to

sleep on that night. La Plante observes, "It would have been far better to keep shelters open 24 hours a day; seven days a week, providing the stability essential for escaping homelessness. Ironically, we would have gotten more people off the streets faster."

Assigned at one point with disbursing an encampment of 75 tents in the center of downtown San Francisco, Steve quickly identified the two leaders after chatting amicably for a while with some of the homeless occupants. "A basic sociological premise is that any group of three or more people will have a leader," he notes, "so I knew my best bet was to find them first." The leaders, however, promptly pointed out that the encampment was adjacent to a round-the-clock vigil protesting the lack of federal funds for HIV/AIDS research and had been there for several months with the mayor's approval. "I was clearly on the horns of a dilemma," La Plante recognized. "It would have been hypocritical of me to break up the homeless camp while letting the vigil remain."

It took Steve a month to negotiate a settlement. Fortunately, the press coverage of the situation resulted in an outpouring of donations from the public that allowed the campers to rent a vacant retail space and La Plante facilitated the move. The vigil, however, remained for several more months until President Reagan could be convinced to provide monies for HIV/AIDS research *and* for programs assisting homeless people in urban areas of the nation. Though his crisis negotiation skills were immeasurably valuable, Steve found his knowledge of sociological concepts such as group dynamics, prosocial behavior, equity theory, and the norm of social justice beneficial as well.

On the heels of successfully disbanding several homeless encampments without a single arrest, Steve was asked by the mayor to investigate the unusual deaths of ten infants that had occurred over a two-year period in San Francisco's foster care system. "It was the most emotional experience I've ever undertaken in my career," he admits. "With the State threatening to take over the operation of our foster care program if we didn't resolve the problem, the investigation became tantamount in my life." As La Plante wrote in his report, three of the deaths were the result of homicide by the foster parents, four of the babies would have died in any event from afflictions like Sudden Infant Death Syndrome (SIDS), and the cause of death for the final three could not be determined by the medical examiner. Being a sociologist, Steve looked to the system for answers concluding that the overriding reason for these deaths rested with the lack of foster care personnel for the workload involved and cited, among other items, the desperate need for new procedures. He was overjoyed when the mayor, after reading his report, furnished funding to expand the staff and implemented every one of his recommendations.

During the late 1980s, at the height of the crack cocaine crisis in urban areas throughout the United States, Steve became the director of San Francisco's Juvenile Hall. As such, he managed a 137-bed detention facility along with a staff of 140 counselors and support personnel. In his first month of hire and to Steve's profound amazement, the city drastically cut his operating budget forcing him to close one of the seven units. Overcrowding was extensive. La Plante was familiar with the correlation between overcrowding and violence so moved quickly to offset inevitable hostility by instituting a policy declaring juvenile hall neutral turf for gang members.

Knowing about the power of symbols from his study of interactionist theory, Steve soon prohibited all gang-related signing, colors, and graffiti. In each of the units, the number of rival gang members was equalized to prevent fighting. "Happily, these changes worked, markedly reducing violence among the youth," he recounts. "I found out later that the gang members were secretly pleased to accept the neutral turf doctrine." Despite limited resources and lack of adequate facilities, La Plante successfully established new programs for the youth including an Omega

Boys Club chapter, art classes, family visitation opportunities, and peer counseling for prostitutes.

In 1991, Steve became the Chief of Public Safety for the Department of Health. In that role, he oversaw the traditional police and security services at San Francisco's main hospital as well as nine neighborhood clinics. He oversaw the budget, monitored contracts, coordinated personnel requisitions, arranged for capital improvements, insured effective communication, and trained staff in disaster preparedness techniques. "Keeping a large, inner city, acute care hospital and trauma center safe is indeed challenging," Steve acknowledges. He credits his knowledge of sociological concepts like definition of the situation, socially constructed reality, and control theory for his success as Chief of Public Safety. While La Plante describes the job itself as fascinating with multiple opportunities for growth, he concedes that he least liked working under non-police managers who did not understand the complexities of health care policing.

For the past 15 years, La Plante remained with the Department of Health working first as an Emergency Medical Services (EMS) and Disaster Specialist and later as the EMS Administrator. This office leads the health and medical responses to any disasters in the city, Steve explains. Therefore, he is responsible for disaster preparedness and response training, planning, and logistical functions for the health department. Steve shares a normal though perhaps atypical day in the life of an EMS & Disaster Specialist.

He received a call at five o'clock one Sunday morning apprising him of a fire at a hotel in a low-income area of San Francisco. When he arrived, the fire was extinguished and 150 displaced, high-risk victims were already on buses bound for the shelter that had been established in a nearby recreation center. The mood was thick as most of the people had left their medications in their rooms when they evacuated. Some were already showing the effects. La Plante negotiated with the battalion chief to have the firefighters go back into the hotel to collect all the medicine they could find. Steve then took the meds to the shelter and with the guidance of a nurse, distributed them to their owners. By mid-afternoon, a medical team arrived to ascertain that everyone was stabilized. According to Steve, the experience was a textbook example of the way in which government is supposed to work in a crisis.

"The value of sociology in disasters cannot be overstated," La Plante points out, "since people act very differently in emergencies than they do in normal circumstances." Concepts such as collective behavior and social contagion are extremely useful in this field. In fact, through the work of Kai Erickson and since Hurricane Katrina in New Orleans, an entirely new area of study called the Sociology of Disasters has evolved. La Plante's knowledge of this area has enabled him to render assistance in numerous catastrophic situations, the most memorable being the 2010 earthquake in Haiti.

Steve reminds students that a major in sociology is particularly conducive to a career in government. With about 40 specialties for sociologists in government alone, the possibilities are almost limitless. Although "government" seems to have become a dirty word, La Plante steadfastly maintains that a career in this area is both noble and fulfilling. Surely, his own experiences speak to this assertion.

As for Clarence, he remained in a coma for five months then died. Although he was white, he was buried in the "colored section" of the local cemetery because the state would only pay for a pauper's funeral. On the day of the funeral, Steve and the mental health coordinator followed the hearse for several miles to a dirt road, then another mile to a perfectly manicured sylvan knoll. But Steve and Maggie continued their ride past this area to the rear of the cemetery — to the "colored section." It was shabby and over-grown with weeds. Two elderly black gentlemen leaned on their shovels. They had arrived earlier in an old, worn-down pickup truck and dug the grave by hand. There was only the prison chaplain, the hearse driver, the two gravediggers, the mental health coordinator, and Steve. "I felt like I had stepped back a hundred years in time to 1879," Steve intones sadly.

Clarence's 80-year-old mother could not afford the trip from Oklahoma to attend her son's funeral. In his letter of condolence to her Steve wrote, "I will be talking about Clarence in my next report to the Federal Court with the intention of forcing the State of Arkansas to create a separate facility for mentally ill patients." Within a year, a 60-bed unit with a full treatment program opened in Pine Bluff, Arkansas. "You see," La Plante observes, "sociologists *do* make a difference."

To learn more about Stephen La Plante and his work, please contact him by email at laplantescurtis@yahoo.com

6

SOCIOLOGISTS IN ARTS AND SPORTS

Arts and sports, in their many diverse forms, are found in virtually every human culture worldwide. For this reason, sociologists consider them both cultural universals. Along with the major institutions, arts and sports reflect the lifestyles and values of their people; serve as a means of socialization for (not socializing among) their young; serve as means of communication between members; and encourage social cohesion. As such, art and sports promote understanding and maintain unity.

This section introduces **William (Bill) McNeece**, a photographer, and **T.D. (Tom) Schuby**, a horserace handicapper. Both explain their draw to sociology (and McNeece, his interest in religion) by way of personal histories. Each then describes how sociology helped them turn hobbies into livelihoods.

WILLIAM (BILL) MCNEECE

For *William (Bill) McNeece,* the road to sociology began on the front porches of his neighbors and extended family members in a traditional Irish Catholic working class community during Detroit's hot summer evenings. There, the little boy would join the adults who gathered after long days in the city's ubiquitous factories to relax and discuss the events of the day. Frequently, conversation focused on the Tigers, Detroit's professional baseball team, or the demands of assembly line labor. Just as often, however, discussion turned to topics that Bill could not understand at the time. He would hear ominous comments like, "they're coming," or a street would be defined as a barrier that had been breached. Buying a home and moving as far away from the old neighborhood as possible soon became the goal not only of his family but that of many others in his community. As McNeece grew older and better informed, he realized that manifest racism was the social force informing those foreboding comments. Conversely, Bill's father had a passion for jazz. Weekends in the McNeece household were filled with the musical sounds of Duke Ellington and Count Basie. The racially integrated Benny Goodman quartet was his father's favorite. "Even as a child, this contradiction between attitude and action did not escape me," Bill muses.

In time, the McNeece household moved out of Detroit to a suburban street lined with small three-bedroom ranch style homes. From his new vantage point, Bill could literally look across the street at another world — that of the middle class. While the fathers on Bill's side of the street wore rugged clothes fit for work with dirt, grime, and grease, the fathers of the middle class wore white shirts and ties to work. Moreover, the families "over there" lived in spacious houses that exuded charm. Another contradiction surfaced for McNeece: social class and its attendant inequality.

As Bill grew older, he learned that his father's family had experienced intergenerational downward mobility. McNeece's great grandfather had been a physician in a small Michigan town; his grandfather had been a pharmacist but was killed in an accident during the Great Depression. As a result, Bill's father sold newspapers and delivered prescriptions to help the family survive. Never having the chance to graduate from high school, he spent his life working for the telephone company, climbing poles to maintain switching systems in the downtown area of Detroit. "From the onset, my dad had other plans for me though," McNeece contends. "When I was eleven years old, he got me to get a job as a newspaper carrier with the understanding that the money I made would be saved for my college education. Upon graduation from high school, however, I was still an immature kid and since it was less expensive than a university, my father decided that I would attend a recently-established community college. I complied since many of my high school friends were going there, too. After our first year, however, I was the only one left; the rest had all dropped out. Some of them were later killed in the Vietnam War."

Given his background, Bill's first sociology class was a revelation. He soon found the discipline spoke to the concerns that had been emerging for him since he began to question the world around him and his place in it. McNeece elaborates, "Sociology provided a language and a theoretical framework that allowed me to give meaning to the social contradictions in my world. This included questions surrounding race, ethnicity, religion, and social class."

McNeece also learned scientific methodology and scientific objectivity (to the extent that objectivity is ever possible, he clarifies). These tools later qualified him to research a flying saucer cult for which he applied concepts like mystagogue, epistemic community, and seedbed subculture to inform his data. His findings helped to explain the religious belief system of the cult members;

what attracted them; what sustained the cult; and what ended it. Though the project lasted several years, Bill confirms its value as he learned about the power of religious belief and the reasoning people will use to support those beliefs.

At the same time, McNeece's study reawakened his long-standing interest in the religious world. "I was raised Catholic," he offers, "and I never assumed religion was destined to just go away as have many social scientists. Since it is an ongoing human activity, I feel it is worthy of study."

As a graduate student at Eastern Michigan University (EMU), Bill focused intently on classes that explored the relationship between religion and culture. At the same time, his longtime interest in photography was also stoked. Initially, this led to separate but parallel paths with Bill teaching both photography and sociology of religion classes concurrently. In addition, he took on photographic assignments that included shots of paintings and sculptures for artists as well as work as a photographer for the City of Detroit. Finally, he combined the two interests into visual sociological research.

McNeece notes that the primary goal of visual sociology is an understanding of the social world through description of cultural and social phenomena in ways that bring greater awareness to the viewer. "What makes images visual sociology is not their content alone but their context since the pictures usually need to be framed by text," he adds. As much as possible, visual sociology has to represent social reality and the pictures must be of sufficient quality to attract the viewers' interest. "Ideally," Bill suggests, "the pictures are made better by the time spent interacting with the groups they represent. This deepens an understanding of the subjects' social world and increases the likelihood of a more representative image."

In collaboration with a distinguished anthropologist, McNeece undertook an examination of the changing religious landscape in the United States that had resulted from immigration since the mid-sixties. As the project's director of photography, he researched his subjects and developed databases then visited each site to photograph the ritual activities he observed. So realistic were his images that admirers assumed he had taken a world tour. Bill enjoyed telling them that he shot all of the photographs locally, in the Detroit area.

His exhibit brought McNeese an invitation to Malaysia for a conference on religious and political conflict. There, he exhibited his photos and explained that research is essential to the photographic stories he tells. To accomplish his goals, he revealed, he first learns about the histories, cultures, norms, folkways, and discords that identify the groups he studies. Social conflict theory, rational choice theory, and feminism are just a few of the concepts he regularly applies in his research whether he is depicting America's new religious reality or religious pluralism worldwide.

Furthermore, Bill elaborated, the research requires a sociological perspective, that is, an understanding of the groups' behaviors from the point of view of the group itself. Often, tension between artistic quality and political content arises. Questions about the inclusion of religious leadership and/or adherents must be deliberated. Consideration of concerns about gender, ethnicity, and social class become significant. Interplay between the quality of the photograph and its contribution to greater understanding is another necessary concern. Most important, Bill emphasized, the text must be accurate and the people represented in the images, respected.

While he continued to work on the religious pluralism project, McNeece coordinated an endeavor titled, "Difficult Dialogues: New Learning across Race, Religion, Culture and Ethnicity." Since the primary goal was the development of critical thinking and articulation skills among students at the University of Michigan, the project presented a variety of perspectives on social issues in a historical and intellectual context. Significantly, the project sought to help students understand that differences on these perspectives matter. "The intent," Bill clarifies, "was not to achieve consensus or to 'feel good,' but to be able to talk with one another effectively and to hear each other truly and respectfully." The project also enriched dialogue between university administration and community leaders which ultimately engaged students in neighborhood affairs and community members in campus events. Bill most enjoyed the stimulating discussions he had with an array of fascinating speakers, community people, students, faculty members, and administration.

McNeece submits that sociology's most significant contribution to his personal life has been the ability it has given him to think critically. "I have found this skill useful in making decisions that were often contrary to mainstream viewpoints," he acknowledges. "Happily, these decisions have led me to places I would have never imagined." He discloses that the first home he and his wife bought was located in the city of Detroit. As that part of the city became increasingly integrated racially, many of his white neighbors moved out. Bill and his wife opted to stay. As a result, they became members of a church that embraced diversity and transcended distinctions between black and white. There, the labels were more likely to designate Haitian-American, Nigerian-American, African-American, German-American, and many others. As a result of Haitian-American friendships, the McNeece couple joined with others in the 1990s to create ongoing medical and educational support for Haiti.

Currently, McNeece is the vice president of Haiti Outreach Mission, an ecumenical and humanitarian NGO (non-governmental organization) that partnered with two Haitian priests, a Catholic and an Episcopalian. As conflicts have arisen between the priests and the groups that support the mission, Bill utilizes his knowledge of Weberian leadership types, bureaucracy, rationality, and authority to help resolve the issues. "Up to now," Bill claims, "the organization has maintained a traditional/charismatic structure.

We've now evolved to the point that we need a rational/legal style. I'm working as a member of the mission to accomplish this end."

McNeece's travels to Haiti also present him with opportunities to photograph the Haitian people in a more representative manner than the usual depictions of its hunger, illness, and devastation. His photos have been exhibited in art galleries around Michigan in an attempt to share social awareness.

Asked how he got his various jobs, McNeece responds: "Most of my career opportunities have come as a result of doing good work initially and having it recognized." On that note, Bill was recently given an archive at the University of Michigan Historical Library which will primarily contain his sociology of religious photographic research materials.

Overall, sociology has given Bill a life he enjoys: "I like the way things turned out," he admits. Although he may retire from part of his teaching load in a few years, he plans to continue his sociological photography and his work in Haiti indefinitely.

To sociology majors seeking advice, McNeece points out that for him, personally, sociology provided the tools to analyze his social experiences, expose some of the myths regarding human behavior, and help him find a path to follow. He believes a major in sociology can provide the same for others.

For more information about William McNeece and his work, please contact him by email at: McNee@umich.edu

T.D. (TOM) SCHUBY

It was inevitable that **Tom Schuby** would become a sociologist even before he knew anything about the discipline. As a student at a private suburban high school in the early 1960s, he was required to research a social problem of his choice for one of his classes. As he traversed the already-decaying industrial city of Detroit, he was struck by the vast discrepancies between opulent wealth and debilitating poverty. In one part of the city, Tom could see yachts docked behind mansions; just a few miles away, he was confronted with living quarters so bereft that the inhabitants lacked even electricity and basic plumbing. A dilapidated shack in which a family barely survived became the focus of Schuby's research which concluded with his prediction of impending rebellion. Much to the amazement of the city's government and business leaders, the Detroit riots exploded in the summer of 1967, a mere three years following Tom's astute forecast.

As an undergraduate student at Wayne State University (WSU) in Detroit, Tom's interest in the acquisition of wealth and the perpetuation of poverty grew even more pronounced as he explored topics such as social stratification and institutional racism in an urban environment. By 1970 in a study he titled "Process of Elimination," Tom correctly identified the impending expansion and gentrification of Detroit's medical center and the WSU physical campus by the twenty-first century. This process, he hypothesized would leave the poor, largely black community surrounding the university in decay and the people, without power. "Sad though some outcomes are," Tom observes, "the ability to use sociological research to forecast results can better prepare us to face our futures." During this time, Tom was introduced to classical theorists such as C. Wright Mills, G. William Domhoff, and Ferdinand Lundberg. In addition, Tom developed collegial relationships with many of his professors some of whom would talk with him for endless hours about the crucial issues of the time: civil rights, the war in Southeast Asia, and the consequences of the growing chasm between the wealthy and the poor. All of these experiences inspired his master's thesis in which Schuby investigated the means by which the 12 wealthiest, aristocratic families in Detroit acquired, maintained, and wielded their wealth, power, and privilege. Tom titled his thesis, "The Divine Right of Property" and later won the Graduate Student Competition Award from the North Central Sociological Association. This marked the beginning of his career as a sociologist.

At the same time that Tom was enamored with various aspects of social stratification, he was equally fascinated by statistics, methodology, and research practices. As a result, he immersed himself in classes like social statistics, political and economic sociology, and a seminar about the power structure of Detroit that would later prove vital to his research perspective. During this period, Tom also joined professional organizations such as the Michigan Sociological Association and the American Sociological Association. These organizations introduced Tom to a widening scope of professional contacts and opportunities that helped him launch his career.

One such opportunity was an invitation to join a group of students who were studying architecture at the University of Detroit and who wanted to build sorely needed low-income housing for the city. Schuby contributed to this team by first designing the questionnaire for the population that the architects had targeted, then by training the interviewers and helping to survey those people in the sample. Finally, he analyzed the data that enabled him to draw conclusions and make recommendations. Tom found that the skills he had used only abstractly in his classes indeed had practical application. He poured over his methodology textbooks to develop the questionnaire, his research notes to hone his interviewing techniques, and his statistics texts to compute correlations. Using his sociological perspective, Tom was able to "get inside the shoes" of those he queried — people who lived in roach- and rat-infested buildings in a neighborhood with no supermarkets, medical facilities, or entertainment opportunities. His sociological imagination allowed him to connect the circumstances of the individuals in this study to the economic, political, and historical structures of the city and even the nation. Schuby's findings then allowed the architectural students to design housing and a community that specifically met the needs of the people who would live there.

In analyzing the data, Tom unearthed a serendipitous finding that was supported by later literature. He determined that using community residents as interviewers dramatically increased the response rate from the sample population. (In this study, community interviewers obtained an 80% response rate while interviewers from outside the community procured responses from only 50% of the sample.) Although Schuby found that the research process can sometimes be repetitive and vexing, he enjoyed working as part of a team. Doing so allowed him to learn about architecture, urban geography, civil engineering, and other specialties from his team members while he hopes he contributed to their knowledge of sociology. In addition, Tom relished the opportunities that interviewing gave him; feeling honored when he was invited into the homes of his subjects, offered a beer or lemonade, and taken into their confidence. Tom muses, "I learned so much from people who are poor, illiterate, and disempowered; people whose everyday existence was so different from my own. I was repeatedly humbled." Most of all, however, Tom liked the surprise element of discovering meaningful data.

Beyond his job with the architectural team during his student years, Tom worked as a counselor to men transitioning from prison to life on the outside. There, he used the sociological perspective to step outside of his own familiar world and into those of the former inmates for an understanding of their emotions and the conditions they faced. In this position, he found it beneficial to understand group dynamics, social role theory, and the influence of social structures such as economics, law, education, race, class, and community on individual actions.

In this job, Schuby all-too-often experienced a sense of failure when men he had counseled were returned to prison or were killed on the commission of a crime. He was saddened and angered by the frequent short-sightedness of the staff, the public, and government officials. He felt constrained by the rigid and sometimes senselessly punitive rules that he was forced to implement. Nonetheless, Tom's enthusiasm would be restored each time one of his clients experienced success, whether it was to obtain and keep a job, return to school, reunite with family members, or simply stay out of trouble for an extended period of time.

While jobs in higher education were scarce by the time Tom completed his master's degree and even established sociologists were working in a variety of non-academic positions, Schuby persisted, knowing that his passion lay in teaching sociology. As such, his typical day would find him traversing the Detroit metropolitan area, teaching a variety of sociology courses concurrently at community colleges and major universities. His classes were filled with a diverse array of students that included streetwalkers, exotic dancers, undercover FBI agents, police officers, nurses, labor organizers, pastors, homemakers, and aspiring Wall Street executives. Oftentimes, any combination of these personalities would sit in the same room together as they explored controversial sociological topics. The knowledge about cultures, mainstream as well as subcultures and countercultures, that Tom had acquired in his own sociology classes helped him navigate the sometimes tense situations that ensued and opened the world of each of his students to those of the others.

"There's almost nothing that I don't like about teaching," Tom acknowledges, "though I'm sometimes exasperated when administration, with little classroom experience of their own, will impose rules and busy work that gets in the way of my ability to teach effectively. I also get frustrated with students who waste their money by coming to class unprepared. But then I see a light go on in a student's face that tells me they get a concept we're discussing and my love for teaching sociology is restored."

At the same time Tom enjoyed teaching, his interest in handicapping thoroughbred horse races had piqued and with it, the realization that his statistical research skills could lead to success in this endeavor. Tom soon discovered that the very foundations of logical theory-building and methodology as well as the ability to ascertain statistical validity could be applied to handicapping the races. In addition, he depends on the sociological perspective to "read between the lines"; to get into the minds of both the horse and the trainer to discern their intent. "For example," Tom states, "I first ask myself why this particular horse is in this particular race. Then I try to ascertain what the trainer is trying to achieve: do they want to win or are they simply exercising the horse that day." Over time, Schuby has managed to turn a leisure time activity into a lucrative source of income thanks to sociology.

Furthermore, by viewing the game of handicapping through the prism of sociological theory and insight, Tom regularly develops racing formulas that he sells to the public and publishes articles in popular horse racing magazines. "Such concepts as groupthink, cognitive dissonance, irrational belief, and social reality come alive at the track," Tom explains. As he applies terms like invulnerability, rationalization, self-censorship, and definition of the situation to the world of horse racing, he expands the uses of sociology. "I like to think," Tom quips, "that I'm introducing sociology to yet another audience, non-traditional as it might be."

Of late, Schuby has become known in racing circles as someone who thinks outside the proverbial box, looks first at the obvious and then delves beneath it, discards tedious rules, and designs the simplest approaches to the undertaking. Schuby enjoys the ability to see an educated guess or a speculation (a hypothesis) through proper implementation (methodology) produce an outcome (result) for which he is financially rewarded. He most regrets the public stereotype that those who bet on horse races are impulsive losers and notes that two of today's leading handicappers hold advanced degrees in literature from Ivy League schools. Tom is also frustrated at times with the public misperception that the horse racing business is exploitative. He admits that there are some who mistreat their horses in the same way some people neglect an expensive car or even a child but the vast majority, he contends, care deeply about the well-being of the horses.

Schuby is currently semiretired from teaching so spends some part of every day handicapping horse races and helping others learn his techniques for success. His average day consists of meeting with his classes in the morning and then advising students who want additional assistance. Then he turns to his "hobby-job," as he calls it, and downloads pertinent racing materials so he can study track conditions, the line-up for the next day's races, and the experts' odds on each of the horses. Tom also considers data on the horses as well as the jockeys. All of this research allows Tom to wager successfully...most of the time! Several times a month, Tom enjoys visiting one of the Detroit-area tracks. Other days, he works on developing racing formulas and writing articles for popular racing magazines.

In the future, Tom plans to write a 12-step program for handicappers in which he delineates strategies and techniques for handicapping with mastery. He intends to direct this product to the serious handicapper who wants to make a living at the endeavor as well as to the individual who just wants to spend an enjoyable day at the track.

If Tom could begin his career anew, he would double-major in both sociology and economics. Why? "Sociology," Tom states, "gave me both macroscopic and microscopic worldviews which have opened numerous doors for me, both professionally and personally. Combined with a major in economics, I could have pursued a career in personal finance, banking, or government service. I might have enjoyed directing foundations or being part of an academic think tank."

Tom offers the following advice to anyone who wishes to turn a hobby or a personal interest into a livelihood: treat it like a job. "It can still be a job you love," Tom insists, "but your hobby must be approached like a job if you are going to make money at it." He also suggests that a person be conscientious about transferring the skills they learn in school and from other jobs to those in the future.

Finally, Tom encourages a student who chooses a major in sociology to consider an additional major or the acquisition of a practical skill. While it is possible for a person to adapt sociology to a multitude of careers as Schuby's background so clearly demonstrates; Tom feels that, "Any additional training will only increase one's career options. Furthermore, sociology provides a greater understanding of world events which is indispensable in our fast-changing global economy and during times of political uncertainty."

To learn more about Tom Schuby and his work please contact him by phone at 586-859-5511 or by postal mail at 22013 Shore Pointe Lane, St. Clair Shores, Michigan 48080. Though Mr. Schuby prefers to correspond by mail, he nonetheless welcomes your inquiries.

7

SOCIOLOGISTS IN MEDICAL RESEARCH

We normally think of health and illness in biological terms, looking to the physical sciences for diagnoses and cures. Social factors, however, play significant roles in defining wellness and sickness. These factors influence who gets what kind of treatment and under what circumstances. Over time, infectious diseases have generally declined in the western world while degenerative diseases now comprise the major causes of death. Both, though, are related to socioenvironmental factors that are the focus of sociological inquiry. Social movements that demand the right to decent health care and wholesome surroundings are also part of sociology's domain.

In this vein, *Janet Hankin* describes her work as a medical sociologist starting with the 14-year period during which she studied the response to mental disorders in primary care settings. She then discusses her investigations of pregnancy outcomes among women living in poverty as well as another series of studies that focused on health disparities among African Americans, all conducted in the Detroit Metropolitan Area.

Diane Binson illustrates how the HIV/AIDS epidemic fueled her career as a medical research scientist in San Francisco, providing her opportunities to engage in meaningful work that promotes social justice.

Through their findings and recommendations to policy makers, both Dr. Hankin and Dr. Binson have been able to improve health status and health care delivery for thousands of individuals in their target populations.

JANET HANKIN

Though sociology courses taught in American high schools are rare, *Janet Hankin* was one of the fortunate few whose suburban Milwaukee, Wisconsin high school offered such a class. There, Janet immediately "fell in love" with the study of deviance, race relations, and social class inequality. Given her fascination with the topics that comprised sociology, she leaped at the opportunity to study the discipline further once she was admitted to Case Western Reserve University in Cleveland, Ohio. There, she pursued their Integrated Graduate Studies program, earning both her BA and MA in sociology during the next four years. Since Hankin enjoyed the classroom environment and the intellectual interchange that it provided, she initially thought she might teach after graduation. Janet's thesis advisor, however, recommended against it. She was too young and too short to be taken seriously, he claimed. Despite his dubious counsel, Hankin took a teaching position at a state college in Minnesota where she stayed for two years, preparing a daunting nine different courses each year. Although she vacillated between a doctorate in sociology and social work, she finally realized that she enjoyed teaching sociology and the opportunities it gave her to apply its theories to the real world. Given this, she pursued her PhD at the University of Wisconsin-Madison.

Hankin arrived at the university to discover that a new program in medical sociology had just been funded by the National Institute of Mental Health (NIMH). She soon learned that medical sociology is a specialization which places health and disease in a social, cultural, and behavioral context. A focus on medical sociology, therefore, would allow her to apply the perspectives, theories, and methodologies of sociology to human health and disease. Janet was immediately intrigued.

She quickly embraced this relatively new area of sociological study as an NIMH trainee and stayed in the specialty for all three years of her doctoral study. Her dissertation examined the use of health services among university students with psychological distress and supported her hypothesis that psychologically distressed individuals are higher users of general medical care than the nondistressed.

Just as Janet was finishing her dissertation, serendipity brought changes to her career plans. Though she had already accepted a position at the Johns Hopkins University to examine issues in health care reform, Hankin could not resist when she was invited to study health care utilization at a health maintenance organization (HMO) in Maryland. In the mid-1970s, she explains, the federal government had developed a keen interest in the operation of HMOs. Simultaneously, the NIMH furnished significant funds for research on mental disorders in primary care settings. The convergence of Janet's background in medical sociology, an HMO anxious to conduct studies, and government funding paved the way for a series of research projects that spanned a 14-year period.

"For some time," Dr. Hankin explains, "policy makers suspected that substantial numbers of patients who sought primary care also suffered from mental illness and psychiatric symptoms." Further, there was evidence that primary care providers failed to recognize these mental health disturbances in their patients. This, in turn, suggested that many patients with these problems would go untreated. Therefore, Dr. Hankin hypothesized that providing mental health care would offset or reduce use of nonpsychiatric services by the mentally ill.

Screening for depression in primary care settings, Hankin found that 21% of her sample demonstrated depressive symptoms though only 15% were recognized by health care providers. In fact, a follow-up study of those same depressed patients one year later revealed that half of them still suffered from depressive indicators.

At the time of this study, there was growing belief that the provision of mental health services would pay for itself as it would reduce the cost in other areas of health care delivery. Hankin tested this hypothesis and found a modest offset effect. On that basis; she recommended that health insurance have comparable coverage for physical and mental illnesses.

In 1986, as a "trailing spouse," Janet followed her husband to Detroit where she obtained a position as an associate professor at Wayne State University's School of Medicine in their Department of Obstetrics/Gynecology. There, she focused her efforts on improving pregnancy outcomes among women living below the poverty line. As such, she evaluated the impact of a program intended to improve access to and quality of prenatal care. In this program, low-income women who had recently delivered an infant themselves were trained to advocate for peers and then accompany them to the clinic for their prenatal visits. The program made a difference, Dr. Hankin is pleased to note. In one especially memorable case, a pregnant woman came to the clinic with her advocate and a translator, as English was not her native tongue. The woman's blood sugar reading was dangerously high. After four hours of waiting, the translator left but the advocate remained. The physician wanted to send the patient home because he was unable to communicate with her but the advocate intervened, refusing to give up until she found a pediatrician on staff who could speak the dialect of the pregnant patient. The pediatrician could explain the dangers of gestational diabetes in terms the patient could understand and the woman gratefully agreed to be admitted to the hospital. Thus, her life and that of her baby were saved.

In 1989, the U.S. Congress mandated that a label be placed on all alcohol beverage containers which warned of the dangers alcohol presents to pregnant women and their unborn babies. Previous studies had already established that birth defects, or Fetal Alcohol Spectrum Disorders, can occur if a woman drinks heavily while pregnant. When the legislature passed this law, they included funding to examine the impact of the warning label so Dr. Hankin oversaw a study of 21,000 pregnant African American women. The findings revealed that the warning labels had only a modest and short-lived influence on the amount of pre-natal drinking that occurred. One reason for the lack of impact, Hankin believes, was that the legislation did not mandate large print or icons on the warning label. Hankin would have liked to see a picture of a pregnant woman with a large red X, for instance. "People don't pay attention to text," she continues, "which is why American cigarette warning labels had less impact than those in Canada. Canadian labels on cigarettes show pictures of people in the intensive care unit because smoking has damaged their lungs."

Disappointing as the results of the study were, they led the research team to design a prevention program targeting women who drank heavily during their previous pregnancy. "Protecting the Next Pregnancy" identified as their target population women who drank at risk levels during their previous pregnancy. Using a clinical trial, 300 women were randomly assigned to either an experimental or a control group. The experimental group received an intensive brief intervention encouraging them to limit their alcohol intake considerably or to abstain completely. Women in the control group were given the standard clinical warning that they could have healthier babies if they cut back or stopped drink-ing during their pregnancy. Hankin's study followed the women for five years and determined that among the women who deliv-ered a subsequent infant, those in the experimental group had babies with longer gestations, higher birth weights, and higher scores on psychosocial motor and mental development measures.

Another of Hankin's projects focused on health disparities among African Americans in the Detroit Metropolitan Area. In collaboration with the Center for Urban and African American Health, she developed a core set of psychosocial and community measures for the research participants. "To study this issue successfully," Dr. Hankin explains, "I needed the means to assess racism, discrimination, coping, stressful life events as well as chronic strains, social networks, social support, self-reports of physical and mental health, neighborhood satisfaction, and attachment to the neighborhood." Hankin also created a neighborhood inventory that was used as a "windshield survey" to study the census tracts in which the participants resided. Trained observers then drove through these neighborhoods, documenting the available resources along with the barriers to adoption and maintenance of healthy lifestyles. They recorded, for example, whether the respondents had access to fresh fruit, vegetables, and safe places to exercise as well as the number of liquor stores, broken sidewalks, and fast food establishments. These measures were then provided to the team of researchers studying hypertension and salt sensitivity; breast cancer survivors' weight gain; and cardiac patients' rehabilitation experiences.

Hankin currently serves on a review team for the City of Detroit examining causes of infant deaths. Based on the team's findings, they will recommend changes that address these causes in attempts to reduce Detroit's infant mortality rate, which is currently one of the highest in the nation and comparable to that in many Third World nations. In a previous study, this team determined that some of the deaths were the result of unsafe sleeping practices and cribs that did not meet safety standards. Given this, the team recommended that free cribs, a video about the proper sleeping position, and training for new mothers be furnished in the postpartum units of hospitals. When the team confirmed that other infants died because the mother spaced pregnancies too close together, it recommended counseling regarding spacing between pregnancies. Other changes have included improved access to prenatal care, more high-risk fetal specialty physicians, and greater provision of social support.

As a medical sociologist working on interdisciplinary teams of psychologists, nurses, physicians, and social workers, Dr. Hankin is responsible for the design, implementation, and evaluation of the studies she undertakes. As such, she directs the sample selection, instrument development, training of interviewers, the data-collection process, data analysis, and the interpretation of results. Moreover, she supervises the interviewers, data entry personnel, and statisticians. Additionally, she translates the results of the studies for clinicians and policy makers. Ultimately, she oversees the evaluation process.

In all of these projects, Janet's sociological skills have been essential. Daily, her familiarity with certain sociological concepts underpins the success of her research. Social stress theories help her understand health disparities in minority group members. Labeling theory is crucial to understanding whether physicians perceive patients as suffering from psychological distress. Hankin's utilization studies apply the concept of the sick role to examine how patients behave when they have symptoms. The concept of illness behavior provides comprehension of the ways in which patients interpret and decide to act on their symptoms.

How has Dr. Hankin's career changed over the years? As Chair of Wayne State University's Sociology Department, she did more administrative work than she had in the past. This limited the amount of time she had for research. Even in this capacity, however, her background in sociology provided her with insights about human behavior helpful to managing a department of academics.

Without a doubt, Janet Hankin finds her career choice in medical sociology extremely fulfilling. From providing data that helps policy makers improve health status and health care delivery to recognizing psychological distress in patients to promoting better pregnancy outcomes, Hankin finds her work extraordinarily rewarding.

"The field, however, is not without obstacles," Hankin warns, "as health care providers often perceive medical sociologists to be spies and interlopers." In one case, for example, she was conducting participant observation research at an adolescent psychiatric ward. Her research ultimately resulted in a paper about the power of lower level personnel such as aides and nurses to resist implementation of a new treatment program. The paper was stolen from the psychiatrist's office and circulated among the "lower level personnel." They read the paper and were furious. Hankin had to appear at a staff meeting, explain her research, and "beg for forgiveness." As a consequence, her next project was restricted to reviewing patients' charts. "Far less controversial," Hankin smiles.

For those sociology majors considering medical sociology as a career, Hankin recommends a solid background in research skills, the ability to write technical papers well, and the knowledge that it is possible to sociologize *anything*!

To learn more about Dr. Janet Hankin and her work, please contact her by email at: ad4388@wayne.edu

DIANE BINSON

Equipped with her double major in math and biology from the University of Michigan (UM), **Diane Binson** returned to her hometown with plans to teach junior high school math. The year was 1965. The world around her was changing with frenetic speed and with it, Diane's personal world was transforming as well.

Binson had been raised in a safe, working-class neighborhood of Detroit; attended its public schools; obtained a fully-paid scholarship to college; and while she was an undergrad, supported herself with a job at a local grocery store not far from campus. During her four years at UM, President John F. Kennedy was assassinated and the Civil Rights Movement became the top story on the nation's radar screen. Diane still vividly recalls the front pages of *The Detroit Free Press* as they routinely exploded with coverage of young civil rights workers brutally killed in states like Mississippi, Alabama, and Georgia. She remembers stories, too, of black men lynched for supposed indiscretions to the white hierarchy of the caste system that still dominated the southern United States. There was also Viola Liuzzo, a white, middle-aged, wife and mother and an assembly-line worker in one of Detroit's many auto plants. Driven by her values to participate in the now-famous civil rights march from Selma to Birmingham, Alabama, she was viciously murdered while driving home with a black man following the protest.

"Exposure to those events began to severely erode my admiration for the United States," Diane muses. At the same time, she was learning about the insidious role of the United States in Vietnam and in other parts of the world.

Although Binson immersed herself in her new teaching job after graduation, she found herself increasingly distracted by the turmoil taking place all around her. Looking for answers, she enrolled at a local university in an evening class titled,

The Sociological Analysis of Deviant Behavior. Diane recalls, "To consider that deviant behavior was socially constructed was an awakening for me; to see deviance in the social context intrigued me. To understand that entire nations could be deviant made me want to expand my experiences; to discover other facts about the U.S. and the world."

This was only the beginning for Binson. Her intellectual curiosity stimulated, Diane finished her one-year teaching contract and hastily left Detroit for the east coast. There, she registered for more sociology courses that summer and then began another year of teaching math. Throughout that year, however, she found herself even more frustrated with teaching; with the confinement of the classroom; and the narrow scope of the curriculum. "It just wasn't enough," Binson concedes. Diane yearned to understand how other people lived and soon found other inquisitive, adventurous teachers with whom she would eventually travel. So it was that she became a math teacher by day; a factory worker by night until she had enough money to bankroll her ventures.

By the summer of 1967, she finally embarked; traveling by planes, trains, buses, and not infrequently hitch-hiking over the next year throughout Europe, the Middle East, and Asia. There, she took part in long, intense discussions with people who lived in those places and participated alongside them in their daily activities. "It was a kind of individualized community engagement and experiential learning course in world sociology," Binson reflects. "Connecting the experiences of so many different people and cultures to sociological concepts like imperialism, social conflict theory, and corporatism was definitely an enriching that experience gave more meaning to my graduate studies." As Diane interacted with peoples from so many parts of the globe, she remained captivated with and appreciative of their cultures, politics, economies, and how they all fit together. These experiences inspired her to broaden her education still further. Finally, she got serious about pursuing a doctorate in sociology. "That was over forty years ago," Binson ruminates, "and I must admit, I don't regret a moment of my choices. Sociology played a major role in developing my perspective on the world and my part in it. It turned my head around and opened up a lens to the world that still shapes my thinking today."

For the last 25 years, Diane has been a research scientist at the Center for AIDS Prevention Studies in San Francisco. In between, there were other jobs — secretary, survey interviewer, research assistant, and sociology professor, all of which brought Binson to her current position. Diane's introduction to professional survey research began as she was working on her doctoral dissertation. She had moved to Chicago a few years earlier and with finances running low, she took a job at a research center. Because the center was connected to the university she was attending, Diane was able to learn survey skills from the leading methodologists of that time. "Best of all, it was a chance for me to work on projects that made a difference; that mattered to me and to my desire for social justice," she acknowledges. Since 1985, the AIDS epidemic has been a driving force in Binson's research.

Dr. Binson explains that by 1981, AIDS (or GRID — Gay Related Immune Disorder as it was known then) had gained the attention of the press but the outbreak was totally (some argue purposely) ignored by the Ronald Reagan Administration. Reagan's Director of Communications, Pat Buchanan, publicly stated that AIDS was "nature's revenge against gay men." Not until 1987 did President Reagan even utter the word, "AIDS" publicly. By that time, 36,058 Americans had been diagnosed with the disease and 20,849 had died. In this milieu of political expediency and stigma, there was scant funding for the kind of health-related studies needed to ascertain patterns of sexual behavior among the U.S. population. Such studies would have tracked the likely projectile of the epidemic and might have saved lives, Binson observes angrily.

Yet, since no government agency had ever asked even basic questions about sexual behavior, it was impossible to know the number of individuals in the United States who were engaged in risky behaviors. Clearly, the need for information about sexual behavior among Americans was dire. Without it, programs that could curb the spread of AIDS were limited. In this context, Dr. Binson began her work in AIDS research.

Eventually, the federal government started to fund pilot studies focused on the human immunodeficiency virus (HIV) and HIV-related risk behaviors. Diane was still employed by the survey center in Chicago at that time and, as part of a team, designed a telephone survey that was conducted throughout the Chicago metropolitan area. "Here we were," Binson calls to mind, "persuading perfect strangers who just happened to answer their phones to answer rather pointed questions about their intimate practices!" She still remembers the reaction she received in 1986 at a national conference where she presented the findings of the research team: "I kept hearing a startled gush of voices in the audience followed by nervous giggles as I read some of the questions we had asked. I must admit it was exciting to be on the cutting edge of work I knew would someday have significant social consequences."

Research on the AIDS epidemic was a turning point in Diane's career as she is still, many years later, working in this area and continues to enjoy it immensely. With the likelihood of a vaccine that could eliminate HIV still years away, the focus remains on prevention. As such, she works daily with psychologists, anthropologists, and other sociologists of many stripes, along with epidemiologists and physician researchers. Together they concentrate their efforts on better understanding the social context of HIV and AIDs-related risks. They analyze data that will give rise to new prevention programs and interventions that address the ever-changing face of the epidemic and will ultimately control the incidence of HIV transmission.

Since it is crucial to the outcome of any research endeavor that findings be shared, Binson's work requires her to publish the results of her research in medical and other academic venues. In addition, she must frequently attend conferences where she is able to collaborate with other interested professionals throughout the world.

As much as Binson enjoys her work, she acknowledges that a career in sociological research is rife with twists and turns. The weeks and sometimes months it takes to write grant proposal requests for funding are often filled with anxiety. Will the ideas attract funding? Is the application clear? Have all the contingencies been considered? What is the budget? Then, once the proposal has been submitted, there is the inevitable wait while it is reviewed. That is followed by even more waiting to learn if the project will be financed. If it is not, the research team has to decide based on the reviewers' comments whether it is worthwhile to revise the grant application and resubmit it. All the while, work on already-funded projects continues: collecting data; working with colleagues to analyze findings and write articles; reading journal articles written by others; solving problems that arise with staff or with data collection and analysis; providing adequate attention to administrative details like budgets and timely reports to the funding source. All this is intermingled with travel to conferences and participation on review committees to evaluate the grant applications of other researchers. "There is never a dull moment in the life of a researcher," Diane smiles wryly. "But that's another aspect I like about this work."

In Binson's experience, careers are not usually planned several years in advance. She states, "I never thought I would end up conducting research on sexual behavior. It is not something I studied for or even remotely conceived as a possibility. Yet, here I am: thoroughly enjoying the work I do." She concedes that for some, having a plan to follow after graduation allows them to focus on their goals. Diane, however, studied the subjects that interested her. "This made the process mine," she explains. "It was more satisfying that way and certainly more fun." Despite this, Binson suggests that the path to career fulfillment probably lies between personal interests and tracking where the jobs are likely to be in the future.

For those considering a major in sociology, she recommends that they take courses in both qualitative and quantitative research methods. "I realize methodology is not as sexy a subject as deviancy, social problems, or urban sociology, for example. Even so, methodology can provide the fundamentals that will underpin an interesting and even lucrative career. Besides, if you apply those research techniques to issues that interest you, you can make the research process fun as well as useful."

As this book was going to the press, Dr. Diane Binson passed away peacefully at her home in San Francisco. Diane had many long-time friends and colleagues who would enjoy sharing information about her and her work with any reader who is interested. One such individual is Stuart Michaels. Dr. Michaels can be reached at Michaels-stuart@norc.org. In addition, Dr. William Woods worked directly with Diane as a medical researcher for many years and can be reached for comment at William.woods@ ucsf.edu

8

SOCIOLOGISTS IN ANIMAL WELFARE, ANIMAL RIGHTS, AND ANIMAL STUDIES

Although sociologist only began to systematically examine the bonds humans share with other species during the last 30 years, this fascinating area of interest gained accelerating momentum by the early 21st century. Not only did university departments start to offer classes in animal–human studies, but books on this subject steadily proliferated. Moreover, major professional affiliations like the American Sociological Association (ASA) approved entire sections and encouraged conference sessions on animal-related topics. The Animals & Society Institute (ASI) helped university departments develop majors and minors in this area of study and continues to provide scholarships for graduate students who conduct research on the animal–human bond. All of these occurrences give academic credibility to this area of study.

Sociologists tend not to research the behaviors of other animals *per se* but in relation to human contact. As such, we look at our relationships at interpersonal, cultural, and institutional levels.

The two sociologists in this section address animal studies, animal welfare, and animal rights in different ways. *Adam Ortberg*, for example, is often described as an "in-the-trenches foot soldier." Using social awareness and tactics like "name and shame,"

he works with the Farm Animal Reform Movement (FARM),
going underground at times to expose wrong-doing. In addition,
Ortberg founded Defending Animals Today and Tomorrow
(DARTT), an organization committed to ending the suffering
of animals in slaughterhouses, research laboratories, and other
exploitative industries.

Trained in law as well as sociology, *Bee Friedlander* chose her
career in animal welfare and advocacy when she joined a small
group of like-minded lawyers to establish the Michigan Attorneys
for Animals, the first association of its kind in the nation. Today,
Friedlander is the managing director for ASI which works on an
international scale to promote awareness of the animal–human
bond through academic research.

ADAM ORTBERG

"It doesn't take a sociology major or even a college degree to see the vast inequities that exist in our world," contends **Adam Ortberg**. From the time he was a small boy, Adam was exposed to multiple disparities and injustices even in his personal environment. He looked on helplessly as his mother was repeatedly passed over for promotions and denied jobs simply because she was a woman. He observed bullies on the playground target minor differences in their victims then play upon them to conceal their own insecurities. As he walked through the cities where he lived, he could see the ubiquitous McMansions clustered together in one section while another neighborhood would be riddled with destitution and crime. Even on his dinner plate, Ortberg witnessed the end results of suffering and human arrogance.

As a teenager, Adam became increasingly troubled by these varied forms of exploitation and oppression. Although he couldn't put words to it then, he eventually realized he was witnessing institutionalized discrimination, hierarchy, and socialization so deeply ingrained in our social system that most people were unaware of their presence. Yet, these conditions plagued Adam. He could not, indeed, would not turn his head and walk away. He wanted to understand the causes and consequences of these wrongs but more than that, he wanted to eradicate them entirely.

These experiences and goals initially brought Ortberg to Notre Dame de Namur University (NDNU) located near San Francisco. He realized his goals of a just world would not be easy to achieve and that he needed a college degree to give him credibility. He first declared philosophy as his major, assuming this discipline would develop his critical thinking skills. However, when he learned of a new major that explored the bond humans share with other animals, he was enthralled. The classes offered in this Sociology: Animals in Human Society major helped Ortberg begin to draw connections between racism, sexism, social class elitism, and speciesism. In fact, it seemed to Adam that every form of oppression he had ever observed was inevitably linked to others in an insidious snare of entanglement.

In 2005, Ortberg became the first student to graduate in the Sociology: Animals in Human Society major. As a parting gift to the sociology department, he arranged for the university library to regularly receive periodicals from a variety of organizations dedicated to animal rights and their welfare on a permanent basis. Adam explains, "This way, more people can have the information necessary to make informed decisions."

Upon his return home to the Washington, D.C. area, Adam accepted a position with Farm Animal Reform Movement (FARM), a national nonprofit organization founded by a Holocaust survivor who dedicated his life to the well-being of nonhuman animals. According to Ortberg, FARM investigates factory farms and slaughterhouses to expose the atrocities committed not only on the meat-producing animals but on the human workers and consumers as well. In addition, Adam states with admiration, FARM actively promotes a plant-based diet. When asked why he thinks FARM offered him the job, he responds modestly, "Besides my major, they liked my enthusiasm for the work."

In a typical work week that generally consists of about 70- hours, Ortberg works with an international base of volunteers and paid personnel. Together, they create and place billboards and flyers in strategic locations to expose the lives of most farm animals around the globe. He designs a variety of websites and works on mail campaigns to promote healthy, meat-free lifestyles. In addition, Adam helps to organize a yearly conference that draws over a thousand participants. "This is the only conference that allows all voices of the animal rights movement to be heard so long as no one advocates injury to a living being whether human or non-human," Adam points out. He is currently working with FARM to develop and implement outreach to

Spanish-speaking communities so they will be informed about the sources of their food supplies as well as a vegan way of life.

"This job with FARM seems like it was custom-made for me," Adam states fervently. "It allows me to work with like-minded people with the same sensibilities and goals that I have. I get to put my values, the theories I learned, and my commitments into action. Since FARM has been a driving force in the animal rights campaign for almost forty years, they have had time to hone the strategies and tactics necessary to make them effective social change-makers. As a result, I've been given a remarkable chance to gain insight into the operation of a successful non-profit and an invaluable set of tools needed to advocate on behalf of non-human animals. This is definitely the place I want to be." Furthermore, Adam enjoys the camaraderie he and the other staff share. He remembers with fondness how the others eagerly helped him refine his less-than-polished web design skills when he first came to FARM.

In addition to his full-time employment at FARM, Adam has co-founded a grassroots, animal rights collective that operates primarily in Washington, DC and Baltimore, Maryland. Defending Animal Rights Today & Tomorrow (DARTT) focuses on combating all forms of animal abuse and neglect inherent in social systems based on oppression and injustice. Adam clarifies that DARTT is dedicated to the philosophy that nonhuman animals should have the right to live free from human exploitation whether in the name of science, sport, exhibition or entertainment, fashion or food. Instead, the organization believes that each individual nonhuman and human animal should be able to live in harmony to the full capacity of their nature. As animal liberationists, Adam and his colleagues feel that, in the quest for profit, monolithic corporations treat animals as commodities that are incapable of thought, emotions, pain, or suffering. Further, DARTT members contend that these economic institutions collaborate with governments for subsidies and protection; subsequently oppressing all animals, human and otherwise.

DARTT uses a variety of tactics to provide a voice for the animals. In addition to leafleting and staffing information tables at appropriate venues, they write letters, send emails, make phone calls, and establish websites to advance their positions. When they are not successful with those techniques, they will organize and protest regularly in front of corporations and businesses that profit from the exploitation of animals. Ortberg explains, "DARTT applies direct pressure to the bottom line of these companies, hitting them in the wallet, so to speak, by encouraging consumers to boycott these enterprises and the employees to question their employers' practices." Some of these strategies Adam has modified from the Saul Alinsky style of community organizing that have been utilized by social justice luminaries such as Cesar Chavez and Reverend Jesse Jackson. Adam stresses the importance of being courteous and well-informed when participating in public outreach. When targeting large corporations with demonstrations and protests, however, he insists that persistence is even more crucial.

Recently, Adam formed another group that he calls the Open the Cages Alliance (OTCA). By joining with like-minded coalitions at conferences and special events, OTCA intends to raise public awareness and inspire activism that will ultimately eradicate not only speciesism but sexism, racism, social class elitism, and environmental destruction. Understandably, Ortberg describes the life of an activist as "busy, busy, busy!"

Though fulfilling on a personal level, Adam confirms that speaking out against an established system has its price. He has been arrested many times by local law enforcement and by the FBI Joint Terrorism Task Force for defending his principles. "It is frustrating to be continuously subject to fallacious charges, illegal strip searches, and malicious prosecution all because we want to exercise our first amendment right for the protection of animals,"

Ortberg admits. "Over and over again, I see Mills' power elite theory come to life as government and law enforcement collude to protect multi-billion dollar corporate interests."

Partly for these reasons, Adams is currently pursuing a career as a paralegal. "If nothing else, I'll have the legal knowledge to defend my rights and those of my colleagues against these forces," he smiles wryly.

Working with FARM, DARTT, and OTCA, Adam uses the sociological perspective and the sociological imagination as he grapples daily with an understanding of other points of view as well as the relationship between private and public issues. In addition, his knowledge of collective behavior, types of social movements, resource mobilization theory, propaganda tactics such as transfer and testimonials, and familiarity with the stages comprising the life course of social movements are all intrinsic to Ortberg's routine efforts. Furthermore, he must also be aware of the role symbols play in his interactions with others. To Adam, for example, a filet mignon represents the unnecessary killing of an innocent animal while another individual might see that same piece of meat as a sign of economic prosperity. Moreover, Adam finds his comprehension of social psychological terms such as group consciousness, group polarization, self-serving biases, and groupthink important to his interpersonal communication which is the core of effective organizing.

Adam staunchly maintains that the grassroots approach to social activism on which his groups' methods are founded is the ideal way to put sociological vision into practice. "Consistently working with members of local communities on issues that concern us all keeps me focused on the wellbeing of the very individuals I'm trying to help, both human and non-human."

Too often, he argues, academics can get comfortable in their offices behind their computer screens. In doing so, they lose sight of the social issues they analyze and the people affected by the policies. Like Karl Marx, Ortberg believes that sociologists must be more than mere observers; in fact, more than even participants. Instead, sociologists must also be social change-makers and visionaries. "Sociology provides the necessary path," he claims, "only the will to take it is required."

In the future, Adam plans to continue his commitment to eliminating exploitation and promoting justice. He recognizes a new social conscience will not develop overnight. He is optimistic, however, that the majority of people, once they are exposed to the underbelly of society with the dreadful suffering that takes place in feed lots, slaughterhouses, fur farms, and laboratories will open their hearts and minds to the plight of living beings, whether human or not. In this pursuit, activists will carry on the slow process of bringing the cycle of violence, inequity, and oppression to a grinding standstill.

Adam takes his cues from history. "Today," he states, "we look at such horrific acts as slavery as archaic, barbaric, and uncivilized. But it has taken a long time to reach this point. I suspect it will take even longer before we see our current treatment of non-human animals the same way." Adam also points out that, historically, the majority of social change has come from grassroots activism, whether it was the formation of labor unions, the quest for women's right to vote, or the acquisition of basic civil rights for people of color. So, too, he believes, the struggle for the rights of animals will come from communities of compassionate people who recognize that the status quo is no longer acceptable.

Adam encourages students in any major; indeed, people of all persuasions to look inward and find what it is in their society that makes them angry, disgusted, or disappointed. "Then channel those emotions into positive energy," he urges. "There are local groups that are already in existence all over the world addressing every conceivable social concern. Find out more about them. Join the groups with which you resonate and get involved in generating the social change you want. Stand up to those responsible for the problems they create and foster."

Ortberg recommends that students consider a major in sociology only if they are not satisfied with simply reading about the world and are not content with life just the way it is. "If, however, a student looks forward to involvement in their community, struggling for their beliefs, and working for the betterment of all living beings or even a segment thereof," he concludes, "then sociology can provide the vehicle to make this possible."

To learn more about Adam Ortberg and his work, please contact him by email at: veegun@speakup.org or by phone at 202-596-9945.

BEE FRIEDLANDER

Both of *Bee Friedlander's* parents were college educated professionals — her mother was a social worker and her father practiced
law. Given this, there was never a question that Bee, too, would
graduate from college. There was never any discussion or pressure; it was just assumed. Upon her acceptance to Ohio State
University, she immediately declared sociology as her major. Why
sociology? Bee recalls she was somewhat of a nonconformist even
in high school. Further, she was fascinated by every facet of
human behavior. Most of all, she wanted to challenge the status
quo, debate weighty issues, and participate in long discussions
about ethical concerns. Sociology allowed her to do so. Though
one of her most memorable projects examined the role of women
in rock 'n' roll and another compared the behavior of men and
women in public restrooms, Bee's favorite classes forced her to
rigorously analyze the social problems of the modern world.

Upon graduation, Friedlander opted for law school though she
was accepted in a master's program for sociology as well.
Traditionally, law had been the domain of men but the times were
changing and more women were entering legal profession. On
a pragmatic note, the three-year law school program appealed to
her while idealistically she believed that, as a lawyer, she could
enact social change that would impact the world. Her decision —
law versus sociology — was not easy, however, and she still
occasionally thinks she should have pursued the latter. Sociology
is, after all, where her heart lies.

Following law school, Friedlander spent several years providing
legal assistance for the City of New York's Department of
Housing Preservation and Development (HPD); the Michigan
Prison Legal System (MPLS); and the United Auto Workers Legal
Services Plan (UAWLSP). In all of these positions, Bee found her
sociological toolbox valuable.

In New York City's HPD, for example, she helped clients who represented over 150 different cultures so had to be familiar with such sociological concepts as ethnocentrism, symbolic interactionism, norms, and customs. In addition, her understanding of alienation, Taylorism, and the iron cage helped her survive the inevitable office politics of a bureaucracy.

As an inmate advocate for MPLS, Friedlander regularly implemented many of the observational and interviewing techniques she learned in her sociology classes. Moreover, her interpersonal skills provided her with the ability to negotiate the tricky fine lines between the prisoners, guards, and prison officials. Bee consistently referred to terms such as differential association, formal authority, and bureaucratic ritualism to effectively perform her job as a lawyer inside a prison. Her work with the UAWLSP sharpened her observations of the social class structure in the United States, the relative social status of professional versus manufacturing employment, and perhaps most interesting to Bee, the fact that occupational status and income are not necessarily congruent.

While Friedlander thoroughly enjoyed transforming the issue facing a client, whether a low-earning immigrant, prisoner, or an assembly-line worker, into a legal construct and then solving the client's problem, she eventually felt boxed in by the legal profession. "I remember thinking toward the end of my career as an attorney," she reveals sadly, "that I had spent most of my time arguing over money."

Although her law degree and legal experience would have proven valuable in the rapidly-growing field of animal law, Bee was forced to acknowledge her disenchantment with the legal profession as a whole. After much thought, she decided to incorporate her sociology background with her passion for animals and obtain the additional schooling necessary to manage nonprofit organizations. At that point, she enrolled in a certification program in nonprofit sector studies where her coursework taught her about grant-writing, fundraising, volunteer management, and theories of leadership. Bee suspects that, except for the business and financial material, she grasped the concepts of nonprofit management so quickly because they are similar to those she learned as a sociology major.

Her year of classes culminated in a three-month-long internship and she chose to work with the Animal Legal Defense Fund (ALDF) in Northern California. "I was fortunate to intern with this group," Friedlander reflects. "I was looking for a chance to make my activities meaningful and ADLF provided this."

For about four years after receiving her certificate, Bee gained more practical experience and enlarged her network of contacts in the animal advocacy and care field by volunteering with a variety of organizations. She also remained active with Attorneys for Animals and the Animal Law Section of the State Bar of Michigan, two advocacy groups she helped to create when she was actively practicing law. During that time, Bee was invited to join the board of directors for the ASI. Friedlander states, "I learned a lot in this period; the most significant lesson being that we need to view efforts on behalf of animals as part of a larger social justice movement. It's crucial to work on 'big picture' issues at the same time we help individual animals in such ways as cleaning litter boxes and mucking stalls. To me, this is the sociological imagination in practice."

Three years later, Bee accepted the position of managing director for ASI where she remained for about seven years. Unlike the legal positions that she obtained by answering advertisements, her job with ASI resulted because she was serving on the organization's board of directors when the position was created.

As the managing director, Friedlander handled a multitude of responsibilities ranging from administration to the promotion of ASI's mission and image. "Since we were a small though international organization, I had to become somewhat of a generalist," she admits. Bee also had to sharpen some of her existing skills and develop others especially in the area of technology. Yet, the variety and the opportunities provided by the challenges were some of the aspects she enjoyed most about this position.

Her day generally began with a review of the finances from which, with the aid of a bookkeeper, she prepared a report at the end of each month. From there, she would often engage in some sort of relationship-building, perhaps with a board member, a key employee, or a group of volunteers. She would often spend her lunch hour grappling with a new computer program or responding to emails and phone messages. The afternoon would typically find Friedlander researching or writing a grant; composing letters of appeal to ASI's constituency; identifying prospects for potential contributions; or working with staff to market the organization's programs and reach new audiences. Her day was likely to end with more relationship-building whether she was coordinating the work of her staff or stewarding donors. "Underlying the accomplishment of these endeavors was the need to comply with the plethora of legal requirements for operating a business," Bee notes. "Even more important was the ability to communicate effectively with a wide array of people about our concern for the well-being of animals."

While no longer the managing director for ASI, Friedlander still orchestrates the Rapid Response Program (RRP) for the organization. This program, Bee explains, is predicated on the AniCare model, which is a psychological treatment plan designed specifically to assess and treat people who abuse animals. While the major thrust of AniCare is to train therapists who will utilize this model, Rapid Response expands this outreach to include the criminal justice system and the general public. RRP does so by first identifying cases of animal abuse most amenable to AniCare's treatment. It educates the public through the media while urging police and prosecutors to take animal abuse seriously. Before an individual is sentenced RRP communicates with judges, attorneys, and probation officers to recommend that AniCare's psychological treatment be ordered. "It is the opportunity to work on change-making programs like this as well as the chance to work alongside people whose values I share that makes this job so unique," Bee asserts.

Sociological concepts like the animal–human bond, cruelty–compassion link, and those that define the entanglements of oppression and domination all comprise Friedlander's normal vocabulary as she informs the human world about other species. Moreover, she utilizes concepts such as perception, emotions, assertion, and conflict negotiation when she finds it necessary to mediate in the occasional rivalries that take place between animal advocacy groups. Furthermore, her knowledge of group behavior, social structures, and group decision-making also helps her understand the human behaviors with which she works every day.

Bee admits she is sometimes frustrated by the lack of financial resources at her disposal. Yet, she enjoyed her job as ASI's managing director and now with their RRP. "I believe I truly found my professional and personal niche in helping animals," she observes.

If she were to start her career over again, Bee would definitely choose sociology for her undergraduate major as it provided her with such a broad backdrop for all of her other choices. If she did enter the legal profession, she knows with certainty she would practice animal law.

As for advice to fledgling sociology majors, Friedlander suggests that they find an area of the discipline about which they are intellectually curious, that provides flexibility they can transfer across the career spectrum, and one they will be able to incorporate into the larger social fabric. "Among other opportunities," Friedlander concludes, "sociology has given me the ability to think deeply about how people relate to animals, the different relationships we have with them, and the context in which to view my own love for animals as part of a large social movement."

To learn more about Bee Friedlander and her work, please contact her by email at: beefriedlander@yahoo.com.

9

SOCIOLOGISTS IN RELIGION

For many, religion gives meaning to life; provides release from daily challenges; offers individuals a sense of identity; and equips society with a moral code. Religion is a cultural universal and a human activity so is, therefore, of interest to sociology. Sociologists want to know how religion affects the behaviors of adherents as well as nonbelievers; how it shapes the overall culture in which it functions; how religion supports and is supported by the other social institutions; and how its belief systems respond to external forces like social change.

In her account, **Danica Wise Hill** shares how sociology helps her in her ministry, using a tapestry as a metaphor to explain the complex relationships that form the human fabric.

DANICA WISE HILL

Danica Wise Hill was initially attracted to psychology because she finds people so interesting and counseling seemed like a personal way to minister pastoral care in the church. It only took one sociology course however, for her to realize that sociology is a means of looking at these complex beings writ large. "Individuals," Danica observes, "are complicated and profound in their own right, but when we examine people in fellowship contexts we see a tapestry of relationships. Each thread is bound up with so many others that it is nearly impossible to appreciate a single thread apart from the whole fabric." Reflecting the theories of social psychologist, George Herbert Mead, she continues, "I've found it is not possible to extricate the individual from the group. We are all social beings. To understand the 'I', we must also understand the 'we'."

Danica admits she found her way to this point by stumbling around, figuratively stubbing her toe a few times, giving up, praying for direction, and then starting again. By the time she graduated, she had a major in sociology combined with a concentration in Christian ministry and several psychology classes to her credit. She had already determined she did not want a career in mental health. So, desperately unemployed and without a plan, she took a few jobs in preschool teaching. Although she quickly discovered that preschool teaching is poorly paid and garners little respect, Danica enjoyed creating curricula that spurred the cognitive and emotional growth of the children. Yet, she was more interested in the big picture of their self-concept development and the manner in which the educational environment, their families, and other agents of socialization influenced their identity formation.

As a childcare director, Danica was responsible for training and supervising teachers, coordinating with parents on behavioral and developmental issues, and complying with licensing requirements. "In this capacity," Danica states, "An understanding of the interplay between social institutions, the prevailing personality of various cultures, norms, and political ideologies helped me understand why an individual child thinks, feels, behaves, and then makes the choices that he or she does. Knowing the 'why' behind the behavior enabled me to know 'how' to respond as well as 'how' the individual can change or mature within and apart from his or her social constructs." Her familiarity with the sociological imagination as well as various kinds of group behaviors along with the generalized other and the looking-glass self helped Danica draw these connections.

Because the national economy rapidly accelerated its downward spiral and especially affected for those with soft science majors, Danica continued to find her career progress stunted. Just to sustain herself and pay her student loans, she worked alternately for a number of years in food service, retail, manufacturing, and clerical administration. At the same time, Hill started and closed three different businesses.

"It was so frustrating," Danica admits. "I had enough sociological insight to see patterns but with no training in business, I could not benefit from those same patterns when I detected them. Adding a few business classes to my undergraduate curriculum might have helped me immensely in those ventures." Even more significantly, she observed that familiarity with the local culture and the state of the larger marketplace has as much bearing on the success of a business as traditional concerns like advertising budget, accounting practices, and customer contact. Danica had moved from the subculture of the San Francisco Bay Area where she was raised to a very different one in the Bitterroot Valley of Montana and then to Portland, Oregon. While she turned to such sociological concepts as social norms, folkways, and mores along with the ecological, functionalist, and social conflict theories to explain the variations, she still found acclimation difficult.

Though Danica managed to support herself for several years with this parade of transitory jobs along with her attempts at business start-ups, they all failed to gratify her on a deeper emotional, self-actualized level. The rumbling dissatisfaction that she experienced along with the four years she had spent obtaining her undergraduate degree motivated her to seek greater fulfillment from her career. Following much prayer for direction, she entered and successfully graduated from seminary school.

Presently working with a church and diocese in Oregon, Danica explains that she views her spiritual work through a sociological lens: "Sociology helps me navigate the Church tapestry so I can reduce tensions, bring people to reconciliation, and teach godly relationship principles within the Church." She uses the theories of Maslow, Erickson, and to a lesser extent Jung, to gain insight into relations between Church members that will then inform her own responses.

In a normal week, Danica trains, mentors, and tutors members of her church and chairs a variety of committees. She participates in ministries to teens and assists youth leaders in piloting their own groups. In addition, she plans, staffs, and coordinates retreats and trains acolytes along with lay Eucharistic ministers. In the past, she served as a delegate at diocesan conventions, taught Sunday school to teens and adults, preached to the parishioners occasionally, and advised the youth drama team.

The most stressful part of her position in the church is the attendant role confusion. She finds questions about authority — who has it; how it should be wielded and to what extent; how others view it — can easily cause frustration among people trying to work together if the perceptions differ. "In some positions, I am the authority," she explains. "In others, I am the subordinate. Either is fine with me but the uncertainty is sometimes exasperating." Danica submits that although power vacuums can be dangerous, confusion about power is equally so. Moreover, she believes that in this post-modern period, more role confusion will be engendered in the workplace and that societies will eventually have to address this lack of clarity. For now, concepts such as anomie, power versus authority, and role expectation provide her with some direction.

Regardless of the job challenges, Danica finds her greatest delight in helping someone attain their full potential and function without her assistance. "That," she emphasizes, "is my goal." She speaks proudly of a 16-year-old girl whom she mentored from timidity to confident command of the youth drama team. From the growth of individuals like this young woman into healthy, functional entities Danica can ultimately observe transformations in the groups to which they belong. She explains, for example, that the role of the acolytes she trained is not really necessary to the events that take place at the altar. However, by valuing and nurturing the contributions these young people make, the Church demonstrates appreciation, develops their self-confidence, and provides a sense of inclusion. On a larger scale, the service provided by these acolytes has an even greater effect on the congregation. When the adult members see the acolytes' contributions as normal and meaningful parts of their own worship, they extend the circle of inclusion. "As such, everything is interconnected," Danica concludes, "and any success, even one that may seem insignificant at first, has far-reaching ramifications."

Over the years, Danica has used a variety of means to obtain the multitude of jobs she held after completion of her bachelor's degree. In some cases, she followed the traditional route of responding to employment ads in newspapers and on-line. For others, she relied heavily on her network of family and friends to recommend her. Most of all, the reputation she established for herself with regard to the quality of her work and her character was immensely beneficial in securing all her jobs, especially those with the church. She muses, "I doubt if anyone would have recommended me if they didn't perceive me as a fast learner and a conscientious worker. It has been worth my effort to build this reputation."

Danica's short-term career plans are directed at serving others in a religion, theology, or pastoral studies department at a college where she can teach in an adjunct capacity or work in campus ministry. She admits, though, that she is also interested in developing parish-based spiritual formation groups and retreat programming. Whatever path she chooses, however, Danica Wise Hill wants to influence the next generation of Church leaders in order to "preserve what has historically been God-pleasing and to correct erroneous doctrine that has crept into the Church."

Asked to ponder what she might do differently if she could plan her career again, Danica replies she would devise a long-range strategy before her first day of class. Then, instead of accumulating a debt of $36,000 in student loans while she spent six years completing her coursework, she would have attended classes on a part time basis while working at a job or at least an internship related to her chosen field. That way, she speculates, she would have had a stable employment history and her career underway by the time she graduated. "It is a beautiful thing to dream big and to pursue those dreams," she cautions, "but those dreams will sour quickly if they don't produce meaningful work that pays enough to cover expenses soon after graduation." She believes this counsel is more relevant to those in the soft sciences than for those in the skills-based or hard sciences because "there is no tangible product when the vocational outcome is people and our culture is product-preoccupied."

Therefore, she encourages any college student to have a back-up plan whether it is a way to use their degree in a manner that produces a concrete outcome or a secondary skill on which they can depend while building their career.

"No one," she adds, "steps off the stage with diploma in hand ready to function as a research scientist, university professor, or therapist. Reaching any worthwhile goal requires the input of time, energy, and some dues-paying." So, while the diploma-toting undergraduate expends the elements necessary to achieving their dreams, Danica continues, he or she can also earn a living and pay their bills using practical abilities if they've acquired them. "Nothing crushes dreams so easily and resoundingly as financial ruin but some early and realistic strategic planning can make those dreams possible," she concludes.

To learn more about Danica Wise Hill and her work, please contact her by email at: twolamps@brightblades.com

10

SOCIOLOGISTS IN TECHNOLOGY AND THE ENVIRONMENT

Few developments in the last millennium have brought such radical changes to our social core as computer technology and global warming. The switch to an information-based, global, service economy has left tens of millions unemployed yet has created new, less physically demanding, and more mind-expanding jobs for others. At the same time, global warming has contributed to mass migrations world-wide as well as to the demise of rainforests, oceans, and tundras once inhabited by unique flora, fauna, and human cultures.

Sociologists agree that any major changes in technology or in our physical environments will eventually, like a game of dominoes, require attendant shifts in social structures and individual lives.

Because of the powerful symbiosis between humans, technology, and nature, sociologists are among those in the scientific community who are exploring ways to contribute to a better quality of life worldwide.

In this section, ***Eileen Monti*** depicts how she assisted journalists faced with job loss when traditional print was replaced by digital means. Further, she notes how a newly created job as a technology specialist helped her realize a fresh and far more satisfying life for herself.

Lakeshia Freedman relates the way her initial introduction to the underwater world, through video technology, inspired her interest in environmental studies and how a serendipitous turn of events made her a sociology major. Freedman takes readers through her series of careers from energy specialist to director of a nonprofit green trust, each one bringing her closer to preserving the natural settings she loves.

EILEEN MONTI

For **Eileen Monti**, her sociology major has acted as a GPS (Global Positioning System) through myriad and wide-ranging careers, giving her an understanding of cultures, large organizations, small groups, social systems, and interpersonal relations.

When she was in high school, it was assumed that if a woman had a career at all, she would be a teacher or a nurse. Neither of these choices appealed to Eileen though she was interested in pursuing some sort of "helping" profession. Social work was emerging as an alternative, so her initial plan as she entered California State University, Northridge was to major in sociology and minor in social work with an emphasis on small group theory. Over the next three-and-a-half years, her attraction to social work waned, but she became increasingly enthralled with sociology. Through this discipline, she discovered a systematic, logical base for understanding people across cultures, social classes, and generations that she has been able to apply to every one of her jobs.

Though Monti's resume now includes a plethora of occupations, jobs in general were scarce when she graduated. With little work experience, she was rejected for job after job. After a brief stint as a middle school teacher, Eileen spent two years as a Peace Corps volunteer in the Philippines.

Up to that point, her cultural context had been limited to the United States but in the Philippines, she had the chance to field test what she had learned in her sociology classes about culture, functionalism, ethnocentrism, and xenophobia.

When Eileen arrived in the Philippines, the Vietnam War was raging. "Culture shock hit me hard," Monti recalls. "Boarding the plane in San Francisco, I was an activist who had openly protested the policies of the U.S. government in Southeast Asia. Stepping off that plane, I was greeted by Filipino students who were protesting against *me* because I represented to them the very government that I opposed!" It took her sociological imagination for Eileen to understand and survive those events.

Eileen submits that the Peace Corps volunteers were actually a living experiment in small group theory so she was able to study them objectively as a participant observer. Eileen was especially interested in how the group responded to their treatment as pariahs in their host country. She noted that after the first year, the volunteers had split themselves into two camps: those who became integrated into the Filipino culture and those who reacted defensively by stalwartly supporting U.S. policies. "The knowledge I had gained about these phenomena in my sociology classes," she states, "helped me ward off paranoia and weather the experience."

Upon her return to the United States, Monti took a position with the U.S. Civil Service, later named the U.S. Office of Personnel Management (OPM). Her background with the Peace Corp benefited her immensely as it automatically gave Eileen preference over other job applicants but it was really her sociology major and the experience of working in another culture that qualified her for the personnel position. Once on the job, she was forced to make a paradigm shift from the small groups with which she was accustomed to the colossal bureaucracy of the federal government. Her studies in organizational behavior and social network analysis helped her understand both the formal and informal structures of the various agencies. Further, she realized that although bureaucracies have rigidly codified procedures, the *actual* work gets done through informal channels and social connections. Monti eventually moved from OPM to the Army Corps of Engineers. Though she was doing the same type of job, she soon understood that the agencies had two distinctly different subcultures and she would need to use another communication style to function in this new environment. Once again, her background in sociology helped her identify the problem and make the necessary shifts in her approach.

After 10 years with the federal government, Eileen left the rigidity with which she never felt completely comfortable and, along with her husband, founded their own desktop publishing business. She found those exciting times as the publishing industry was undergoing dramatic changes due to the advent of digital tools. Typesetting, plate making, and offset printing were all affected. As a result, businesses were retooling and the people in those professions required retraining. Eileen observes, "Even though it was only in a small way, I was able to participate in the massive social and economic changes that were being brought by technology." During that time, Monti also taught college extension classes in desktop publishing applications. Most of her students were older workers who had been sent back to school by their employers. They shared with Eileen that they either had to learn digital word processing, page layout, and printing or lose their jobs. For some, she remembers, it was not a problem but for others the pressure to change was overwhelming. She realized she was seeing the microscopic level of a major social shift.

Eileen progressed from the home-based desktop publishing business to working with large digital publishing and website production companies. There, she took part in the rapid growth of new companies that had been started by far-sighted and creative individuals. From her background in organizational sociology, she could see that the companies most likely to survive were those with owners who had both the talent to create and foster a new enterprise and then manage it successfully once it was large enough to be traded on the stock market. Those entrepreneurs without the latter talent sometimes survived by selling their start-up company to an established firm while older companies often sustained themselves by purchasing start-ups. This required employees to be constantly aware of changes in their field and vigilant about the undercurrents in their organization. More important, they had to be flexible enough to move easily into an acquisition or to a more stable company. Eileen recognizes that because sociology provided her with the ability to gather and compare data then hypothesize her findings, it was easier for her than for many others to accurately predict an organization's chances of survival. She could then adjust accordingly.

Family responsibilities required Monti to move from Washington State to northern California just as the computer industry began its decline. Jobs in the field had become increasingly limited and since she was new to the Bay Area, she had few connections. Therefore, when the opportunity presented itself, she opted for yet another career shift, taking a position as the jail librarian for a county facility. She found that the same knowledge of institutional structures and subcultures that helped her in previous jobs aided her work in the prison system and with the prisoners themselves. She soon observed that the inmates had a hierarchy and rules of their own that were considerably less flexible than those of society-at-large. "It was interesting to me," Eileen comments, "that for some, this unyielding structure provided so much security that they would purposely get re-arrested just hours after their release so they could go back to an environment that felt safe to them."

Eileen took pleasure in the interesting stories the prisoners shared with her and, as an avid reader, the fact that she had to first read every book she approved for the inmates' use. Nonetheless, the gloomy, depressing atmosphere that blanketed the environment coupled with increased oversight and constraint required by the correctional setting eventually extracted their tolls. In the computer/internet industry, Monti had been a project manager with considerable freedom and independence accustomed to directing teams of creative professionals. As a librarian in a county jail, she was required to report frequently and in detail to her supervisor so that regulations were accurately followed, inmates' rights were respected, and her personal safety was ensured. For someone used to the inventive spirit of internet development, it was an adjustment Monti was not willing to make.

As such, Eileen sought out another career, this time, as a farmer. Leaving the San Francisco area, she put down roots in a small town in eastern Oregon where her friends still farm with draft horses. There, she connects with the earth and her animals, the cycle of planting and harvesting, and the change of seasons she enjoyed much earlier in her life.

Even though her town of 315 people is 54 miles from the nearest traffic signal or perhaps because of it, Eileen is intricately linked to technology. She explains that immediately upon her arrival, she was recruited to work at the local newspaper. Though that job focused primarily on secretarial and billing functions, she was soon swept into a digital environment that brought the newsroom into the 21st century. On the heels of that position, she was hired by the local school district as their technology specialist. There, Eileen oversees equipment purchases, repairs existing hardware, and teaches classes for staff, faculty, and students in all the grades.

Monti's future plans focus on linking technology to rural advancement. Already she is working with local and county groups to bring area-appropriate employment opportunities to the county. "Since there are few livable wage jobs available," she elaborates, "most of the youth leave the area as soon as they are able. If we can retain some of the young families and even attract a few more, there is potential here for a thriving little environment." The community has already held a series of meetings to discuss potential employment options. Eileen proposes the expansion of the school district's offerings with technical tracks in instrumentation control; wind power engineering; organic farming; and equestrian/horsepower farming. These ideas would all strengthen the financial base of the region, thereby guaranteeing its viability. In addition, their implementation could also bring students from outside the area which, in turn, could generate local income by providing boarding services. "All of these advancements will, of course, require an innovative technological foundation," Eileen realizes.

To this end, Eileen is already involved with others in the chartering process and establishing relationships with community colleges in eastern Oregon. If this effort is successful, Eileen will then apply for available grants to help the county achieve its goals. Personally, Monti dreams of enticing a major software company to move their technical support services to Pine Valley, Oregon. She is certain that any company can win customers if they offer tech support "from people who speak their kind of English." In all these endeavors, Eileen is using the knowledge of community organizing, organizational process, and social change that she acquired in her various sociology classes. Asked what she might do differently if she were to start her career over again, she replies contentedly, "Can't think of a thing!"

Eileen advises students to consider the sheer range of careers that sociology offers. "Look at me," she invites. "I went from the Peace Corp to government services and then to publishing. I worked as a jail librarian, a farmer, and back again to technology. Some of these things, I did concurrently. I've never been unemployed and I've never been bored. I credit that, in part, to my sociology major. A good working knowledge of sociology is a powerful and versatile tool that will enable you to move ahead into any future you want."

To learn more about Eileen Monti and her work, please contact her by email at: eileenmonti@pinetel.com

LAKESHIA FREEDMAN

As an inner city kid who grew up in the projects of Miami where she attended its public schools, **Lakeshia Freedman** was never expected to finish high school let alone college. Certainly, the odds were against her. "I don't remember anyone in my family who ever encouraged me even though, for some reason, I always got good grades," she laments. "Maybe it was my near-sightedness that saved me. I couldn't see beyond the end of my nose so I buried myself in books. The other kids made fun of the coke-bottle eyeglasses I had to wear so I never got caught up with the gangs, drugs, or pregnancies that were all-too-common in my neighborhood." Lakeshia does recall, however, her seventh-grade science teacher and credits him for the direction her life ultimately took. "Mr. Jackson," she smiles at her recollection. Freedman explains how he piqued her interest in the natural world on the first day of class with a video about coral reefs. "I never knew that anything so beautiful actually existed," she explains. "And to find out they were right off our coast; about twenty miles away, was absolutely mind-boggling. Of course, twenty miles was a world away for someone like me."

Even so, Mr. Jackson continued to command Freedman's attention with his focus on the rainforest, the arctic, swamplands, and other wilderness areas around the world. She soon found she enjoyed unraveling the cause-and-effect relationships in nature and was particularly captivated by a lesson about wolves in Yellowstone National Park. "I was baffled by how their reintroduction reduced the overabundance of elk which, in turn, allowed the grasses on which the elk grazed to multiply. This was responsible for preventing more soil erosion." There were dozens more lessons like this that began to make Lakeshia feel hopeful, even empowered, for the first time in her life. She realized that changes could be made to situations that had seemed inevitable and fated to her before. That, Freedman contends, was a turning point in her life. "I don't imagine it hurt that Mr. Jackson was black, either," she ponders ruefully. "Before him, it never occurred to me that a black man could be a scientist *or* a teacher."

Though no other teacher impressed her quite so much for the next five years, the die had been cast. Lakeshia took science classes whenever she could, often endearing herself to the teachers by staying after school to assist them and immersing herself in their extracurricular projects. While Freedman maintained good grades, she had little hope of attending college until she confided her dream to the pastor of her local church. Pastor Streeter introduced Lakeshia to a businessman who had achieved a modicum of success in her community and to the chapter president of the National Association for the Advancement of Colored People (NAACP). Together, the three men arranged a scholarship that would cover her first two years of college. Lakeshia also remembers tearfully that the pastor took up an additional collection every Sunday from his congregation that went into the college fund he helped her establish.

Petrified of leaving the only home she had ever known and yet desperate to broaden her horizons, Lakeshia purposely applied only to colleges outside the state of Florida. Ultimately, she decided on the University of Wisconsin (UW). Once there, however, she found herself struggling mightily to keep up her grades, especially in her biology and chemistry classes. Freedman soon realized that even though her academic success was impressive at her public high school, it was not adequate to compete with students from far superior school systems. "I was devastated," she reports, "until my advisor suggested I try the environmental sociology major that the university had recently introduced."

Lakeshia quickly learned that environmental sociologists use a wide variety of sciences — both physical and social — to study issues such as the socioeconomic and political organization of food production, the global impact of water privatization, and the disproportionate burden of environmental harm on marginalized populations.

Still hesitant about changing her major, Lakeshia reluctantly enrolled in the prerequisite sociological theory and research methods classes. There, she learned about some of the early pioneers in the environmental movement and the ways in which they used the sociological lens to study the relationship between people and the natural world. In successive classes, Freedman examined why 14% of the world's people are malnourished and more than one-third do not have access to clean drinking water. Further, she investigated the impact of globalization and homogenization on small towns and atypical cultures. In still another class, Lakeshia studied the effects of industrial pollution on the health of humans and other species.

Finally convinced she had found her niche in an environmental sociology major, Freedman analyzed the results of laws and social policies on wildlife extinction, the consequences of mountain-top removal on rural poverty, and the implications of overpopulation. Before she graduated, she absorbed herself in classes about community organizing and community development strategies. "I lapped up all this information like a puppy at mealtime," Freedman laughs, "but on a personal level, I benefited most from all the teamwork in which we sociology majors had to engage." She points out that she hadn't come to college with many social skills and was too self-conscious to pursue friendships. Working together with others who shared mutual interests, however, made friendships flow more easily. "For the first time in my life, I had friends," she remarks quietly. "I also developed acquaintances who have provided me with recommendations, referrals, and resources that have been valuable throughout my career."

Graduating with honors, Freedman took her first job with an advocacy group committed to ending American dependence on coal. "This dependency has resulted in deforestation, mountain-top removal, poisoned waterways, death of wildlife, and the elimination of once vital communities," she explains. As an energy specialist, Lakeshia offered a variety of services to commercial enterprises that included free energy efficiency assessments. During the assessments, Freedman noted technological and behavioral energy use practices for which she would research alternatives. Once her report was complete, she would return to the businesses and advance her recommendations. If the company chose to pursue her plan, she would report the decision to the local utility so they could issue incentives once the work was completed and inspected.

States Lakeshia, "I found that financial incentives and the promise of bigger profits convinced these businesses to comply almost every time." Freedman most enjoyed the fact that each client was unique and that she had the latitude to address them as individuals. "That's where my sociology background came in handy," she maintains. "I was careful not to stereotype. Instead, I would closely observe the clients' behaviors and make careful notes to myself so I'd be able to interact more constructively in future meetings."

Though Lakeshia submits this approach often made the difference in the decision-maker's acceptance or rejection, she acknowledges she was often viewed with suspicion despite her best efforts. "I realize that some people will always be cautious about change of any kind. Still, it was hard not to personalize their rebuff," she observes.

After three years as an energy specialist, Freedman was promoted to project manager. In this position, she directed the work done by the contractors who installed the technologies once a company had capitulated. "In all honesty, I only got this promotion because I worked harder, put in more hours, and produced more compliance than any of my co-workers," she recognizes. The job actually called for an advanced degree.

With that motivation, Lakeshia returned to school a short time later to obtain her master's degree. There, she learned about diffusion theory; risk perception; and chaos theory. Along with the data collection and interpretation skills she honed, these concepts helped Freedman immensely in her next job as a human rights trainer.

Lakeshia had sensed early in her life that low-income communities of color and particularly women in those locations suffered disproportionately from environmental injustices ranging from greater pollution to health risks. She had often thought about assisting communities like these at some time in her life and this new position gave her the chance to do so. As such, she organized workshops whereby community leaders learned to build strategies that would bring legal, policy, and political changes to bear on the inequities. As part of her approach, Freedman facilitated collaborations with social activists and academics that could provide the community with information, support, publicity, and credibility. Moreover, she taught leaders how to mobilize letter-writing campaigns, create websites, and garner the attention of political representatives. "This was the hardest job I ever loved," Lakeshia quips, paraphrasing a slogan from the Peace Corps. "Seriously though, it was exhausting; frustrating; demanding, and yet, incredibly exhilarating. I loved watching the confidence of a community grow and the people exhibit a new-found sense of empowerment. I enjoyed prepping an individual to speak in front of a politician or businessperson and then see them flourish."

On the other hand, Freedman confesses that her personal safety was sometimes jeopardized as people who opposed the changes she advocated sent her hate-mail and tried to intimidate her in public. Once again, her sociological training and concepts such as standpoint theory, stability-change dialectic, cultural lag, relative deprivation, and especially, conflict theory all helped her understand the challenges that social change can represent. "This is especially true when a threat to money and power is involved," she submits knowingly.

Currently, Lakeshia is the director of a nonprofit trust that acquires and restores land for public use. Her work consists largely of the policy development necessary to provide green areas, trails, and access to the natural environment. "These will be the parks of the future," she predicts. "As suburban sprawl takes more and more open land, people will still need places to go where they can connect with nature. These spaces, though small, will provide them." On occasion, Lakeshia manages teams of engineers, botanists, ethologists, and landscape architects for projects that restore prairie lands, reintroduce wildlife, plant flora along roadways, and eliminate non-native vegetation. Sometimes her work requires alterations in a natural area and even the creation of an artificial ecosystem. She cites an example of a wetland area she helped redesign as a water purification structure.

Freedman is challenged, almost daily, to fairly address the needs and desires of multiple jurisdictions since the parks, trails, waterways, and the transportation to reach these sites usually involve many towns and counties. Therefore, she has to be familiar with the policy issues and concerns of each municipality as well as the personalities of the opinion leaders. She is adamant that the success of her work is totally dependent on partnerships as these partnerships allow for a holistic approach to environmental preservation. "We have to bring together multiple scientific disciplines, the general public, and politicians that often come to the table with different missions, stakes, and distinctive sets of constraints and regulations. It is my job to help them achieve some measure of agreement on each project we undertake. The process can be long and arduous but it is far superior to litigation," she stresses. Lakeshia frequently calls upon concepts such as social ecology, popular epidemiology, social constructionism, and even eco-feminism to help her reach the requisite collaboration and consensus. In a typical month, Freedman also addresses public forums, youth groups, and other interested parties who request her expertise.

Asked about future plans, Lakeshia responds that she would someday like to work with an international organization to promote environmental justice. "Presently, the majority of this work has focused on the United States, Canada, and Western Europe," she explains. "So much still needs to be done in Asia, India, Africa, South America and Eastern Europe that there is a colossal contribution we environmental sociologists can make." Eventually, Freedman would also like to operate an eco-tourism company that allows her to share her love for nature in an ecologically-sound manner. "My graduation present to myself was scuba-diving lessons," she reveals. "At first, I only dove in the lakes near my home. Then, I finally got to directly experience the coral reefs off the Florida coast, the ones that originally captured my interest in nature when I was in seventh grade." Since then, Lakeshia has engaged in whitewater rafting, hiked through redwood forests, and camped in the Adirondack Mountains. She has visited the Florida everglades, the Amazon rainforest, and the Canadian arctic. "All these opportunities have allowed me to see awe-inspiring beauty but they have also made me acutely aware of the work still needing to be done. Saving the Florida panther, the polar bear, the river dolphin, in fact, all the endangered species is mandatory for the survival of our planet and our species," she insists. "I want to be a part of that effort."

Given the chance, what might Freedman do differently? "Lots of things about my childhood," she discloses wistfully, "but in my career? Not a thing! Even though I resisted a major in environmental sociology at first, it turned out to be the best decision I could have made. As a result, I've worked with some phenomenal activists whose dedication never fails to re-ignite my passion. I've been interviewed by newspapers, magazines, radio, and television. I've testified in front of the Environmental Protection Agency (EPA), the Department of Energy (DOE), and once, I even spoke to a Congressional Committee. How many girls from the projects can say this?"

As for advice to a potential sociology major, she suggests simply, "Be flexible." More than a specific "how-to" approach, Lakeshia maintains that sociology provides a broad, general foundation that can be useful in any number of professions. She, herself, has met sociologists working in all sectors of the economy.

Regarding her focus on environmental sociology, Freedman concludes, "I initially declared this major because I was awed by nature's beauty and grandeur. Sociology gives me the means to preserve what I love."

Tragically, soon after this vignette was completed, Lakeshia Freedman died from a fall and snake bites she sustained while hiking through the Appalachian Mountains. My sincere sympathies are with her colleagues, co-workers, friends, and loved ones. Should you like to learn more about Lakeshia and her work, please contact me, Dr. Cheryl Joseph, by email at cjoseph@ndnu.edu or by phone at 650-355-0969.

11

SOCIOLOGISTS IN SOCIAL SERVICES

Sociology offers excellent preparation for careers in the social services. As a multidimensional field, social services advance the welfare of vulnerable populations, fulfilling hundreds of needs that range from housing to food, employment to medical care, child care to education, and elder assistance to veterans' benefits. Usually, these services are underwritten by government and non-profit organizations. Although the services and populations discussed in the next three vignettes are by no means exhaustive they are, nonetheless, representative.

Laura Barulich, for example, has enjoyed helping female parolees reconnect with their children after incarceration and has also worked with mentally ill adults. Upon completion of her master's degree, Laura plans to work with women-at-risk, helping them establish and achieve their life goals.

For *Lynnett Hernandez Kinnaird*, a career in the social services exposes her daily to the injustices of racism, sexism, ageism, and other able-ism along with the consequences thereof: poverty, family violence, gang warfare, and community dysfunctionality. Yet, she has designed and implemented programs of which she is justifiably proud because they have made differences in the lives of individuals, families, and entire communities.

Kathleen Soto takes us through her various positions from her work with homeless individuals to military veterans who are dually diagnosed and developmentally disabled children living in group homes. Kathleen had enjoyed the flexibility provided to her in roles such as program coordinator and consultant. Currently, she assists senior citizens and special needs clients obtain and keep low-income housing.

LAURA BARULICH

As a recent graduate of Sonoma State University, **Laura Barulich** is excitedly poised on the starting block of her career. Nonetheless, she is convinced she has already found her home in sociology. Raised by a stable, loving, and supportive two-parent family in a middle-class suburb of San Francisco, Laura initially planned to enter the medical field. She quickly found herself disinterested in those classes, however, and took an Introduction to Sociology class partly to meet her general education requirements but mostly for diversion. Fascinated by the breadth and variety of issues sociology embodies, she changed her major by the end of that semester. "I loved learning about all the different demographics, cultures, and lifestyles and was especially captivated by the courses in deviancy and mental illness," Barulich explains.

Following graduation, Laura worked first as a child care counselor for a drug and alcohol treatment facility. Her particular branch served women on parole. If the women had custody of children less than 13 years old when they came to the center, the children were allowed to live with the mother onsite. While the women attended classes or searched for jobs, Laura planned activities and implemented schedules for the children. The mothers were required to work in the child care center for a few hours a week as a condition of their treatment so Barulich supervised the women as well. In addition, Laura taught parenting classes to the mothers, going over a standardized curriculum with them and overseeing their groupwork, homework, and quizzes. "That was weird at first," she acknowledges. "There I was just 22 years old. I was not a parent and yet I was teaching mothers how to raise their own kids!" Initially Barulich was intimidated but as the women began to respond positively, the classes became her favorite part of the job.

At times, Laura found the job challenging and frustrating. "The children at the facility had experienced more adversity in a few short years than I probably will in my entire life," she observes. She recounts how many of the kids had been bounced around from one foster home to another then dumped back with their biological mothers. Some had not seen their mothers in years. Most saw their fathers infrequently at best and some did not even know who they were. These children had not been well-socialized and only knew how to express their fear, anger, loneliness, and other uncomfortable emotions through temper tantrums. "It was exasperating to deal with a child in the throes of a tantrum knowing their circumstances," Barulich reveals.

As difficult as these children could be, however, Laura submits that they were also fun. She built bonds with the kids and particularly enjoyed watching them build relationships with their moms. She remembers one four-year-old girl in particular who was being reunited with her mother after a two-year separation. It was problematic at first as the little girl missed her foster parents but ever-so-slowly, she began to adapt. "It was rewarding to watch them achieve little steps toward forging a bond and to know I facilitated some of the process," Laura reminisces. Barulich found her interactions with the women at the facility rewarding as well. "Though some distrusted me at first, most warmed up after a while and would seek me out to talk. I'm sure I learned more from these women and their experiences than they could have ever learned from me," she admits.

After a year, Barulich took a position as an assistant coordinator where she worked with mentally disabled adults whose diagnoses ranged from bi-polar personality to schizophrenia to clinical depression. There, she planned and implemented daily activities designed to help this population socialize effectively. As such, the clients played games, engaged in art activities, took part in group discussions, and joined field trips. She describes her work with this demographic as "demanding but rewarding."

Barulich enjoyed the challenge of engaging her clients in group activities and conversation especially since they were typically withdrawn. "There was one client in particular," Laura notes, "who was so introverted that he escaped to a chair in the corner all by himself every time he came to the center. I was delighted when I persuaded him to help me with the dishes at the end of each day, all the while prompting him to talk about his life. Eventually, I encouraged him to participate in various art projects until he agreed to make a square that depicted his handprint for a quilt the other clients were assembling. He died just a couple months later. Not only do I have that small piece of him but it feels good to know he enjoyed himself during the months I knew him." While Barulich liked working with this population, she admits the clients could be loud, rude, confrontational, and mean especially when they were not taking their medications. Laura also found it difficult at times to gain the trust and respect of these clients, all of whom were considerably older than she.

Laura contends there are numerous sociological concepts her knowledge of which helped her perform successfully in these two positions. With both populations, she observed the stigmas and labels that her clients endure. Moreover, she saw the impact of childhood deprivation, especially among the children, and was reminded, sadly, of the Harry Harlow studies. She watched the effects of the various socialization stages as well as that of inadequate socialization unfold before her. The nature—nurture debate, Cooley's looking-glass self concept, and Mead's role-taking theory came to mind for Laura whenever she witnessed clients deciphering how to interact appropriately. Moreover, her classes on mental illness taught her about the medicalization of deviance, mental disorders, and even the social functions of deviance and mental illness. Barulich shares, "This background helped me comprehend the barriers my clients face and to respect them profoundly for the struggles they have to fight."

Currently, Barulich is pursuing her master's degree in social work and upon graduation plans to focus on women, particularly young mothers. She observes, "I've seen the potential so many of them have that could benefit not only them and their children but their communities as well." Laura would like to be part of the efforts that help these women realize their promise.

Asked for her advice about choosing a career path she replies, "Use college to find your direction. Study what you enjoy because it will open doors to a career that is satisfying and fulfilling for *you*. It may not be the career your family and friends would have chosen for you but it will be the work and life that *you* enjoy."

To learn more about Laura Barulich and her work, please contact her by email at lkkramer@gmail.com or by phone at: 650-520-6772.

LYNNETT HERNANDEZ KINNAIRD

Even as a child, **Lynnett Hernandez Kinnaird** was intrigued by myriad cultures and lifestyles she observed all around her. She was curious about the choices people made and the consequences they incurred as a result. Kinnaird was also troubled by the limited life-chances she saw imposed on certain individuals. In particular, she calls to mind her speech therapist, a young woman who was wheelchair-bound and accompanied by a canine companion. Lynnett had no idea then how this woman would influence her future goals and career undertakings.

As such, Lynnett began her educational journey double-majoring in sociology and psychology. She was intent on developing the skills that could one day help her challenge and change the social labels, stereotypes, and stigmas that afflicted not only her personally but many others as well. Kinnaird reflects, "College opened doors for me, teaching me to think critically and analytically. I learned to be patient with a world that was not progressing fast enough for my taste. At the same time, college enhanced my thirst for social justice. In that atmosphere, I could express my ideas openly, finding support and guidance instead of prejudice." Lynnett contends it was through her college experiences she found the voice necessary to advocate for members of her community who would otherwise not be heard.

The community-based learning and research classes in the sociology department's curriculum provided Kinnaird with an understanding of a world outside her own; a world where abject poverty and constant crime were real. Lynnett was especially touched by the struggles that the children in the neighborhood faced: struggles like hunger, drug-addicted parents, language difficulties, and inferior education. "Even in broad daylight, these kids would commonly see drug deals and prostitution taking place right outside the doors of their rat-infested apartments," she recalls. Lynnett soon recognized she was more frightened than the kids and that she would eventually have to "walk into the lion's den" if she was going to have any influence. As a result, Kinnaird learned to facilitate interpersonal relations and build social networks based on common concerns. She learned to design programs that aided the community and, she is proud to say, some still operate in that neighborhood. Moreover, she continues to use those programs as blueprints for others she has since devised.

Following completion of her bachelor's degree, Kinnaird joined Americorps while she pursued a master's degree in psychology. At the same time she studied the dynamics of a healthy family system in the classroom, she developed programs for children in desperate need of positive role models. First hand, Lynnett observed socio-logical concepts such as resiliency theory, attachment, and survival mechanisms. "For many of these children, just getting to school each day was a major accomplishment," she recognizes. "But they had a quest for learning and a drive to enrich their lives. They were not afraid to speak their minds and they were thirsty for whatever knowledge I could give them." Though Lynnett enjoyed the opportunities to guide these kids; to teach them reading, lan-guage, sports, even lessons about their cultures and those of others, she also found her work frustrating. "Limited support from the Americorps director and facilitators; constant changes in the criteria for participation and inadequate access to safe space were all problematic," Kinnaird admits.

After a year with Americorps, Lynnett undertook a job with a group home for teenagers dually diagnosed with mental health issues as well as substance abuse problems. "What a challenge!" she recalls. "I was responsible for six girls and had to learn fast how to communicate with them. With six of them and two female staff members all together in one house, the dynamics of family living were very real!" Each day held many and varied lessons for Kinnaird. She discovered how traumas encountered at a young age can break the bonds of trust and emotionally cripple an individual for life. On the other hand, she observed that the presence of trust built compassion and allowed healing to begin. Though she had studied concepts such as the pathology of normalcy as well as theories like cultural transmission and social learning, she was surprised by the girls who, because of the chaotic homes in which they had been raised, were completely unresponsive when she approached their conflicts calmly and rationally.

Lynnett emphasizes that no day in the life of a group counselor could ever be considered typical though she characteristically conducted room searches and drug tests, removed boys hidden in the girls' closets, and called the police several times a month. When emotions left by past experiences boiled over, Kinnaird was frequently the object of a girl's anger or their shoulder on which to cry. Above all, Lynnett tried to bring a sense of normalcy to lives that were otherwise fraught with chaos and violence. Although she admittedly "took a couple of emotional hits in the process," Kinnaird found an approachable demeanor and positive attitude the most effective tools she had for attaining this goal. "Nonetheless," she observes, "the dilemma between heart and head is constant in this line of work."

Upon completion of her master's degree, Kinnaird remained at the group home so she could continue the process she had started. "I was the constant support, the stability, and at times, the sole responsible person in the lives of these six girls for almost a year," she explains. "They had become comfortable with me and started to respond to various interventions I'd used. I found that art, music, and narrative therapies worked especially well with them and they were slowly opening up. I wanted to see if these girls could transition successfully once they left the facility and what strategies best helped them heal." Besides, she added, she had become so involved in the daily functions of the operation with all the different shifts she worked and the nights she stayed onsite that it felt like her second home. Despite the emotional satisfaction she derived from working with dually diagnosed teenage girls in a group home setting, Lynnett concedes that the job had its disadvantages as well. "The relentless changes in administration, the lack of consistency in supervision, and the acute shortage of personnel to cover the shifts all meant the girls didn't get the solo interaction they deserved," Kinnaird submits.

Difficult as it was to leave, after two years Lynnett accepted a position as an intern therapist working for a family care agency in a largely Latino community. She began with a program that offered direct care and case management to families referred by Child Protective Services (CPS) and was immediately made responsible for 10 families whose offenses ranged from minor allegations of neglect to major charges of abuse. Here, she found her ability to speak Spanish fluently a crucial tool in the therapeutic process. Lynnett contends, "Not only did our common language make verbal communication easier but it bonded us to the knowledge of a shared culture that made my clients feel understood instead of persecuted. As a result, they were largely responsive to my suggestions." Through these experiences, she found sociological concepts such as symbolic interactionism; cultural relativity; cultural convergence, and the Sapir–Whorf Hypothesis come to life.

Kinnaird admits this work, like that of her previous job, was emotionally consuming and that at times she succumbed to compassion fatigue. Yet, she also found it satisfying to participate in a family's healing process and make reunification possible in preparation for a healthy life together.

When county budget policies closed this project, Lynnett stayed with the organization and was promoted to direct care therapist. In this position, she worked intensively with family programs based in the school system. These schools, ranging from elementary through twelfth grade, were notorious for the family violence, drug use, depression, self-esteem issues, and gang affiliations that their students suffered. "Every day presented a new challenge," Lynnett remembers. "I mean, how could I provide therapy for a child at a school site when his or her entire environment was sick? How could I reach kids who already had numerous negative encounters with therapists and social workers? How was I going to engage a child who was as emotionally locked up as Fort Knox? Well, I found ways. I relied on some of the concepts I'd learned in my undergraduate sociology classes for starters — concepts like value judgment, stereotypic threat, and referent group. Then I turned to some of the intervention strategies I'd learned in my master's program. In doing so, I let the kids know it was safe to talk with me about their feelings so that I could help them address their hurt, anger, and frustration."

During the three years Kinnaird worked in this program, she felt fortunate to have consistent support of the school staff and principals to design programs that benefited the children. More than that, she is grateful she was accepted by her community because it provided her with people who not only appreciated her work but contributed to her efforts. And best of all, "I have a very supportive husband," she smiles. "That makes up for a lot of stress and disillusionment."

Even so, working in this environment exposed Lynnett, first hand, to the injustices of social class, social status, powerlessness, and poverty. Notwithstanding the programs, services, and actions she advanced or the social networks she established, Kinnaird is clear that these conditions can dispiriting. "It is tough to see the juvenile justice system fail youth, families, workers, and the entire community. At times like these, I had to reflect on the hard work I had done and the progress that resulted."

Eventually, however, dwindling program dollars and changing ideas on the part of school administration forced Kinnaird to consider a transition in her career. She recalled the wheelchair-bound speech therapist of her childhood and her youthful desire to help people with disabilities. This brought Lynnett to her current position as a service coordinator with a regional center that serves the developmentally disabled population. Recommended by a former colleague, she was then interviewed by a panel of district managers who questioned her knowledge of social systems, therapeutic interventions, and additional community resources. "With each new job," Lynnett points out, "the interviews were more intensive. Fortunately, I could always rely on the knowledge I'd gained in my previous positions along with the theories and concepts I'd learned in school."

In the capacity of service coordinator, Kinnaird assists families with children from four to twenty-two years old who are attending school. She acts as a combination of social worker, therapist, and advocate for individuals and families who must consistently face challenges of immobility and inability, discrimination, and the attendant emotions that inevitably arise. Lynnett's day usually begins at seven in the morning with a plethora of meetings that involve individual clients, their families, educators, and representatives of the court. These meetings allow her to follow up on the progress an individual is making on their treatment plan, link the client to services they need, check on educational growth, locate care providers, and discuss conservatorship with family members. Whatever time is left after these meetings is consumed by report-writing. Lynnett estimates that about 40% of her job is occupied by this activity.

Though Lynnett thoroughly enjoys her exchanges with the clients, she is frequently aggravated when their needs go unmet because of insufficient funding and a lack of concern for the issues her clients must confront daily. "Here is where I most readily see some of the sociological concepts I learned about as an undergrad," Kinnaird remarks. "Routinely, the privileged and the elite in this country benefit at a cost to the poor. Programs and services for my clients get cut at the same time I read about large corporations and businesses getting subsidies. I witness ways in which undocumented immigrants are pitted against those who are here legally, all in the struggle for a few crumbs."

As much as Kinnaird enjoys her career and appreciates all that she has learned from her work, the most significant revelation has been society's treatment of the disabled, special needs, and medically fragile populations. "On the one hand, we are so technologically advanced, we can see what is going on in every corner of the globe," she argues, "yet we blind ourselves to the needs of those in our midst because they are somehow different from us. Maybe they make us uncomfortable or maybe they require more time and effort than we are willing to give. But my clients, just like any of us, just want to fit in; be accepted and loved." Given this, Lynnett asserts that her greatest challenge is reshaping the minds of the general public and removing the social stigmas put upon those without the voice to defend themselves.

Toward this end, Lynnett is completing her certification as a Licensed Marriage and Family Therapist (LMFT) so she can specialize in counseling special needs and disabled populations. She feels this group commands little recognition and could benefit immensely from the therapeutic process.

Having made excellent use of her sociology degree, Lynnett recommends goal-setting to any student. "It may be necessary to recalibrate from time to time but having a place to start will get you back on track quicker." For those who pursue the care-giving professions, Lynnett encourages them to take the time necessary to rejuvenate and tend to their own needs. "It's like a flight attendant says in the onboard safety message: 'Place your own oxygen mask securely in place before attempting to help others around you.'"

To learn more about Lynnett Kinnaird and her work, please contact her by email at: lkinnaird01@gmail.com

KATHLEEN SOTO

Silicon Valley's upper-middle and lower-upper social classes kept **Kathleen Soto** insulated for her entire childhood and some of her adult life as well. Though her family sometimes skated around the fringes, she was never exposed to the desperation and need that poverty creates. The only African-Americans Kathleen saw were on television and in movies; the Latinos she observed worked at the local Taco Bell. "It felt so plastic," Kathleen states emphatically. "I had this feeling I was living inside a well-kept secret."

Following graduation from high school, Soto went directly into the corporate world as an assistant to the human resource department for a large engineering firm. There, she was exposed to a variety of occupations and their attendant lifestyles, working with everyone from the CEO of the company to the janitors who cleaned the offices at night. She was confronted with a host of personal and cultural issues in this role but was forced to adapt. Yet, each situation she handled prompted questions about the ubiquitous inequities. Soto wondered, for example, why individuals from one race or ethnicity were treated differently from those of another. She questioned why certain occupations were overrepresented by a particular culture or gender. When Kathleen took her queries to her father, a prominent and highly respected businessman in California, she was told that "certain kinds of people just do certain jobs better."

That was the eighties, Kathleen acknowledges, and her father's thoughts in this regard were commonplace. Something about his response, however, irritated Kathleen. After ten years in corporate America, she entered college hoping that she would find more satisfying answers to her concerns.

As a twenty-eight-year-old student at a private school in Northern California, she found herself immersed in a pool of cultural diversity. A Caucasian female, Kathleen soon became friends with people younger than her and representing an array of races, ethnicities, religions, and social classes. With her first sociology course, she found herself stepping into a world rife with poverty, plight, and pain. Further, she found herself resonating with the university's mission of social justice.

Kathleen recalls that she had always felt compassion for victims of wars, apartheid, famine, and the Holocaust. Yet, she learned from her family that careers in social work and service to others were not "proper." *That* was about to change! With each sociology class she took, Kathleen learned that the well-being, indeed, the very survival of a society depended on individuals acting collectively on behalf of the greater community. Kathleen realized this meant extending assistance to those weakened by the demands put upon them.

It was a qualitative research project; however, that most significantly challenged all that she had previously known. For an entire semester, Kathleen, along with three traditional age students from her class, spent their weekends and many of their evenings in the Haight-Asbury or hippie district of San Francisco. There, they hung out with the homeless population that resides in its doorways, parks, shelters, and on its sidewalks. To gain the trust of the people they wanted to learn about, Kathleen would assemble her dorm mates every Friday evening to make peanut butter and jelly sandwiches that she and her research group would take with them on their weekend sojourns to The Haight. There, they would spend hours sharing the sandwiches and engaging in conversation with the homeless.

Kathleen recalls an occasion when two police officers approached the group and threatened them with a fine for offering food to people with whom they were personally unfamiliar. "It turned out," she clarifies, "that an ordinance had just been passed in San Francisco prohibiting the distribution of food to more than six strangers. Of course, we realized it was just a way of getting the homeless to leave the area, but then an officer explained that some unscrupulous person could also use food as a vehicle for poisoning the homeless. That was another mind-blowing revelation for me — that anyone could hate someone else so much!"

Notwithstanding the ideas she had learned from her family, Soto quickly found that the homeless were not a disparate or dangerous bunch. Instead, these individuals had joined together as a community that protected each other, watched over each other's possessions, and established a strict code of rules that they enforced among themselves. She spent time talking with the young mother who had escaped a violent home with her two children and nothing more, the teenage boy whose family evicted him for being gay, the military veteran who had turned to drugs to quell his nightmares of war, and the middle-aged woman brought to destitution by the costs of her illness. She met others driven from their homes by high costs of housing in the Bay Area and a limited supply of housing available to those with meager incomes. She learned that many of the people only started abusing substances *after* they had been on the streets awhile. The drugs and the alcohol helped them cope with the accompanying effects of homelessness like cold, hunger, loneliness, and fear. Increasingly, Kathleen realized there were few differences between her and the homeless people she had grown to know save the adversities they suffered and their lack of stable housing. Even more disturbing was her recognition that most people in the United States are only a paycheck or an illness away from homelessness.

"This entire project was a defining moment for me," Kathleen admits. "When I watched people on the way to their jobs or their homes averting eye contact with a ragged, unclean, and obviously desperate individual, I had to acknowledge that I had never really noticed homelessness before either. Yet, by stepping out of my comfort zone, I had the richest and most rewarding experience of my life."

Despite her family's disapproval of her work with the homeless, Kathleen felt honored when the sociology department at her school invited her and her group to present their findings at a meeting of the Pacific Sociological Association the following spring. That opportunity convinced Soto to major in sociology.

Aware that she would be more marketable in the social services sector if she established a work history while still in school, Kathleen took a position as a vocational counselor for the Veteran's Administration during her last two years of college. Her clients were mostly recovering addicts with dual diagnoses such as depression or schizophrenia coupled with Post Traumatic Stress Disorder (PTSD). In this capacity, Kathleen provided emotional support, guidance in the job search, help with applications for college and reunification with their families. The majority of her clients were also homeless, so Kathleen found some of the hands-on lessons she had learned in The Haight along with her knowledge of pathology of normalcy, absolute and relative poverty, and the medicalization of deviance useful in her new job.

Following her position with the Veteran's Administration, Soto worked in long-term care facilities conducting psychosocial assessments; addressing the general needs and well-being of the residents; and assisting with end-of-life issues. While the pay was poor, Kathleen received satisfaction from providing palliative care to those who might not otherwise receive it.

Soto was approached by her next employer with an offer of an administrative position at an intermediate care facility for developmentally disabled children. There, she managed two group homes with a total of 12 children and 21 employees. In addition to conducting psychosocial assessments, Kathleen monitored the children's goals, met regularly with state agencies and medical personnel, and maintained standards regulated by the state and federal governments. "This was, by far, the toughest yet most rewarding job I ever had," she notes enthusiastically. "These children were confined to wheelchairs and yet, they filled their worlds with laughter. Learning to feed or dress oneself was considered a huge accomplishment." Kathleen fondly shares one event out of many that she treasures: "Everyone in the facility was tense because the state agency was evaluating their operation. The children had been seated for dinner and the surveyor was scrutinizing every possible aspect. One little girl with cerebral palsy had never spoken before but suddenly as the surveyor approached her table, the girl flashed an enormous smile and shouted, 'Hi!' Then she repeated it." To Kathleen, experiences like these represent the essence of medical social services. "It is not about adulation or prestige or pay although I did earn a *very* good salary in this position," she asserts. "It is about helping people achieve their goals and seeing their successes no matter how insignificant they might seem to others."

Soto does acknowledge that her job was difficult; however, noting that she typically worked 13 to 14 hours a day and would frequently be called to the hospital in the middle of the night when one of the children was ill. These demands affected her health adversely after a few years and she resigned so she could recover.

During that time, Kathleen worked as a consultant to a variety of long-term care facilities assisting them with their assessments and producing documentation for the state evaluations. She would typically work with an operation for a week or two until she satisfied their needs. Then, depending on her health, she would either work at another facility or take time to recuperate. "The best part of consulting was the ability to set my own schedule," Kathleen points out. "When I felt healthy enough to work, I did; when I was too weak, I didn't." She admits, though, that working independently requires considerable self-discipline and effective time-management skills.

Soto is now employed as a program coordinator for a nonprofit organization that helps senior citizens and special needs clients obtain and maintain low-income housing. In doing so, she delivers programs that educate her clients about financial and health issues as well as the various benefits available to them. She makes referrals to appropriate agencies and advises her clients of their rights. Further, she advocates on their behalf when necessary and insures their rights are not violated. This work demands that Kathleen understand numerous sociological concepts like life cycle needs, primary and secondary group functions, institutional ageism, and stigmatization of illness.

A typical day for Soto depends on the facility at which she is working. If she is at a senior property, she might start by managing the distribution of groceries to their low-income clients. Following this endeavor, Kathleen will probably contact other agencies on a client's behalf or help them fill out the forms necessary to apply for benefits. Alternately, if she is working at a special needs facility, Kathleen is likely to spend some of her day in the computer lab teaching clients the skills they need to work and live. Then, she is usually available to help with practical matters like filing applications or providing emotional support. Regardless of the facility at which she is working, Kathleen generally spends part of her day scheduling or delivering programs that educate clients so they will ultimately be able to make independent choices.

Each time Kathleen was looking for employment, she would turn her search into a part-time job in and of itself that she would start every day upon her return home from work. She typically sent out five to ten resumes daily until finally, the interview offers would materialize. "I think circulating your resume whether on websites or among social and professional contacts is always beneficial. Nowadays, of course, Facebook and LinkedIn are invaluable for staying in touch with people who might be potential employment sources." In addition, she has joined several business and social groups over the years with the goal of staying connected to like-minded individuals in her field. "These are the people likely to call me when they have a special project or a job position to fill," Soto explains. If Kathleen's health were to improve, she would return to school for a master's degree without hesitation. As it is, all of her work must be supervised by a medical social worker with an advanced degree.

Kathleen concedes that without her first sociology course and the attendant research project with the homeless people in The Haight, her life would be remarkably different today. Kathleen does take credit, however, for the courage necessary to step outside of the world she knew so she could begin her life change. She encourages other students, whether sociology majors or not, to do the same.

To learn more about Kathleen Soto and her work, please contact her by email at: ksoto@aol.com

12

SOCIOLOGISTS IN SOCIAL WORK

While social work is not synonymous with sociology, the two have been considered "sister disciplines" since the founding of the sociology department at University of Chicago alongside the establishment of Hull House. Sociology majors would take courses at the university from professors like Robert Park, Louis Wirth, and Florien Znaniecki. Then they would work alongside luminaries such as Jane Addams and Ellen Starr providing meals, housing, education, and multiple other services to largely immigrant populations in Chicago's poorest neighborhoods.

Though sociology has traditionally been defined as the scientific study of human social behavior and social work as efforts to improve conditions of disadvantaged individuals, groups, and communities, the advent of public sociology and community engagement as a mode for learning have pushed the discipline further into experiential practice. Conversely, social work has, over time, developed its own theories, methodologies, and professional code of ethics. Even so, there remains considerable overlap between the two.

As a result, large numbers of undergraduate sociology majors pursue a master's degree in social work (MSW) and/or certification as a Licensed Clinical Social Worker (LCSW). Increasingly, those with MSW or LCSW degrees will undertake a doctorate in sociology.

Christina Risley-Curtiss began her career in an urban, African American community of South Carolina as a Volunteer in Service to America (VISTA). Since then, she has held numerous positions dedicated to improvement in child and maternal welfare as well as impoverished communities-at-large. Dr. Risley-Curtiss presently co-directs a training project in public child welfare at Arizona State University (ASU) and evaluates programs for the State of Arizona. Christina is one of the first in her profession to design courses about the bonds people share with animals, to provide certification for professionals in the treatment of animal abuse, and intervention for youth who abuse animals.

Jana Whitlock shares how her quest to become bilingual so she could counsel her Latino clients more effectively led her on travels throughout the world. She reports she found sociology as valuable in Thailand where she taught scuba diving to tourists as she has in Salinas, California where she now practices.

CHRISTINA RISLEY-CURTISS

Given her family culture and her gender compounded with the era in which she was raised, *Christina Risley-Curtiss* is surprised she has a career at all! She was born into a middle-class family and spent her childhood on an idyllic 100-acre, non-working farm in rural Connecticut during the 1950s. Her father followed in the footsteps of his father with a rewarding practice in veterinary medicine. Risley-Curtiss recalls that he was internationally recognized for his expertise on milk production and often traveled to South America where he helped wealthy landowners there increase the output of their own milk cows. Frequently, her father would take Christina with him on calls to local farms and once, when she was 13 years old, she accompanied him on a visit to Venezuela.

Though a college graduate, Christina's mother was a full time homemaker. Christina suspects she would have enjoyed a professional career, however, as she was a creative and confident woman who even served in the U.S. military during World War II. When offered a promotion, though, she declined because she would have outranked her husband had she accepted. Upon her return to civilian life Christina's mother was discouraged from a career pursuit by Christina's dad.

As both of her parents were intelligent and generally progressive, however, Christina recalls numerous spirited discussions about topics like racism, sexual assault, nuclear war, and communism. "It was around the family dinner table that my interest in social relationships and social problems emerged and my passion for social justice was born and fed," she ruminates.

Surrounded by an array of animals and a family sympathetic to the well-being of others, Risley-Curtiss quickly developed an interest in both. "I identified with animals at a very young age and with the human underdog as well," she reflects somberly.

Her family always assumed that Risley-Curtiss would attend college and impressed upon her the importance of learning for its own reward. Both were secondary though, in the mind of her parents, to finding a college-educated husband who was expected to support her. Moreover, her degree was intended to secure her a job to fall back on should Christina "have" to go to work. Christina shrugs at the memory. "That's just the way it was in those times," she muses.

Upon entering University of Connecticut, she planned to be a history teacher but resonated with the first sociology course she took. Captivated by all the social issues she studied in that class, their connections to each other, their causes and the consequences, Risley-Curtiss graduated with a duel degree in history and sociology. She had also found that college-educated husband and was married soon after graduation. The marriage lasted just three years; however, thereupon Christina joined VISTA (Volunteers in Service to America) and moved to Columbia, South Carolina. "Finally!" she rejoices, "I was on my own!" It was the mid-1970s in the midst of President Lyndon Johnson's War on Poverty.

The VISTA experience brought her into direct contact with urban life in an African American community and with "doing social work." After being trained as a community organizer by the Association of Community Organizations for Reform Now (ACORN), she helped organize and direct programs for adults and children in low-income neighborhoods. She was also loaned out to the South Carolina Social Services Department (DSS) where she authorized requests for food stamps. This position eventually led to a job with DSS as a caseworker for the state's Aid to Families with Dependent Children (AFDC) program.

Although she liked her clientele and her co-workers, she hated being part of a system that encouraged poor people to manipulate it just to obtain basic resources. Risley-Curtiss explains, "Sometimes people would exceed the income eligibility limit by just a few dollars. I would either have to refuse them food stamps

or suggest they 'spend down' their savings in order to qualify."
She particularly recalls an elderly woman who had to spend all
the money she had saved for her funeral just to meet the criteria
for food stamps. "That was frustrating," Christina concedes. "I
never knew whether I was actually helping or just exacerbating
poverty. In addition, I became an unwilling sounding board for
racist and negative views against the poor. I generally came to
view the state services as inefficient, ineffective, and unethical."

After two years as an AFDC caseworker, Risley-Curtiss transferred to the foster parent licensing unit. From there, she became
an intake worker for Child Protective Services (CPS). As a licensing agent for foster parents, she conducted in-depth studies of
the home life whenever a family applied to be foster parents. She
made recommendations for approval or denial and found families
for children who needed placement in foster care. Moreover, she
recruited families to be foster parents and served as the DSS
liaison to the state foster parent association.

As an intake worker for CPS, Christina answered phone calls
charging child abuse and neglect then secured and screened the
information to determine if the circumstances met the criteria for
citing child maltreatment. If it did, she would complete a report
and pass it along to her supervisor who would then assign the
case for investigation. Both as a caseworker and an intake worker,
Christina found her knowledge of concepts such as the biopsycho-
social model, bonding, social support, and especially boundary-
setting beneficial.

Eventually acknowledging she was unsure of her skills as well
as her ability to help her clients actually improve their lives,
Christina returned to school, this time at the University of
Tennessee in Nashville to obtain her Masters of Science in Social
Work (MSSW). Concurrently, a previous interest of hers that
stemmed from a sociology paper she researched as an undergraduate was rekindled. In that paper, she compared the incarceration

experiences of men and women. As a result, she requested an internship at the Tennessee Women's Prison.

Upon completion of her MSSW, Risley-Curtiss began working for the State of Tennessee Department of Human Services (DHS) in child welfare. As her education at University of Tennessee had been financed by a pre-employment stipend from DHS, she had a commitment to fulfill. With her degree, she moved quickly into the State's training division as a manager where she worked for the next two years. "I thought I would love this work," Christina reflects, "but I missed the direct contact with clients." Therefore, after satisfying her contract with Tennessee's Department of Human Services, she returned to South Carolina where she worked first as an investigator for CPS and then as a supervisor. Later, she was recruited as the District Director of Public Health Social Work for the state's public health agency, DHEC. In this position, she supervised social workers engaged in family planning, home health care, and high-risk maternity cases.

While Christina enjoyed her colleagues, she abhorred the bureaucracies that frequently hindered her efforts, typically to the detriment of the clients. She remembers with annoyance a number of issues in service provision that were all-too-common to many agencies at that time. "For example," she reports, "there were no programs for poor women that provided health exams unless they were pregnant or going to family planning clinics. In the maternity and family planning programs, male partners were rarely, if ever, included in the women's visits. In fact, the only programs provided for men were examinations for sexually transmitted diseases. Additionally, when a woman in the high-risk maternity program had a miscarriage, her case was automatically closed with no further contact encouraged." Christina instituted the practice of having her social workers write the woman a note of condolence. "It was the least we could do in an extremely emotional circumstance," she maintains. Sociological concepts such as empathy, *verstehen*, and gender role socialization were indeed helpful in this position.

During her time with DHEC, Risley-Curtiss also chaired a committee that encouraged the involvement of social workers in family planning. Additionally, the committee trained women in assertion so they would have the communication techniques they needed to avoid sex without condoms.

After eight years of social work practice, Risley-Curtiss again returned to school, this time for a PhD in social work at the University of Maryland in Baltimore. The experience allowed her to test some of the assumptions she had made about her clients while working in various capacities. She wanted to know more, for instance, about the mechanisms children use to feel safe in dangerous environments and how such children learn to trust. She was curious about the means that allow some to survive traumatic childhoods and become functioning adults while others cannot. She questioned the impact of generalized dysfunction and concepts like associational theory. She wanted to investigate the correlation of poverty to deviance versus causation theory.

With her doctorate completed, Risley-Curtiss accepted a teaching position at Arizona State University (ASU) where she remains at present. In this position, she has continues to nurture her interest in the development of child welfare programs. She is a co-director of the Child Welfare Training Project, an undertaking that educates MSW students who plan to work in public child welfare. Moreover, Dr. Risley-Curtiss has worked with a variety of state agencies as a program evaluation research consultant. In this capacity she designed and implemented evaluations to identify the impact of state programs on prenatal health care for low-income women. She also helped the state child welfare agency evaluate the effect of a legislatively mandated health care pilot project for foster children.

Beginning in 2003, Risley-Curtiss began to observe how her personal relationship with animals and social work practice were correlated. If social workers were supposed to look at people in interaction with their social environments, she reasoned, they needed to take companion animals into account as they increasingly permeate our lives. Therefore, she designed and taught a course for social workers that she titled "Animal–Human Connections." Since that time, Christina has been able to combine her desire to help people in need with her love for animals by developing programs and teaching others about the bond humans share with other species.

In this endeavor, she collaborates with an international animal welfare organization to provide an online certificate program for professionals in the treatment of animal abuse. Further, she created an assessment and diversion program that intervenes with children who abuse animals. "Undertakings like these are vital to reducing violence both toward animals and people," Dr. Risley-Curtiss argues. "Plenty of research has demonstrated a disturbing association between cruelty to animals and violence toward people. If we can detect and eliminate brutality perpetrated on animals, we may ultimately be able to save thousands upon thousands of lives both human and non-human."

A day in the life of Christina Risley-Curtiss generally begins somewhere around sunrise when she feeds the cats, chickens, her greyhound, and the horse that claim residency on her land. After a quick breakfast, Christina's paid workday begins. During the academic year, her schedule involves email correspondence, meetings, preparing course content, reading papers, evaluating assignments, and teaching. In the fall semester she adds her online program, Animal-Human Interactions for the Professional Treatment of Animal Abuse, to her regular teaching load. Many days, she works from home and on other days from her office at ASU in downtown Phoenix. There, she squeezes in research, writing, and consultations with her community members about animal–human issues.

Risley-Curtiss enjoys the flexibility of her job along with the opportunities it gives her to research and work on the cutting edge of her field. She admits, however, that such work can be lonely. While the interdisciplinary nature of animal–human studies compensates somewhat, she would love to have more colleagues with whom she could collaborate. In hindsight, Christina wishes that she had merged her interests in child welfare and animal-human interactions sooner.

In the future, Dr. Risley-Curtiss will continue to integrate animals into social work practice. Further, she plans to design an instrument that measures the empathy of children for animals and promote effective models for the treatment of animal cruelty.

For any sociology major considering a career in social work or child welfare, Christina implores them to understand that they *must* be advocates for their clients. To that end, they *must* learn effective advocacy strategies if they hope to obtain the resources necessary for their clients. "Advocacy for vulnerable individuals as well as social change is the heart of good social work," Risley-Curtiss concludes. "It is the reason I became a social worker and why I hope others will, too."

To learn more about Christina Risley-Curtiss and her work, please contact her by email at: Risley.curtiss@ymail.com

JANA WHITLOCK

Jana Whitlock entered college as a business major intent on making *lots* of money when she graduated. Within a few weeks, though, she was bored with the accounting, micro-economics, and marketing courses she was required to take. Her roommate, by contrast, was ecstatic about her sociology classes. Every day, she would fascinate Jana with the array of issues they discussed in her sociology classes, topics to which she could relate. By the following semester, Jana enrolled in her first sociology course. Always the rebel, she researched witchcraft for her term paper, mildly surprised that her professor approved the topic. Uncertain how she might use a major in sociology to earn a living, however, she tackled another course that introduced her to a San Francisco neighborhood plagued poverty, prostitution, drugs, and crime. Then she undertook an internship at a group home for the mentally ill. Finally, by applying some of the principles she was learning in her classes to the realities she faced, Jana realized she could use sociology in dozens of occupations. She had discovered her niche.

With her bachelor's degree in hand, Whitlock returned to her hometown where she immediately found a position as a counselor at a group home for residents with a variety of diagnoses. There, she supervised the daily activities of the residents. By fine-tuning the trust-building techniques she had learned in her social psychology class and implementing skills such as active listening along with strategies for managing dialectical tensions, she built a rapport with the residents. Unfortunately, the pay was barely above the minimum wage and Jana quickly realized she would need an advanced degree to progress. As such, she sought admission to a graduate school in California's central valley.

While waiting for acceptance, Whitlock took another job at a residential treatment home for teenage girls and obtained a certificate in Drug and Alcohol Counseling. At the treatment facility, Jana encouraged her clients to establish goals then helped them develop independent living and money management skills. Once she was accepted in the Masters of Social Work (MSW) program to which she had applied, she interned at an outpatient drug and alcohol treatment center. There, she executed assessments and interventions utilizing strategies such as support, clarification, confrontation, information delivery, demonstration, and negotiation. In addition, she prepared clients' charts and made appropriate referrals, co-facilitated Twelve-Step substance abuse groups, and assisted clients with ongoing plans that addressed the management of their problems.

Asked what she found most challenging about this internship Jana responds, "It was definitely the fear of the unknown. I mean, what did I know about the life of a heroin addict or a schizophrenic or a teenage prostitute who already had two children? How could I connect with them and relate to their issues? I worried that I wouldn't be able to help them. I was also afraid that my own entrenched biases would emerge." Most of all, Whitlock was fearful that the group would physically attack her. After all, she had already experienced an assault at another facility.

The following year, Whitlock took a position at a county mental health facility where she administered psychosocial assessments and provided clinical diagnosis. She co-facilitated a group of women suffering from depression and individually counseled other patients with various sorts of mental illness. To identify and define these problems, Jana turned to concepts like relationship-building, interpersonal communication, and interviewing techniques which she had initially studied in her undergraduate courses.

She allows that the hardest part of this internship was the ambiguity surrounding her role and the lack of clear structural procedures. Jana credits her supervisor and some of the other therapists for their guidance. Because of them, she soon overcame her apprehension about working with mentally ill individuals who often spoke gibberish and responded to voices in their heads. The crisis interventions required of her, however, still continued to frighten her: "I couldn't imagine how some people could be in the horrific places that they were." Furthermore, Whitlock was still uncomfortable facilitating therapy groups and doubtful about her ability to provide useful council. Finally she realized that with time and practice, she was improving. With that, her confidence skyrocketed.

Upon graduation, Whitlock again went back to her hometown where she focused her work on children. She quickly found a position in a dual diagnosis program as a relief counselor though, once again, at a far lower salary than she had anticipated. She supplemented that income while gaining experience with elementary school children as a counselor in a prevention and assistance program. There, she conducted screening assessments and referred children along with their parents to appropriate resources when they were needed. Focusing primarily on a play therapy model, Whitlock occasionally found it necessary to provide crisis intervention and to collaborate with Child Protective Services (CPS) on behalf of her young clients. After a year Jana again returned to school, this time for a license in clinical social work (LCSW).

With this degree, Jana reasoned, she could go into private practice and make enough money to finally move out of her parent's home! The only obstacle was the 3200 supervised and unpaid hours she had to accumulate for this credential. She began with an internship at a community counseling center where she delivered in-clinic counseling, psychotherapy, prevention services, and intervention for individuals, families, and groups. Whitlock responded to crisis calls and walk-ins while also providing school-based counseling services. Later in her internship, she provided substance abuse counseling to children and adolescents. At the same time, she worked closely with family members at risk for child abuse. Whitlock notes, "Families raising the children of their relatives such as grandchildren and younger siblings are particularly stressed out. I helped them most by connecting them to community resources like welfare, food, clothing, counseling services, and transportation."

In all of these situations, Jana observed the dire need for counseling in the Latino community and the value of her bilingual abilities. Though she managed on the Spanish she had learned in junior high and high school, she still found the communication frustrating. In addition, she determined that there were very few bilingual therapists in an area that was overwhelmingly Latino. Once again, Whitlock returned to school but in this case, it was to improve her Spanish language skills.

Through a news magazine published by the National Association for Social Workers (NASW), she found a six-week intensive immersion course being offered in Quetzaltenango, Guatemala and off she went! Upon her return, she continued with night classes at a local community college before setting out on another venture, first to Cuernavaca, Mexico then back to Guatemala where she was hired as the coordinator of the Spanish language school she was attending.

Jana followed these undertakings with travels to Europe that started in Switzerland where she reconnected with a man she had met in Honduras while taking an advanced scuba diving course. From there, they proceeded to Germany, Denmark, and finally, to Spain.

Whitlock eventually returned to a counseling center in Northern California at which she had interned previously, intending to open her own office in a nearby town. There, she planned to provide bilingual therapy to clients referred primarily by the schools. Life has a curious way of turning plans on their heels, however, as Jana found out when her Swiss boyfriend proposed an offer too good to refuse. "Come with me to Thailand," he implored, "and help me teach scuba diving classes to tourists." So, off she went on yet another adventure! Once there, the two worked together in a business that offered snorkeling and diving expeditions while they immersed themselves in the customs and rituals of the Thai culture.

By that time, Jana was feeling increasingly comfortable in cultures and environments very different from her own. As a result, she and her friend resumed their travel after an extended time in Thailand. Vietnam and Cambodia were their next stops. There the couple lived history, seeing firsthand the devastation the Americans had inflicted on the land and the people. "The ravages of the Pol Pot regime, which killed two million Cambodians from 1971 to 1974 remains sadly apparent as well," Whitlock conveys. Jana reflected on such concepts as the power elite theory, military-industrial complex, and totalitarianism to help her explain the heartless atrocities she observed.

The Philippines beckoned next followed by Yap and Palau, two Micronesian Islands in the South Pacific where their planes were met by bare-breasted women offering flowered leis. While delighting in the customs and folkways of these cultures, Jana was sobered by the toll that World War II and now, global warming has taken on these islands. Hong Kong, Macau, Guam, and Singapore rounded out the couple's itinerary before they vacationed on the Riviera and then returned to Switzerland. A few months later, Whitlock came back to California to complete the hours required for her LCSW.

Despite the kindness of the people they met throughout their travels, Jana reports that the couple's lack of proficiency in any of the Asian languages made travel in that part of the world difficult. "I kept hearing the voices of my sociology professors talking about symbolic interactionism and how the daily activities of people create the words they use," she laughs. Nonetheless, she maintains that the venture was definitely worthwhile: "Even in hindsight, I wouldn't give up any part of my travels for different experiences."

Whitlock considers sociology excellent preparation for the consistent adjustments and adaptations that were necessary. "The sociological perspective continually reminded me to look at the world from the viewpoint of others while concepts like cultural universals, socialization, and linguistic relativity were constant reminders of our common humanity," she notes. "Furthermore, sociology removed some of my stereotypes and forced me to utilize cultural relativity instead of being ethnocentric whenever I experienced an event outside of my comfort level." Jana would remind herself that although some universals exist in all cultures, there are legitimate reasons for the differences. "Furthermore," she continues, "I remembered that cultures are human-made instead of genetic and that I had to be socialized to believe my culture does things the 'right way' but that, in fact, there is no one right way. There are usually several."

Eventually, Jana finished the hours required for her LCSW degree but was frustrated with her job as a family caseworker. Mexico called to her and she went, planning to open a dive shop in Playa del Carmen. A series of misfortunes and missteps, however, eventually dissuaded her and she returned to California after several years to renew her therapy practice with Latino children in school settings.

Back at home, Whitlock is experiencing the inevitable reverse culture shock. She is slowly adjusting to the hectic pace and learning to drive again after years of walking and taking buses everywhere she went. She is living alone and misses the community inhabited by the ex-patriots and local people she grew to know and love. "It will take me awhile to acclimate to my primary culture," Jana suspects.

In hindsight, Jana wishes she had stayed in Guatemala longer to study Spanish and taken even more opportunities to travel. "Most people don't understand why I lived outside the U.S. for so many years. They listen to my stories but they can't relate to them," she laments. "I try to tell them I am a different person because of my travels. Travel has given me the best education

possible and sociology provided me with a foundation to understand and adapt to cultures different from my own."

What sort of person makes a good sociologist? Whitlock
responds: "If you find yourself fascinated by other cultures, wonder why some families are so dysfunctional and more families are
not, or ask why some countries are so wretchedly poor in the face
of obscene wealth, then you have the makings of a successful
sociologist."

To learn more about Jana Whitlock and her work, please contact
her by email at janaita@yahoo.com

13

SOCIOLOGISTS IN COMMUNITY ORGANIZATION, ADVOCACY, AND ACTIVISM

Many argue that the quest for social justice resides at the heart of sociology. Certainly, sociologists are frequently found in activities organized around social causes and change; as activists and leaders in social movements; and as advocates for a just and peaceful world.

Carolina Cervantes works as a community organizer to improve conditions and opportunities for the people in her own Latino neighborhood. Taking the reader through a typical day in her life, she points out how she uses myriad sociological concepts to understand the strategies by which her community allows its own subjugation on the one hand and yet will engage in liberation efforts on the other.

Megan Scott began her career with AmeriCorps in Baltimore, Maryland where she provided job and personal growth training to unemployed women living below the poverty line. Through her MSW program, she was thrown into the fray of community organizing. She learned, by applying theory to practice, how to work effectively with residents, activist groups, and elected politicians on issues such as birth control and emergency contraception availability. Taking her experiences with her to Maine, she has since organized grassroots coalitions related to tobacco use concerns, underage drinking, and other public health issues.

Karen Schaumann first used her sociology major to organize poverty-stricken communities in southeast Michigan to protest draconian cuts in welfare benefits. At the same time the cuts were imposed deindustrialization, the North American Free Trade Agreement (NAFTA), and the Personal Responsibility and Work Opportunity Act (PRWOA) eliminated jobs by the thousands in that part of the United States. The successes Schaumann and her allies experienced motivated her to take their cause to state and national lawmakers, bureaucrats, and even to the United Nations. Inspired by the tactics of the Civil Rights Movement, Schaumann helped to organize a bus tour which joined together protesters from across the United States. Karen argues that with massive unemployment enmeshed with home foreclosures, evictions, and the sorry lack of affordable housing, the fight for economic justice remains as much a concern today as it was at the end of the twentieth century.

With his discharge from the U.S. Navy in 1947, Lincoln Grahlfs began his relentless advocacy for the abolition of nuclear weapons and war. This was prompted by Grahlfs's own assignment to an atomic bomb site during wartime and the subsequent health problems he suffered. Further angered by his government's blatant dishonesty and the disdain it demonstrated for the Micronesian culture during World War II, Lincoln has engaged in a lifetime of social activism that includes prolabor, anti-racist, and anti-war issues. Grahlfs discusses his participation in the historic Flint (Michigan) sitdown strike that supported the United Auto Workers' labor union and the American Civil Liberties Union (ACLU) chapter he helped to form when African Americans were denied housing in his neighborhood. Now, at 93 years old, Grahlfs continues to fight tirelessly for the rights and benefits which U.S. service men and women deserve.

CAROLINA CERVANTES

"*You* go to a uni-ver-sity?! But you're Latina!" These unguarded words from a 14-year-old Mexican American stung the ears of **Carolina Cervantes** as they further fueled her motivation to earn her college degree. The assertions were not *just* words; they represented statistics, emotions, experiences, and barriers. They reflected the lack of collective pride that Carolina had felt as well when she was a teenager. Still, she defied the statistics and overcame the barriers to graduate, *summa cum laude,* from a "uni-ver-sity" just a few years after hearing the prickly assertion. Carolina attributes much of her success to the influence of three extraordinary women — her mother, her aunt, and her grandmother. Despite the challenges of being immigrant single mothers who spoke broken English, they all raised resilient and proud Latina daughters. Carolina considers her experiences within her family, community, and career instrumental in defining her life purpose.

With her first sociology course as a college freshman, Carolina realized her passion for the discipline. Asked in that class to analyze a current issue within the sociopolitical context of her own life, she chose education and began a volunteer placement at the local middle school she herself had attended. The school had been predominantly comprised of Latinos, African Americans, and Pacific Islanders when Carolina was a student and remained so almost a decade later. As part of her research, Cervantes compared the academic profiles of schools on the east side of this San Francisco suburb which included the school where she was volunteering, to schools on the suburb's west side. "I was appalled to learn the extent to which the youth in my own community were underserved," she admits angrily. "It was so blatantly obvious that the 'rich and white' went to the best schools which were on the west side while the 'poor and brown' like me were in the low-performing schools on the east side." Since her district did not have a high school, the students were bused to the west side where the vast majority of the east-side students were placed in the community college and general education tracks.

As a result, Cervantes notes, 65% of the students of color in that district dropped out of high school before graduation. This research project familiarized Carolina with concepts such as at-risk, low-income, and relatively deprived — terms that were used to classify these youth and, she realized, herself as well. The epiphanies she experienced from this study propelled her to declare both sociology and psychology as majors so she could understand how and why her community and those similar to it are oppressed while others prospered. Furthermore, she wanted to know about the means by which individuals come to accept as well as cast off their own domination.

Following graduation, Carolina began work as a community organizer and found her academic background in sociology crucial to discerning the underlying systems that affect the communities with which she worked. Marx's social conflict theory and his concept of scarce resources helped her understand the existence of poverty and power while C. Wright Mills provided her with the sociological imagination to explain the connections between society and the individual. "This concept," Cervantes comments, "continues to give me the sociological lens through which I conduct my everyday work." Furthermore, Mills's power elite theory helped her understand how a privileged few have created the vast inequalities she regularly observes as well as the ways individuals unknowingly enable this small but powerful group to maintain their control. Cervantes observes that, "Community organizing is a vehicle for challenging the existing power structure and dismantling the oppressive sociopolitical system that thrives on the powerlessness of its people." Therefore, she feels it is essential that she apply theories and concepts such as these to the realities that she faces daily.

Through organizing, Carolina learned the art of effective listening and the skills necessary to develop dynamic leaders. She then taught others in her community to operate with finesse in the public sphere, thereby enabling "ordinary" people to find and use their own voices. Moreover, Carolina taught others the value and techniques of grassroots organizing. "At the core of grassroots organizing," Cervantes believes, "is the ability to use interpersonal conversations to build relationships, to surface sociopolitical issues of common concern, to research solutions together, then to gain consensus and support for the remedies in the public arena." To date, Carolina has worked successfully with her community on such problems as gang violence, immigration policies, adequate health care, and affordable housing.

As a community organizer, a typical day for Cervantes consisted of four or more visits to the homes of community members. During these visits, they would discuss the problems that concerned them. These might include their lack of health insurance, insufficient youth programs for their teenagers, and lack of advocacy regarding immigration issues. Each of these meetings typically lasted about an hour or two and generally took place in the evenings or on weekends since most of the people in Cervantes' community worked long hours and had more than one job.

When Carolina was not meeting with community members, she was usually preparing for upcoming meetings and training sessions with the leaders in the community. In addition, she would conduct research that helped in her discourse with public officials, gathering political intelligence and researching the social issues themselves. "When we were preparing for community action with a politician," Cervantes elaborates, "the three or four months leading up to the action would consist of *very* long days and weeks. We would sometimes work as much as 12 hours a day as well as most weekends." One of the most successful actions in which she participated brought together over 500 community members, the city mayor, and the county sheriff. This community action forced the city to assist with funding for affordable immigration legal services and garnered agreement from the county that no deportation arrests would be made without a warrant.

Carolina admits that while community organizing can be fulfilling and exhilarating, its very nature makes it stressful. Long hours, working against angry opposition that refuses to acknowledge the hardships others face, and lack of support from outside the community can physically and emotionally drain the most dedicated organizer. This, in turn, contributes to high rates of burnout. Yet, a victory over a problem that previously plagued her community, an uplifting conversation with an associate, or evidence of a community member who overcame a personal challenge always reenergized Cervantes.

A particularly important component of Carolina's work focused on training others to function effectively in multicultural environments. To prepare herself, she initially examined the areas in which she herself might be a target for oppression. In this respect, she looked at all the statuses she occupied: she is a bilingual, educated, Catholic Chicana from a traditional Mexican working-class immigrant family. She then looked at how each of these statuses influenced her behavior, her world view, and how others responded to her. In doing so, Carolina found sociological concepts such as socialization, collective consciousness, and sociological perspective as well as racism, sexism, and social class elitism to be pertinent. Cervantes recalls that this exercise was extremely useful for addressing prejudices toward and within her own community.

"During my first week on the job," she continues, "I talked with a Latino leader who believed only white people could successfully mobilize Latinos because 'we look up to them.' Even though I vehemently disagreed with him, I still had to understand why he felt that way if we were to work together productively. As we talked further, certain themes emerged. For one, this man was conditioned through his own statuses to believe that people of color are 'less than' whites. I was amazed and saddened. Yet, additional conversations with other Latino leaders revealed this common thread among them." Applying concepts like the self-fulfilling prophecy, scapegoating, projection, and neocolonialism helped Carolina further understand the impact of oppression and to openly discuss the dysfunctions of racism. In this way, she could open the doors to healing and empowerment.

Several of the community members have reminded Cervantes of her own family. Using the principle of shared experience allowed her to create connections, deepen relationships, build trust, and nurture interdependence. With this foundation, she was able to challenge destructive thoughts and encourage growth among potential leaders who previously felt incompetent. "I've been for-tunate to witness the transformation of people," she states, "from passive to bold, from self-conscious to confident, from feelings of inferiority to pride. I've watched a sense of being 'less than' slowly dissipate as positive, collective images formed. My own identity was fortified by being a part of this change."

Carolina eventually left her job as a community organizer to pursue a master's degree in Marriage and Family Counseling with an emphasis in Latino Psychology. With comparatively few Latino therapists currently in practice, she argues that many needs of her community are not met. "Latinos tend to stigmatize therapy and the attrition rate among those who do enter therapy is high. I sus-pect this is due in part to the lack of Spanish-speaking, affordable, and culturally competent therapists," Cervantes speculates. "Furthermore, I believe Latinos tend to distrust psychology and therapy because these practices hinge on a Western male model based on individuality that either invalidates Latino values or pathologizes them." She offers this example: a 40-year-old Caucasian man who lives at home with his mother would be encouraged to move away and pursue an independent lifestyle. In contrast, a Latino of the same age who lives at home would be thought normal as it is common in his collectivistic culture to put mother and family first.

Carolina's goal, therefore, is to provide some of the care she deems necessary in her community but in ways that respect Latino beliefs. She acknowledges wisdom in the words of Steven Biko who theorizes that "the most potent weapon of the oppressor is the mind of the oppressed." Nonetheless, Cervantes also contends that only in combination with sociopolitical involvement people of color can liberate themselves from the insidious impact of domination.

Cervantes's future plans focus on the pursuit of a PhD that will allow her to conduct and advance research on the psychological, sociological, and the political components inherent in domination and liberation. Ultimately, Carolina will become involved in traditional politics most likely beginning as a city council member. She plans to continue her struggle to cultivate leadership and ensure that the voices of communities of color are not only heard but respected.

Cervantes suggests that those who practice sociology remember that the learning which occurs in the field will undoubtedly be reciprocal. "The people you are trying to help will have just as much to teach you as you have to share with them," she advices. "Take those lessons back to your classrooms so that other students can benefit from your experiences."

Additionally, Cervantes recommends that sociologists learn a second language. "In our multicultural world," she predicts, "it will become mandatory that we are fluent in more than a single language. For one thing, it shows respect for another culture when one attempts to speak that language and therein, the ability to communicate effectively becomes greater." To Carolina Cervantes, communication between people, whether one-on-one or as whole cultures, embodies the essence of sociology.

To learn more about Carolina Cervantes and her work, please contact her by e-mail at: ixcana@ymail.com

MEGAN SCOTT

For **Megan Scott**, racial epithets and stereotypes were ubiquitous in her childhood home. "Even as a kid," Megan reveals, "I felt there had to be more logical explanations for the behaviors of people than the ones I was given by my family."

Scott started college as a psychology major, reasoning that this discipline would provide her with the tools necessary to help other people. With her first class in sociology, however, she was instantly attracted. Megan explains, "I had finally found a school of thought that reflected my own. Sociology explained the world in a way that satisfied me and confirmed my speculation that a person's social environment plays a major role in the way they behave." Furthermore, the fact that sociology could involve her with the people she was studying in the environments that shaped their personalities appealed to her. "We all have unique stories," Scott maintains, "and sociology would provide me with the means to discover, understand, and appreciate them." Certainly, she acknowledged, helping people on an individual level was valuable and necessary. Then again, she thought she personally could make a bigger impact if she could change social structures instead of modifying individuals to fit environments that were often toxic. She realized that would be possible with the macroscopic approach sociology provides.

When her undergraduate education was completed, Scott joined AmeriCorps choosing a program that took her to Baltimore, Maryland. She lived there for a year with nine other volunteers in an old, rundown convent. She admits that she is not certain what caused the greatest culture shock — moving across the country, working in an unfamiliar city as complex as Baltimore, or living with nine very different strangers. In all of these situations, however, her sociological understanding of the nature and stages of culture shock helped her adjust.

During her first year, Megan worked at a job training site preparing unemployed and underemployed women who lived below the poverty line for the workforce. The primary goal was, of course, to help the clients eventually sustain their families financially, Megan explains, but as working women they would also be positive role models for their children. Scott helped the women finish their high-school education and supervised two after-school programs. Most of her students were African American, single mothers, and not much older than Megan herself.

She quickly found that all the women she met *wanted* to work; they wanted a better life for themselves and their children. "This reality was so different from the picture of welfare moms driving expensive cars that is painted by so many people. This includes members of my own family," Megan claims. "I think it must be easier to stigmatize these women than to acknowledge that our institutions, especially our economic and political structures, are broken. I observed how difficult it is for women without adequate food, housing, education, health care, or childcare to enter the job market and earn a living wage." Megan credits such sociological concepts as Oscar Lewis's culture of poverty, the Davis–Moore Thesis, and the feminization of poverty with helping her understand the structural inadequacies that maintain poverty. Similarly, concepts like blaming the victim, projection, and frustration–aggression theory permitted her to cope with the attitudes perpetuated by mainstream ideology.

Scott loved Baltimore so much that she reenlisted with Americorps, spending that year at a large nonprofit organization. Megan was instructed to develop a comprehensive manual intended to help the organization recruit and use their volunteers more effectively. She spent her days observing how the current volunteers were being utilized, learning about the organization's many programs, and researching the best practices for volunteer recruitment and management. Scott suspects the completed, all-inclusive manual "is now collecting dust on some shelf somewhere." In hindsight, she realizes it was not what the staff needed or wanted. "Had I conducted a needs assessment first, however informal, I could have redirected my efforts and provided the organization with a useful document. Lesson learned," she concludes. As it was, Megan experienced such concepts as bureaucracy, alienation, and Weber's iron cage as well as the fervor with which people can resist unwanted change.

Following completion of her second year with AmeriCorps, Scott left to pursue a master's degree in social work (MSW) at the University of Maryland. She selected this particular graduate program because it offered a nonclinical tract in community organization as well as a specialization in social action and neighborhood development. Since she wasn't drawn to academic research or teaching in higher education, she reasoned that an MSW would be the most logical way to build on her background in sociology. Largely because of her previous experience with AmeriCorps, Megan was placed at an agency with which the university was collaborating on a local political campaign.

As such, she had the opportunity to work closely with elected officials. The issue in question was extremely unpopular with the neighborhood residents, however, and Megan argues their opposition was well-founded. "Over and over," Scott elaborates, "the people would tell us how groups just like ours would come into the neighborhood intent on 'fixing it.' Then the funding would run out, the groups would leave, and the community would be unable to sustain the projects. Therefore, they would see no benefits and even worse, the neighborhood would be left more disadvantaged than before." Given this history and the skepticism that understandably accompanied it, it was not possible for Megan and her colleagues engender any support.

In retrospect, Megan understands that, "We were outsiders to this community and we were telling people that something of theirs was broken. We were proposing solutions without listening and learning from them. I mean, they were the experts on their own neighborhood! And here we were, trying to tell them what they should do. We needed to hear from the community members so that we could build trust. Yet, we were trying to organize a community around an issue they had not initiated and were not convinced they wanted! Another lesson learned!"

In the second year of her MSW program, Scott was placed in the Public Affairs Department at Planned Parenthood of Maryland. She worked with a lobbyist and a grassroots organizer studying the legislative process as she followed Planned Parenthood's often controversial issues through their course. In this position, Megan's normal day involved examining bills of interest to the organization and familiarizing herself with the research that supported their stances as well as those of their opposition. Scott often accompanied the lobbyist to public hearings and meetings with legislators. In that capacity, she got her first taste of testifying before state politicians and is justifiably proud that she could present the testimony she prepared on the Emergency Contraception bill. Scott sometimes found it challenging to counter misinformation and stubbornness and to display patience with the snail's pace at which bills moved through the legislative process. Nonetheless, she was always exhilarated by the passion that could consume people on all sides of an issue.

Finally, she had found her calling! She clarifies, "I recognized that so much of our lives are significantly influenced by those few we choose to represent us in government. Through this internship, I learned that elected officials need our involvement. They are just normal people who, very often, do not know any more about an issue than we ourselves do." Megan admits that she initially found this fact terrifying but then it motivated her to stay involved in public policy. With her background in sociology and community organizing, she felt she could objectively analyze the many facets of an issue that too often go unexamined and unheard. She contends that the sociological imagination allowed her to understand how issues affect not only individuals but also the world-at-large.

Most of all, she realized how critical it is to share that information with those who control the funding and make the decisions that impact lives.

With graduate degree in hand, Megan moved to Maine with her new husband. It took her a few months to find a job because she was "from away" and wasn't familiar with the regional subculture of the state. In the end, however, her educational background and training helped her secure a position as a grass-roots organizer for the Maine Coalition on Smoking or Health (MCSOH). "MCSOH," she explains, "is a coalition of voluntary and public health organizations that work together on tobacco-related concerns." At the time Megan worked with them, the agency was primarily concerned with protecting the share of the money awarded to the state in a celebrated tobacco settlement. While Maine properly used the funds for health-related prevention programs, the monies were in constant jeopardy of being redirected to fill other, unrelated State budget needs.

Scott felt strongly that, as a grassroots organizer, she needed to make it as easy as possible for community members to be involved in policy issues. "It can be intimidating to work with legislators and other key decision-makers," she acknowledges. "Therefore, I furnished people with the tools that would make them comfortable doing so. As such, I was constantly available to answer questions and provide the groups we were organizing with talking points, research, contact information for local legislators, and training sessions." Ultimately, Megan developed rapport with the staff of Maine's 31 community health programs. She traveled across the state to meet with them and their volunteers; building trust and support for the primary goals of MCSOH.

In addition, MCSOH worked to ban smoking in public places. "This work was grueling in an area dominated by libertarian views," Scott disclosures. "Many business owners believed that the bar culture was rooted in the customers' freedom to smoke while they drank. There was wide-spread fear that bars would go out of business if smoking were banned. MCSOH, on the other hand, supported the right of workers to an environment that did not compromise their health." Although Megan enjoyed working in a common cause with others who shared her values, she found it equally frustrating that the health of our society's labor force seemed secondary to business interests. Despite the difficulties, however, the education Megan helped provide to communities, the media, and legislative officials along with tireless organizing, coalition-building, and time she reluctantly spent in smoke-filled bars herself eventually produced a statewide ban on smoking in public places. "It was thrilling when we finally prevailed," she enthuses. "And for the record, not one bar in the state went out of business because of the ban!"

Since Megan's position with MCSOH was funded solely by a grant, she was not surprised when the monies evaporated and she found herself out of the labor force again. Because of the connections she made within the public health community by that time, though, she was quickly hired as the coordinator of the Maine Association of Substance Abuse Programs (MASAP). Megan worked on issues that involved underage drinking. As with her previous position, she aligned closely with community groups and coalitions furnishing them with the information and tools necessary for their members to become involved in the legislative process.

In this case, however, Rice had to navigate carefully between the impact of policies on local communities and their effect on state-level organizations, legislative officials, and the state government bureaucracy. To do so successfully, Megan worked closely with state legislators as well as their constituents educating them both about current research and providing feedback regarding the proposed policies. "It was a constant dance that required me to know my sometimes disparate audiences; meeting and accepting them where they were; then demonstrating the reality of the policy's impact on their locale," Scott explains.

"The work was exhausting and stimulating all at the same time," Megan reports, "but I had found a career that I was passionate about." Scott acknowledges that working on the same issues year after year and making the same points to counter the same misconceptions over and over again was tiresome. She often found opinions about alcohol could be fierce and soon realized she had to tread lightly or she would be easily dismissed as a prohibitionist.

Conversely, she was always invigorated when she convinced a legislator to vote for public health; when one of her opinion pieces appeared in print; when a community leader found the confidence to testify on an issue; and when she herself had the chance to confront alcohol industry lobbyists.

Eventually, Megan left MASAP to raise her two young daughters but plans to return to the public health policy arena in the near future. She wants to focus on environmental concerns since she finds the sheer beauty of her state so magnificent. Scott realizes she needs a job that matters; that makes the world a better place. She dreams that one day she will have worked herself out of a job because the social issues she addresses will no longer exist. Being a realist, however, she guides her children toward social consciousness and involvement in the hope that they will eradicate whatever problems she cannot.

For those who choose a major in sociology, Scott maintains they will be able to see the world from a different perspective. "You will always be more than just a volunteer or an activist because your analysis will flow from your sociological imagination. You will be able to broaden the perspectives of those with whom you live and work. You will be able to explain the social structures and conditions that affect people's lives. By listening carefully to others, you will be able to formulate the issues underlying what appear to be personality differences. Your understanding of prejudice and ethnocentrism will allow you to build bridges where others see chasms. Your sociological understanding and especially, your activism will provide direction and inspiration to those who have not had the privilege of your education."

To learn more about Megan Scott and her work, please contact her by e-mail at: meganrice26@gmail.com

KAREN SCHAUMANN

Like many who eventually pursue a degree in sociology, *Karen Schaumann* came to the discipline in a roundabout manner. Armed with a BS in political science that she received from Eastern Michigan University (EMU), she set out to find a fulfilling career. As an undergraduate honors assistant to the political science department chair, Karen had already garnered research skills from her study of German émigré social scientists. She had also been exposed to the critical approach of the Frankfurt School of Sociology and found it immensely interesting. In addition, she was privileged to secure an internship with a Democratic Senator from Michigan while she concurrently conducted research on New England style town hall meetings for mayor of a suburban Detroit city. "Somehow," Schaumann recalls, "I thought I'd be able to find a job as satisfying as my assistanceships and internships had been. I was sadly disappointed."

After a stint as a telephone interviewer and with only limited job prospects on the horizon, Karen was gratefully recruited by the chair of the sociology department at her *alma mater* for graduate school. Since she had already acquired substantial research skills, Schaumann also received a financial assistanceship for which she was expected to tutor undergraduate students in statistics. The funds, she expected, would pay her bills and allow her to feed her children while she was attending grad school.

At the same time, Schaumann was hired by a criminologist who had just published a social history on homelessness to help him prepare an anthology. "As a sociology student, I was learning about social structure, bureaucracies, stratification, and social movements. As a single mom, I was learning about social structure, bureaucracies, stratification, and social movements," Karen notes. "Consequently, my education was formal and academic at the same time it was concrete and real, informed as it was by the Welfare Reform era of the President Bill Clinton administration."

Schaumann vividly remembers how the poor, especially women and children, were demonized at that time. The then-governor of Michigan ruthlessly slashed welfare payments to thousands of recipients, effectively leaving them homeless while nearly 5000 public housing units sat vacant in the city of Detroit alone. Schaumann was compelled to join other single parents and low-income women in alliance with regional and national anti-poverty organizations to debunk stereotypes of "welfare mothers driving pink Cadillacs." Armed with statistics and other hard scientific data, she worked with college faculty and community activists to establish teach-ins. She reasoned that once the stereotypes were dispelled with facts, the attitudes of the nonpoor would be more sympathetic. "We were right," Karen beams. "As we brought academic rigor and innovative research to bear on the question of poverty, we garnered increasing public as well as political support."

In collaboration with Legal Services of Southeast Michigan (before Congress severely restricted their activities), Karen and her allies created a social services advisory board to help providers assist their clients. They first designed a client satisfaction survey for welfare recipients (a novel idea for that time) to determine the effectiveness of the welfare delivery system. "The data provided a solid and credible quantitative foundation for our advocacy," she states. "You have to know what the problem is before you can solve it."

These experiences merely validated for Schaumann that which she had learned in her sociology classes. Concepts like relative and absolute poverty as well as the feminization and racialization of poverty became part of her world as she witnessed firsthand how robotics, runaway shops, outsourcing, the incarceration binge, chronic unemployment, and homelessness are intimately inter-twined. When the state government began locking hundreds of people made jobless by these forces out of their homes *every day*, Schaumann helped to organize a "tent-city" movement in

Michigan. The organizers dispersed warm coats, blankets, and food to those from the cities hardest hit by the factory closures and subsequent job losses. "These small gestures often made the difference between survival and death in the subzero temperatures common to the Michigan winters," Karen explains. "Most people were kicked out of their homes with only the clothes they had on their backs. Once evicted, they could not return to collect any of their personal belongings."

Having already learned the value of bringing awareness to the general community, the tent-city movement made public the private pain experienced by the poor. Large newspaper chains, owned and operated as they are by wealthy conglomerates, were typically reluctant to cover these sorts of stories. To counteract this impediment, community groups that were sympathetic to the plight of the indigent and outraged by the merciless treatment broke the blackout by marching to the state capitol. They held sit-ins, speak-outs, forums, and other kinds of peaceful protests at television news stations. These were tactics the organizers had learned earlier from their study of the civil rights movement and Dr. Martin Luther King (another sociologist, Karen enjoys pointing out).

"By using the media to our advantage, we successfully focused attention on issues surrounding poverty and connected with the general public," Schaumann argues. "We addressed the sorry state of the health care delivery system and the rapid decline of education for the poor. We spoke to the connection between discrimination and unemployment. In doing so, we garnered support from labor unions, civil rights activists, educators, and public health workers."

The following year Karen, along with a diverse alliance of individuals, established a state-wide coalition that held a "State of the People" address on the steps of the capitol building at the same time Michigan's governor delivered his annual "State of the State" address. "Even with all of our marches to the state capitol, the media attention, and the public support we were gaining, our encouragement to 'Fight Poverty, Not the Poor,' seemed to fall on deaf ears among our elected officials," Schaumann remembers. "Cut after devastating cut in the social safety net passed through the legislature as we watched conditions worsen in poor neighborhoods." In addition, passage of the NAFTA along with the PRWOA forced millions more desperate individuals into low-wage service sector jobs that deflated their earnings further. Coalitions of labor, nonunionized service workers, and low-income workers successfully passed local ordinances that required city employers to provide a living income. Yet, they were unable to stem the tide of corporations that rapidly moved their production to other parts of the world where they could pay pitiful wages.

As financial cuts deepened Schaumann, along with representatives from the National Coalition of the Homeless, the National Organization of Women (NOW), and the National Welfare Rights Union, delivered testimony on welfare reform to key members of the House and Senate, the Department of Agriculture, the Department of Health and Human Services, and an official of President Clinton's cabinet in Washington, D.C. The group gave high-level bureaucrats who were, by nature of their positions, largely disconnected from the everyday lives of the poor, a realistic view of low-income life. Using qualitative data, they put human faces on anonymous numbers to demonstrate the impact that welfare reform had on living, breathing human beings. "The continuous loop of data collection and application was intentional," Karen reports. "We deliberately moved between community members and meetings, academic organizations, conferences, and politicians on the premise that social policy construction in a democracy requires the participation of all citizens."

As a result of her work with the indigent, Schaumann was later asked to participate in a study of homelessness in Michigan. In the capacity of regional coordinator for a major county in that state, she organized and facilitated focus groups consisting of service providers, homeless people, and social activists. "This kind of inclusiveness has typified my career," Karen maintains proudly.

Schaumann acknowledges that her training in sociology gave her a macro-level perspective with which to understand her micro-level reality. "C. Wright Mills' sociological imagination was not lost on me," she comments. "Along with the lessons I learned from my low-income upbringing, I was able to connect my personal biography to history. I had learned from direct experience as had my mother and grandmother that the voices of poor people are seldom heard unless they organize together for change. Not being part of Mills' power elite leaves far too many out in the cold — whether former auto workers, women escaping domestic violence, or the working poor."

With sadness, Karen admits she and her allies were unable to have any significant impact on the national policy level even though they had the support of many renowned scholars and activists. At the state level, however, she rightfully claims some significant victories. For example, when the State of Michigan violated the Federal Violence Against Women Act (FVAWA) by implementing welfare reform requirements that contradicted those of the FVAWA, Schaumann worked with the Michigan Poverty Law Program to reinstate protection for countless women trying to escape dangerous domestic situations. "Some of my most gratifying moments came from representing poor people before administrative judges," she states. One woman, a quadriplegic mother, had lost her Medicaid benefits when her son turned 18 years old. Instead of referring the woman to the appropriate alternative program, her caseworker told her indifferently to "have another baby so you'll be covered for the next 18 years." This left the woman without any medical insurance at all. Karen remarks humbly, "I never failed to be inspired by the dignity of these women in the face of hardship and hostility. I always felt honored to help them."

When low-income students at EMU realized the retention rate among their population was lower than that of their wealthier counterparts, they appealed to Schaumann for the sociological understanding she could provide. She quickly realized that many of the low-income students did not know they were eligible for food stamps. Therefore, she helped the students organize "Know Your Rights" forums. In addition, she convinced the university's department of social work to create websites with useful information; set up workshops to help individuals navigate the social service bureaucracies; and provide referrals to necessary services. Karen is pleased to say that, as a result of these efforts, the number of low-income students who graduated from the university grew substantially.

"These micro-level victories were sweet," Schaumann discloses, "but we saw and continue to see great tragedy as well." She remembers the mother whose children were taken by Child Protective Services because she got off work late and missed the last bus to the childcare provider. Unable to retrieve her children from the system, she committed suicide. Other women, she recalls, lost their children when the welfare reform program required them to work afternoons. She cannot forget the house fires that occur all-too-frequently when heat is turned off for nonpayment during frigid winters or the children who are accidentally burned by scalding water that has to be heated on the stove for bathing. Etched in her memory are the countless battered women who endure yet another beating when the abuser appears at the door with a bag of desperately needed groceries. "The horrors of poverty are all too real," Schaumann insists. "While NAFTA and welfare reform were dreams-come-true for employers, they were nightmares for poor, low-income, and working class people. Much of the former middle-class is now living this nightmare, too."

Seeing the devastation that welfare reform exacted compelled Schaumann and her allies to take their cause to the United Nations where they held public hearings, wrote press releases, invited local and state officials to attend, collected personal accounts about the impact of these reforms, and organized the "March for Our Lives." With the Center for Constitutional Rights, Schaumann legally challenged welfare reform before the United Nations in an international forum. Moreover, she testified before the Universal Declaration of Human Rights that welfare reform resulted in violations to economic human rights, presenting evidence to the personal tragedies endured as a result of welfare reform and an unresponsive economy. "We found that poverty and unemployment are, apparently, great equalizers as the women, men, and children who joined our cause represented a cross-section of racial and social class backgrounds," Schaumann reflects. "Together, we spoke on behalf of the people whose hard work was no longer sufficient to feed and clothe their families. We campaigned to ensure that, in the future, no one in this country would have to worry about their next meal, the security of their job or their shelter, their health care, or the education of their children."

Karen believes that careers in sociology are expanding and will continue to do so because the contributions sociologists can make are not only in demand but also crucially necessary to the humanity of our world. In her case, she found concepts such as deindustrialization, corporatocracy, social movement life cycle, and social conflict theory useful to her endeavors but points out that sociology provides a unique analysis helpful to understanding any human activity.

Schaumann reports that tent cities have resurfaced in Michigan and around the nation while more people are impoverished daily. Yet, thousands continue the battle for economic justice. Among them is Karen Schaumann.

To learn more about Karen Schaumann and her work, please contact her by e-mail at karenschaumann@yahoo.com

LINCOLN GRAHLFS

Lincoln Grahlfs admits that he is so mindful of the adage, "Eternal vigilance is the price of freedom," that he is disturbed that so many Americans follow blindly, accept whatever they are told as truth, and label as traitorous anyone who questions government policy. Yet, he confesses, up to the age of 13, he was on the path to becoming that same way. So how did he come to be a professor of sociology, an advocate for peace, and a spokesperson for military veterans exposed to nuclear warfare?

Grahlfs experienced childhood in the New York City of the 1920s and 1930s where he encountered people representing all variations of nationality, race, and religion. In his mind, people were people, and he had been instructed to give everyone equal respect. At the same time, however, the adults in his family maintained a subtle social distance from certain kinds of individuals. Like most American cities in those days, New York practiced both residential (or *de facto*) as well as legal (*de jure*) segregation. In his childhood naiveté, Lincoln thought this living arrangement was a combination of economic stratification and a desire to live among one's "own kind." To Lincoln, therefore, that was just "the ways things were." While his family members did not think progressively about race or integration, he does credit his parents with one thing: they always encouraged him to question. "They might not have provided the best answers," he recalls, "but at least they encouraged inquiry." Doubtlessly, Grahlfs was learning an earmark of sociology at a very young age.

With his admission to Ohio's Antioch College in 1940, Grahlfs was convinced by his father to study engineering. "This was one of many times that I unwisely accepted his advice," he reflects. Immediately bored with the curriculum, he frittered away his time and dropped out of school at the end of his freshman year.

A year later, as the military draft was nipping at his heels, Lincoln joined the navy. Largely because of his proficiency in math, he was assigned to work as a quartermaster. In that capacity, he maintained navigational charts, publications, and instruments, regulated the ship's clocks, trained helmsmen and lookouts, and handled visual communications.

"It was best job in the world," he allows. "I'd been fascinated by ships and the ocean since I was a little boy so I enjoyed my work; I was good at it and I was given recognition for it. I knew my job better than most of my superior officers so they were reluctant to hassle me. Near the end of my enlistment, my commanding officer offered to recommend me for promotion if I would re-enlist." But Grahlfs refused. Why? Because, in his own words, he didn't relish the idea of keeping the guns polished for the next war. Besides, he had observed actions on the part of the U.S. military that he could not justify.

Nonetheless, Grahlfs readily admits that his 6 years in the navy profoundly influenced the course of his life. After surviving 3 years of wartime service, he was assigned to a unit where he partook in atomic bomb tests at Bikini Atoll. Grahlfs swears that, "Contrary to official government statements, neither I nor most of the other participants volunteered for these tests. In fact, most have had health problems related to that involvement ever since." Grahlfs himself was hospitalized with a radiation-related illness less than a year after his assignment to this unit. As a result of this experience, he has been a relentless advocate for the abolition of nuclear weapons since his discharge from the navy.

Immediately following his release from the hospital, Lincoln was sent to Guam and delegated to a ship that provided logistical support for the natives on the outlying territories of Micronesia. He observed firsthand how the U.S. authorities demonstrated little understanding or regard for native culture, effectively undermining the indigenous culture and their economy. Along with his experience in Bikini Atoll, this event helped to shape the individual that Lincoln Grahlfs became.

When he dropped out of college in 1941, Lincoln had every intention of eventually returning though he didn't expect it would take him 9 years! With the help of the GI Bill and a veterans' scholarship from the State of New York, however, Grahlfs finally resumed his education. "When I did, I was a completely different person; I was a serious student with a purpose," he discloses. "My time in Micronesia had given me a genuine appreciation of cultures and a disdain for the ethnocentric myopia behind many of our country's policies. I wanted to do something about that calamity."

As a result, Grahlfs pursued his bachelor's degree in sociology at Hofstra College on New York's Long Island and immediately after graduation, entered Columbia University where, in 1955, he was awarded an MA in sociology along with the Certificate of the East Asian Institute.

Lincoln's master's thesis was largely prompted by the Micronesian people who frequently asserted that the Japanese had treated them poorly while under their occupation. Using the archival research method, Grahlfs concluded that the reaction of the native population was determined by the extent to which they felt included in Japanese life and this varied considerably from one part of Micronesia to another. "For instance," Grahlfs elaborates, "on the island of Saipan, the indigenous population was relegated to 'living on the sidelines' of a thriving metropolis. As such, their resentment of the Japanese was high. By contrast," Grahlfs continues, "since Palau was the Japanese colonial capital of their South Sea enterprise, some Palauans were employed in the administrative complex while others were hired as servants by Japanese officials. Therefore, they were able to share in the more sophisticated lifestyle of the Japanese and were not treated so much like 'outsiders.'" Grahlfs found the application of the sociological imagination, power elite theory, and social marginality helpful in conducting this study.

In the summer of 1956 while Lincoln was working on his PhD, an unexpected correspondence gave his career path new direction. He received a telegram from the president of Wilkes College in Pennsylvania offering him a 1-year teaching assignment in the sociology department. That telegram ultimately resulted in a lifetime in academia that spanned over four decades at five different colleges.

"If I thought my job in the navy had been the best possible, then certainly college teaching was a close second," Dr. Grahlfs maintains. "I never thought I wanted to teach but I was soon enjoying the give and take of classroom discussions."

After fulfilling his 1-year contract in Pennsylvania, Grahlfs arrived in Flint, Michigan, to teach at their local community college. He quickly ascertained that Flint was the ultimate "company town" operated under the thumb of the General Motors Automobile Corporation. Moreover, it was the fourth most racially segregated city in the United States at that time. "During my nine years in Flint," Lincoln reflects, "I truly emerged as a social activist." He soon joined the local Unitarian Church and discovered that several of its congregants had been leaders in the now-famous Flint sit-down strike of the mid-1930s.

Together, these friends founded the Flint chapter of the American Civil Liberties Union (ACLU) and Grahlfs became its chairperson. They also launched a vigorous campaign for an open housing ordinance. "On some occasions when black people moved into previously all-white neighborhoods, they were threatened by beatings, vandalism, and arson. I was one of the whites who would sit with them in their homes through the tense evenings." Grahlfs continues, "In certain neighborhoods where there was documented racial discrimination, we would have a black couple go into a restaurant and sit down. Then we would have a white couple go into the same restaurant a few minutes later. If the white couple got served first, we would report the incident to the authorities." He also recalls that he and a black colleague lobbied the administration of Flint Community College for 3 years before they got permission to team-teach a course on race relations. The results proved so positive that they were asked by the city's police department to conduct the same course for their personnel.

In 1966, a telephone call once again altered the course of Grahlfs's life. The long-time chair of the sociology department at University of Michigan had received a grant from the National Science Foundation to develop sociologically oriented curriculum materials for use in secondary schools. He asked Grahlfs to evaluate all the materials before the final publication. Upon accepting the offer, Lincoln spent the ensuing 3 years developing test materials, analyzing test results, and traveling around the country to observe classroom sessions where the materials were used. As much as Grahlfs enjoyed this work, it all came to an abrupt halt in 1969 when the Nixon administration drastically slashed funding for educational research. So he returned, once again, to academia with a series of short-term teaching assignments that took him from New Jersey to Maryland and finally to the University of Wisconsin (UW).

During this time, Grahlfs had established himself as a civil rights activist, an advocate for peace, and an opponent of nuclear weapons and his reputation preceded him to UW. Whenever there was a potential story about these issues, the local news media would contact him for comments and analyses. As such, he gave numerous interviews to journalists, radio announcers, and television anchors. Grahlfs was also among the early cadre of professors who taught courses that addressed war as a social problem. These classes were so well-received that he was later invited to present the material through weekly broadcasts on Wisconsin Public Radio.

Lincoln was eventually forced to admit that his lack of a doctorate was inhibiting his academic progress. In one case, he had been denied tenure and in another he was not promoted despite his considerable reputation as a social researcher. So in 1988, he enrolled at the University of Michigan where on April 28, 1995, he became "Dr. Grahlfs." He was 72 years old.

For his doctoral dissertation, he obtained information through questionnaires and interviews about the attitudes and recollections of military veterans who had participated in nuclear weapons testing during World War II. In doing so, Grahlfs provided insight into the lives of roughly one quarter million men who had been largely overlooked. The results of his study revealed that the majority of veterans simply wanted the U.S. government to openly acknowledge it had willfully denied the dangers of exposure to radiation. Asked why his study remains significant in the twenty-first century, Grahlfs submits that millions more veterans from wars in Korea, Vietnam, and the Middle East have also neglected, abandoned, and refused recognition for the risks they took. "Furthermore," he adds, "these tragedies will continue as long as we allow our government to conceal the suffering of our nation's most patriotic citizens."

Professor Grahlfs acknowledges that his teaching career has allowed him to carry out multitude activities that underpin his personal values. He was an early protester against the Vietnam War, for example, and following the 1971 massacre of innocent students at Kent State University in Ohio, he helped organize two busloads of students from New Jersey to participate in the ensuing March on Washington (D.C.).

In addition, Grahlfs has frequently used his expertise in sociological methods to design, develop, implement, evaluate, and oversee social research projects. While he was at Washington College, for instance, the National Center for Health Statistics (NCHS) hired him to recruit, train, and supervise interviewers who determined the effectiveness of the health-care delivery system in rural areas of Maryland. After moving to Wisconsin, he was approached twice more to work with NCHS, in these instances as an interviewer. In one study he assessed the organization and procedures of group medical practices and in the other he evaluated nursing homes in Northern Wisconsin and the Upper Peninsula of Michigan.

In the years that followed, Lincoln was hired to assess a federal program intended to help low-income homemakers improve the use of their limited dollars. Grahlfs designed a research plan, hired an interviewer, and proceeded with the program evaluation. The assessment revealed that the amount of funding the families received was not sufficient to meet even minimal financial needs. On another occasion, he was approached by an attorney concerned that his client could not get a fair trial in the county where the alleged crime took place. Grahlfs constructed a survey that ultimately demonstrated need for a change of venue.

At various points in his career, Dr. Grahlfs interviewed respondents for a number of organizations, including the well-known Gallup Poll. "Being a sociologist has opened doors to some fascinating opportunities, both personally and professionally," Professor Grahlfs concedes. "Doing research on my dissertation, for instance, I was humbled and inspired to be brought into contact with hundreds of groups vying for global peace and the abolition of nuclear arms."

More significant than his research, Grahlfs believes, is his activism in antinuclear and radiation survivor organizations. On more than a few occasions, his willingness to speak out has gained him the attention of the federal government. In one case, he was invited to provide testimony before the U.S. Department of Energy. He pointed to documentation of genetic consequences caused by radiation exposure reporting that 21% of his respondents had children or grandchildren who were born with some anomaly. He revealed that his own daughter experienced multiple problems with her endocrine system as a teenager and was dying of cancer at the time of the hearing.

Two years later, Lincoln was appointed to an advisory group that is part of the National Cancer Institute (NCI) wherein he updated the tables used to estimate levels of risk for developing cancer from exposure to radiation. Grahlfs later joined the NCI's Communication Development Group which was tasked with revealing that extensive fallout from nuclear tests in Nevada had exposed large segments of the population to thyroid problems including, but not limited to, cancer.

At 93 years old, Lincoln has retired from teaching but still devotes much of his time to writing, advocacy, and activism around those causes with which he resonates.

Asked about the value of a sociology degree, he recalls a renowned cardiac surgeon who, upon learning of Grahlfs's profession, remarked, "As a sociologist and an educator, you have the potential to save more lives than I have saved in my long career in medicine."

Dr. Lincoln Grahlfs summarizes his life thusly. "As a freshman at Antioch College, I was familiarized with the words of Horace Mann who declared, 'Be ashamed to die until you have won some victory for humanity.' I can honestly say I am not ashamed to die. However, to the extent that there are any victories for which I can take credit, I have to share that credit with many others. Furthermore, I believe that struggles are never won in finality. The gains must be defended constantly and repeatedly. Thus, the need for eternal vigilance."

To learn more about Dr. Lincoln Grahlfs and his work, you may contact him by e-mail at flg17@sbcglobal.net or by phone at 314-355-2651.

14

SOCIOLOGISTS IN EDUCATION

Given all the career possibilities you've just read about, perhaps you are still drawn to the educational environment. The truth is, a large number of sociology majors do spend their careers in college classrooms either through careful planning or through happenstance. Others pursue nonacademic careers during the day and share their experiences with classrooms full of inquiring minds by night. Many more seek out scholarly opportunities after retirement. In these times, working as a sociologist in the world of higher education does not necessarily mean the traditional podium, power point, or monotone lectures.

Sister Roseanne Murphy, for example, engaged her students in community service long before the practice went mainstream. Using popular best-selling books instead of weighty academic tomes, bringing subject matter experts into her classrooms, and requiring internships of majors planning to undertake careers in social work, Sr. Roseanne brought new depth to old topics. More than that, she arranged travel programs to Rome, Mexico, the Holy Land, and beyond. She taught classes at many of the sites abouts which her students were learning.

A "street teacher" in the Chicago School and Elijah Anderson modes, *Don Stannard-Friel* teaches most of his classes in the field *sans* sophisticated technology, classroom walls, and rigid expectations. The result of this style is profound and meaningful learning that better prepares students for the realities they are likely to face in their future careers and personal lives.

SR. ROSEANNE MURPHY

For *Sr. Roseanne Murphy*, a Catholic nun in the Notre Dame de Namur teaching congregation, the decision to major in sociology was not so much a matter of choice but of practicality and mandate. As a registered nurse when she entered the religious community, she was first required by her order to complete her undergraduate major in Social Welfare at Mount St. Mary's College near Los Angeles. Following that, her community sent her to Stanford University because of its geographic proximity to the convent. She obtained her masters degree in sociology and began to work on her doctorate in sociology as well. When she received a research fellowship from the University of Notre Dame in Indiana, however, she got transferred there to finish her terminal degree. Upon completion of her formal education, Sr. Roseanne continued to teach at Notre Dame de Namur University (NDNU) where she has remained since.

Sr. Roseanne explains that the decisions for her to pursue advanced degrees in sociology were made by her order based on the desperate need for trained social workers in those times. So great was this need, in fact, that in 1963 President Lyndon Johnson announced that he could easily hire 250,000 social workers on-the-spot if only they were trained and available. Further, it was widely acknowledged that sociologists could prepare them.

In that same decade, Sr. Roseanne recalls the consequential shifts in the existing social order that were occurring almost simultaneously. The nation reeled from the senseless assassinations of John and then Robert Kennedy as well as Martin Luther King while the Civil Rights Movement begged people to end the racism still rife in this country. Caesar Chavez and Dolores Huerta united farm workers in California as employers in all industries were forced to improve working conditions. Four students at Kent State University in Ohio were murdered by the National Guard and young people everywhere were rebelling against all kinds of authority. The "Summer of Love," the "Peace Movement," and the "Hippie Culture" evolved. With the Haight-Ashbury community and its "love children" in close proximity to the college where Sr. Roseanne taught, she watched many of her students become enchanted with this lifestyle. The "generation gap" abounded as students frequently took on the cause for social change in sharp contrast to their parents who feared and resisted those same changes. At the center of this tumult was the War in Vietnam. As it raged, students on campuses across the country (indeed, around the world) became increasingly conflicted about US involvement.

Being a small college, NDNU did not experience the dramatic conflicts that erupted on larger campuses, but Murphy was, nonetheless, at the forefront initiating classroom discussions about the sociohistorical roots of the conflict, meanings of patriotism, and the rights of conscientious objectors. She exposed students to conditions most had not even known existed through books like *The Other America* and documentaries such as *Harvest of Shame*. Newspapers, magazines, and television exploded with coverage of these conditions and students could see the transformations unfolding in front of them. "It was a time of frustration but also of hope," Sr. Roseanne remembers. "The students were living in one of the most rapidly changing periods in decades. Vast numbers were drawn to sociology for explanations of the causes and solutions to the turbulence they observed. In fact, it even became a status symbol to major in sociology not just at our college but at schools throughout the nation. At NDNU, sociology became one of our most popular majors."

Dynamic classroom discussions ensued as Murphy used sociological concepts like anomie and alienation to explain the disintegration of social norms in the absence of new rules. She noted the dysfunctions of the free love lifestyle that left its participants directionless and lonely. She discussed the angst in this culture that underlay the increasing numbers of LSD drug trips being taken.

"It was a heady time to be teaching sociology," Sr. Roseanne recalls wistfully.

Noting an almost-desperate search for purpose and values among her students, she combined sociology with her religious background to produce a class that fostered awareness of religious influence on perceptions of life, death, suffering, and individual actions. Concurrently, Sr. Roseanne designed a concentration in Christian Ministry for sociology/behavioral science majors who wanted to work in congregations as youth ministers or on university campuses as campus ministers after they graduated. Later, as she observed the changing roles of women in contemporary society, she created a class that spoke to concerns of women who were living these very social shifts. The appropriately titled *Women in Transition* course encompassed the study of identification issues and patterns of change for women seeking equality in the rubrics of their lives.

The college's strategic location in the midst of numerous human service agencies that minister to the needs of vulnerable populations encouraged Murphy to launch an internship requirement for sociology majors intending to pursue social work as a career. In doing so, she provided the early template for the community-based learning philosophy on which the mission of the school now rests. Additionally, she was one of the first professors at NDNU to invite subject matter experts to directly share their experiences with her classes. The exposure to the guest speakers and the internship experience helped students determine if careers in sociology or social work would be the best choice for them.

Sr. Roseanne has been described as a "natural" teacher and she admits that she lights up whenever she enters a classroom. Although she expresses frustration with immature students who do not take their educations seriously, missing classes or coming unprepared, she finds it a genuine pleasure to watch students grow in their understanding of human behavior and social change.

As the department chair for 37 years, Sr. Roseanne represented the faculty members in her department to the larger academic body while maintaining rigorous academic standards. Her knowledge of small group dynamics, prosocial behavior, and informational as well as normative influences helped her achieve success in this position. Convinced that collaborative decision-making enabled faculty to take responsibility for the directions in which the department would embark, Murphy always made certain that each faculty member was valued and every opinion acknowledged. Moreover, as chair, Sr. Roseanne extended knowledge of sociology to high-school students in the vicinity of the university by organizing debates, writing contests, and art exhibits on topics such as war and racism. "In addition to increasing awareness of the discipline," Murphy concedes, "these events were great marketing and recruitment tools as they stimulated the interest of potential students in our university as well as our major."

With the sociology major firmly established under Murphy's direction, travel beckoned. Answering the call, she organized a semester-long course wherein students lived at the congregational headquarters just outside of Rome. She hired teachers appropriate to the endeavor and designed the curricula for the courses. In addition to studying ancient history and learning to speak Italian, students took Sr. Roseanne's classes in comparative cultures where they familiarized themselves with concepts such as cultural universals, stereotypes, culture bearer, and cultural relativism. She recalls, "It was an ideal educational experience because the students could immerse themselves in the actual places we were studying." Sr. Roseanne has led several more excursions to Europe, Mexico, and the Holy Land since that initial trip. Each time, she has been grateful to sociology for her understanding of the ways in which culture shapes individual personalities and social norms. In addition, she contends that knowledge of sociology helps an educator comprehend the influence of culture on learning styles and the impact of prejudice, poverty, and family dynamics on learning ability and outcomes.

In her travels, she has observed that sociology majors tend to be more compassionate and understanding of various customs while non-sociology majors are often more judgmental. Sr. Roseanne maintains that sociology has helped her personally in opening up to subcultures and countercultures even in the United States. "Learning about other cultures," she comments, "has always fascinated me. I don't necessarily accept the customs of these cultures but I recognize that they fit somehow into the overall social structure repugnant though they may be to me personally."

In 1987, Sr. Roseanne was invited to deliver a paper about Julie Billiart, the Foundress of her Congregation, at a conference in Namur, Belgium. As she researched the life of Billiart, Murphy became so inspired by this woman's life that she decided to write a biography about her intended for modern audiences. She traveled to Belgium and France to research her topic, refreshing her sociological research skills to explore the history of Billiart's time and apply a social analysis. "I had to understand the French Revolution and the role of women at that time to successfully write, *Julie Billiart: Woman of Courage,*" she concludes.

On the basis of this account, Sr. Roseanne was later approached by the sisters of her congregation to write the biography of Sr. Dorothy Stang, who had also been a member of the Namur community. In *Martyr of the Amazon: The Life of Sister Dorothy Stang*, Murphy wrote about this nun who helped landless peasants in the Brazilian Amazon fight against exploitation by powerful logging and ranching enterprises. For nearly 30 years, Stang gave her life to protect the rainforest and its indigenous people. Her efforts culminated in her assassination by vile and voracious developers who, in 2005, arranged for Sr. Dorothy's murder. While writing about Stang's life, Sr. Roseanne lived in Anapu, the village where Dorothy had also lived and worked among some of the world's poorest people. There, Murphy states, "Oscar Lewis' culture of poverty concept came alive for me as I observed how the values of the impoverished farmers who only wanted freedom, independence, and dignity contrasted so sharply with our consumer society where people complain if they don't have the latest technological devices." Murphy also saw C. Wright Mills's power elite theory materialize before her eyes as she analyzed the interplay between the political, economic, environmental, and judicial realities of the Brazilian Amazon. Sr. Roseanne feels both humbled and proud that this book was later made into a documentary video and an opera that have reached audiences worldwide.

In recent years, Sr. Roseanne has served NDNU as its Executive Director of Planned Giving. In this capacity she nurtures relationships with alumni, helping them to think about their future plans for the distribution of their assets in ways that benefit the greater community good. She finds her use of concepts such as the sociological perspective, social exchange theory, communication competence, and conversational orientation essential to doing this job effectively. At this point in her career, a typical day for Murphy consists of contacting alumni; attending receptions and reunions; visiting alumni in their homes; engaging them in campus activities when appropriate; and acknowledging donations.

Asked about her advice to a fledgling sociology major she responds, "Since sociology is a study of human relations, it is happening all the time, all around us. Therefore, it is never irrelevant." She asserts that a sociologist can help others become more understanding, tolerant, and accepting of the human experience and thereby grow more compassionate themselves.

To learn more about Sr. Roseanne Murphy and her work, please contact her by e-mail at rmurphy@ndnu.edu

DON STANNARD-FRIEL

Known affectionately as "Dr. Don" by his students and "The Professor" by the prostitutes, addicts, felons, and transvestites with whom he regularly interacts in San Francisco's infamous Tenderloin neighborhood, **Don Stannard-Friel** uses a decidedly non-conventional approach to teach sociology. He explains his strategy by way of personal history.

Having "stopped out" of college for four years, Stannard-Friel returned to student life after hitchhiking across the country from New Jersey to San Francisco. During that time, he enjoyed a plethora of on-the-road adventures; engaged with and became a part of the diverse city that is San Francisco. He joined in the emerging civil rights movement and fully immersed himself in the Haight-Ashbury hippie culture just as it was emerging as the center of the 1960s Cultural Revolution.

Eventually returning to his studies, Don was introduced to sociology for the first time and he recalls, "exposed to its powerful way of explaining what was going on in the world around me." In January 1968, he transferred from a community college to San Francisco State University (SFSU) just in time for an impending student strike. The strikers demanded ethnic and Third World studies, more faculty of color, increased access to higher education, and public opposition to the war in Vietnam War. Once again, his sociology classes helped him assess and understand the social inequities that surrounded him. More significantly, Stannard-Friel admired the public sociology embraced by many of his professors. As such, he participated alongside them in the controversial strike and soon after declared sociology as his major. The discipline quickly became his passion, his career, his life work.

Inspired by his professors at SFSU, Dr. Don continued to study sociology at the masters and doctoral levels, simply because he enjoyed its worldview and found it such a powerful tool for critiquing and *changing* a society that was clearly taking a new direction in history. "Frankly," he admits, "I had no idea what I was going to do with my professional life. I just knew I wanted to continue these exciting studies and be a part of the change-making." At the time, however, Stannard-Friel was certain he would never teach the discipline because the very thought of public speaking struck fear in his heart. Then, a former professor at SFSU convinced him to teach an Introduction to Sociology class. Terrified at first, Dr. Don eventually found that he loved teaching sociology nearly as much as he liked learning about it.

Much of Stannard-Friel's work at the university where he teaches today is based on a community-based service model not unlike the one which he practiced at SFSU during the years of the student strike. "I like this modality because it takes education beyond the walls of the classroom," he explains. "It requires a person to become part of the social arena in order to understand it. Moreover, it is an intimate approach to teaching as the line between teacher and student becomes blurred by the experiences they share with the community." Even the titles of his courses hint at the unique and exciting nature of their content: "The Inner City: The Good, the Bad, and the Ugly," "Lives of the Poor and Infamous," "Exploring the Inner World of the Inner City," "Streetwise Sociology," and "The Promise of the Inner City."

All of his courses embrace one of the fundamental tenets of community-based engagement, Stannard-Friel stresses, in that learning is viewed as a two-way street rather than just an outpour-ing of charity. This, he also makes possible through "Tenderloin U," a concept he created over 20 years ago. This venture forges collaborations between his students, neighborhood service provi-ders, and somewhere around 60 "street teachers" who range from artists and clergy to city government officials and business owners to those who live, quite literally, on the streets. Using this model, he intends for students to learn as much from the community members as they will teach them. This premise helps to assure mutual respect and increased understanding of the similarities shared by seemingly disparate individuals.

Dr. Don initially exposed students to the Tenderloin neighborhood with a class titled, "A Week at the Seneca." The Seneca is a resident hotel for homeless individuals in the center of this poverty-infested, crime-ridden neighborhood. Eight students and four faculties lived in single rooms where a shared toilet and shower were located at the end of a long hallway on each floor. There were no kitchen facilities or utensils, linens, towels, or cleaning supplies. Only a bare light bulb hung from the ceiling of each 8/10 foot room and a sagging mattress perched atop a squeaky bed frame. Supplies as essential as toilet paper were strictly rationed. Sleep was difficult because the small windows in each room were located next to fire escapes that led directly to an alley below. Drug deals were regularly transacted while violence erupted spontaneously and often. During that week, students assisted at soup kitchens, witnessed drug rehabilitation programs, engaged with families who live in the neighborhood, and participated in meetings where conditions that impact homelessness, poverty, and powerlessness were discussed. In the evenings, the group observed life on the streets from hotel windows. They saw degrading displays of sex-for-drugs, the sight of men in BMWs cruising for prostitutes and narcotics, and vicious beatings all-too-commonly played out.

Although the week was decidedly a study of social stratification, institutional oppression, and deviant lifestyles, it alternately demonstrated the power of family, ethnic values, activism, and astonishingly, almost inexplicable hope. During the periods of consistent reflection that Stannard-Friel conscientiously structured into the week, one student concluded, "The entire experience was as unsettling as it was enlightening. I knew I could go back to my college dorm in a nice, quiet, safe, and pretty suburb after five days. But many of the people here are stuck through a series of regrettable circumstances. Though a lot of them have given up hope and are just trying their best to survive another day, others perform mundane back-breaking labor, day after day but receive only minimum wages at best."

The enthusiasm sparked by unique courses has spearheaded several smaller projects that invite students and faculty from departments other than sociology to participate as well. One such outgrowth is *Miracle on Ellis Street,* a yearly holiday event in which collaboration with the Theatre Arts Department produces scenes from *A Christmas Carol* for 200 or so inner city children and their largely immigrant parents. A partnership with the Athletic Department brings lacrosse and volleyball clinics to the youth in the Tenderloin each spring while the children in that neighborhood anxiously await "Halloween in the Tenderloin" every October. At that event, Dr. Don's students staff booths where the community kids line up for apple-bobbing contests, pumpkin carving, and various other games. So that they can trick-or-treat safely in an area where violence is far too common, the college students spend part of the semester researching addresses where the children will be protected and welcomed. They then mark these establishments with balloons early in the day and the children are directed to those sites.

Stannard-Friel has also created a mechanism whereby residents of the Tenderloin can enroll in four of his classes and obtain university credit for doing so. Almost completely funded by the university, this certificate program allows community inhabitants to acquire a full semester of academic credit and learn about research that helps to inform their own living situations. Most of all, these inner city occupants are empowered as experientially informed individuals who bring valuable lessons *to* the classes of traditional college students.

Dr. Don is quick to point out that not all students excel in this modality. He contends that those who do typically possess a prior understanding of the social forces impacting the community. They've learned these either in previous classes or more likely from their own life experiences. This usually provides them with the level of maturity, sense of responsibility, and deep commitment necessary to success with this kind of education. The students who do benefit from community-based learning frequently indicate that their encounters have been not only eye-opening but life-changing.

About his draw to "street teaching" Dr. Don comments, "Community-based learning has been a powerful learning as well as teaching experience for me. The wealth of information that can only be found on the streets, the value of direct learning for the students, and the power of service as a tool to understanding has reinvigorated me even after 45 years as an educator. As a senior in college and for much of his graduate studies, Stannard-Friel worked as a mental health counselor in a locked psychiatric ward. He got this job not because of his sociological background or his knowledge of psychiatry but because his previous positions as a bartender and a cab driver required his ability to manage physical confrontations when they inevitably arose. As ideas about inpatient psychiatry changed in the mid-1970s, community-based facilities were expected to replace large state institutions. Although the promise of community mental health expansion was never fulfilled, there was a still need at that time for young men who could handle oftentimes violent patients, especially in the drug-saturated Haight-Ashbury where Don worked.

Once there, however, Don was able to appreciate the often conflicting paradigms that underlie sociology and psychology. Further, he could apply the sociological perspective to his understanding of the occurrences that took place on the mental ward. "This experience opened my mind and helped me understand the relativistic perspective of sociology especially as it relates to mental illness, deviant behavior, and the social construction of reality. I often found myself in conflict with the dominant perspective on the ward," he admits. Eventually, Stannard-Friel became so frustrated by what he perceived as a form of oppression on the ward that he left the job and took a teaching position at SFSU.

While on the faculty at SFSU, Don also taught classes in a men's jail, in a women's prison, and on an Army base. He took on these opportunities largely out of financial need as a poorly paid lecturer with a growing family at home. The experiences, however, proved to be life-altering, he concedes. As with his work in the mental hospital, Stannard-Friel became immersed in worlds of which he was not a part and was ultimately made aware of the social forces that shaped the lives of the individuals in these circumstances. By getting to know some of the life histories of the mental patients, jail inmates, and even the Army personnel, Stannard-Friel claims he came to truly understand how society actually directs many life choices by limiting or re-channeling them.

Some of his mentors in college, such as Ed Lemert, who helped to develop labeling theory, and John Irwin, a prominent criminologist who did prison time as a young man, gave Don the sociological tools to understand what was happening around him. In addition, he could see the relevancy of some older theories like those of Robert Merton that address the "systematic denial of the means to reach society's goals." Stannard-Friel claims that these events, as much as any others in his life, shaped the community-based learning pedagogy he uses today.

For nearly 38 years now, Stannard-Friel has made NDNU his academic home. In addition to teaching sociology, Stannard-Friel also acted as Dean of Faculty for nine years. In that position, he managed the strategic plan for the campus and led faculty efforts to fulfill planning goals. "I consider this applied sociology," he comments, "as the role involved organizational dynamics, interpersonal communication, paradigm conflict, and process facilitation." As much as he enjoyed the work even with its inherent challenges, Dr. Don eventually felt called back to the classroom.

In 2007, Stannard-Friel was asked to direct the university's newly created Center for Social Justice and Community Engagement. Named for Dorothy Stang, the Notre Dame nun who was murdered in the Brazilian Amazon while helping impoverished farmers obtain basic human rights, the center became a focal point of the university under Don's direction. As such, it now connects NDNU to the community-at-large through partnerships, a speaker series, seminars, publications, volunteer opportunities, and immersion programs. "I'm proud that I could be a part of endeavor," Stannard-Friel states humbly.

As for his future plans, Dr. Don will retire soon from the hands-on work in his Tenderloin classroom. Instead, he will write about the transcendence he observed in the lives of many who resided there. "Through their own eyes, minds, and hearts, I want to share their stories," he reveals.

On a final note, Dr. Don suggests that any fledgling sociologist identifies his or her passion within the discipline. Is it deviant behavior? The animal–human bond? Stratification? Family studies? "Then find meaningful ways to contribute to the world by following that passion."

To learn more about Dr. Don Stannard-Friel and his work, please contact him by e-mail at don@ndnu.edu

PART II

The great aim of education is not knowledge but action.
— Herbert Spencer

15

SNIPPETS FROM THE FIELD

While nearly 40% of all undergraduate sociology majors do pursue graduate school within 2 years of receiving their initial degree and still others do so at some point later in their lives, a substantial number of them find fulfilling employment without an advanced degree. Some, you've already read about in Part I, below are statements from some other satisfied majors.

**

"When I started college, I planned to study fire safety and was determined make firefighting my career. My family was politically conservative so the sociological perspective quickly opened my eyes to a different way of seeing the world. I found myself working with low-income, at-risk youth as a part of my required internship and, to my surprise, thoroughly enjoyed these kids. As a result, I joined Americorps after graduation and was placed in Baltimore's inner city where I taught teens from a violence-ridden neighborhood. Following that year, I moved with my new husband to Nebraska where I continue to work as a family teacher at Boystown. I am responsible for a house full of at-risk adolescents to whom

I provide treatment for all their needs — emotional, academic, physical, and spiritual."

"I was drawn to sociology by my very first course when we discussed how we can be social change-makers who create a 'better tomorrow.' In later on-site classes, I observed concrete extremes between the very wealthy and the very poor. I saw how many of the poor looked a lot like me — olive-skinned with brown eyes and dark hair. I wanted to make a difference in their lives. So for my internship, I chose to volunteer at a youth center near my home. There, I worked with teenagers facilitating workshops where I taught them all sorts of life-skills. I remain with that same organization today as their Director of Education. I knew I found my calling in life as soon as I walked into that agency and met the kids. I got hired there because they knew my work by the time I completed my internship."

"When I took a sociology class about organizational behavior, I started to think about starting my own business. Classes on interpersonal communication made me admit I have a facility for working well with people and making them laugh. I'd always been interested in women's health and the childbirth process. So soon after I graduated, I got my credential as a doula or birth attendant and began working with women from the early stages of their pregnancies through their deliveries and then, after the births. I have to interact not only with the women but with their husbands and with the medical staff so my communication skills as well as an understanding of different cultural and social class norms have proven critical to my business success. A sense of humor and a flair for story-telling (or oral history, as sociologists call it) during

those final days of pregnancy and those long hours of labor helps, too!"

"I always knew I'd have to start earning my own living as soon as I finished high school so I went to beauty school in my senior year. Hairdressing came naturally to me but I got little satisfaction from it until three African-American women taught me how to work with textured hair. Later, I trained as a cosmetologist and hairdresser in Europe and consulted for cosmetic manufacturers. I wrote instructional manuals; conducted seminars; and managed beauty professionals. So, how has my sociology degree helped me? I now understand that beauty is a social norm; a cultural universal or what I call an 'image ritual' that represents far more to a person than simply a haircut or make-up. It is a huge part of an individual's self-concept. In addition, Durkheim's work on social currents has given me the tools to consider the flow of business and what people are likely to buy. This actually helps me predict fashion trends which, in turn, give me an edge on my competition. Furthermore, sociology has provided me with a desire to promote socially responsible beauty and to interact responsibly with my community. This gives meaning to my life. Finally, I've found self-acceptance from obtaining my degree. Today, I own and operate a stylish beauty spa that caters to men and women, young and not-so-young, some with textured hair and some with straight hair."

"I was initially attracted to sociology when I realized the relationships it shares with so many other disciplines that interest me. Following college, I worked as a market researcher where sociology helped me understand the decisions consumers make. My knowledge of social systems and the roles these institutions play in people's

lives aided me in understanding industry trends, functions of consumerism, and business practices. After a few years, I entered the paralegal profession where I currently conduct legal research and write. In both of these positions, the analytical skills I developed in my sociology classes assisted me immensely. In fact, I've found a large number of law students and lawyers majored in sociology as undergraduates."

"Soon after graduation, I left for London (England) where I've had opportunities I had just dreamed about before. For example, I've worked with the Metropolitan Police of London on some major research projects and shadowed detectives from Scotland Yard. Those projects have allowed me entry into many of the most famous (and infamous) prisons in the United Kingdom where such notorious criminals as the July 7 Bombers and the major players in the Irish Republican Army (IRA) are housed. And I've only begun my career in criminal justice!"

"I graduated during a slow economy and soon moved home to Maui where I was quickly hired as the manager of concierge services at a major hotel on the island. Everyday, I'm able to talk with people from a variety of countries around the globe. The skills I learned in my sociology classes help me to trouble-shoot 'people problems,' resolve conflicts, and maximize our guests' enjoyment during their stays."

"I've been interested in demography since high school when I did a research assignment on the cultural composition of my neighborhood. I would have majored in demography in college but my school offered no such major. Sociology, however, prepared me well for work in this field. Since I graduated from college, I've worked with

the U.S. Census Bureau tabulating the numbers of people living in various communities along with numerous characteristics about them. From the numbers, I can see trends and patterns emerge that allow me to forecast the future. Best of all, by getting accurate counts I feel like I'm contributing to a fair distribution of government monies for schools, roads, and other improvements."

"After graduating, I took a position as a one-on-one counselor in a small residential home, working with children who were emotionally disturbed as a result of abuse, neglect, and/or abandonment by their families. I helped to build school-based services that provided early intervention, prevention, and capacity-building. I also championed the rights of children by raising awareness of issues impacting their well-being. At the same time, I focused on a soccer career and am lucky to have played semi-professionally and professionally for four years. Sociology helped me see sports as a microcosm of the larger society."

"Since college, I've been assisting low-income communities build partnerships between the families that live there and the schools their children attend. I've also worked with city agencies to determine if the low-income elderly are being appropriately served. Most recently, I've been participating in a study to investigate the startling increase in applications for government subsidies among the 18–24 year-old demographic."

"My sociology major prepared me to work with an organization that assists incarcerated adults, their families, and inmates upon release. As the director of prisoner services, I develop, coordinate and oversee programs intended to build responsible citizens who contribute to the

community. I see families suffer when a loved one is incarcerated because they are often left without such basics as rent money, emotional support, transportation and even food. I'm proud to be a part of an organization that assists a category of people society often forgets."

"Upon graduation, I took a position a case manager with a group home that provides a quasi-family setting for children who have been abused and neglected. I work as part of a team to facilitate support, recovery, training, and recreation for special-needs children and to establish healthy interactions with their families when it is desirable and possible."

"I came to college with no clue what I wanted to do with the rest of my life (or even, how a degree could help me) and was drawn to sociology because I figured it would provide me with a general background. I'd always been able to earn a living as a mechanic and enjoyed working with my hands but knew that, one day, I'd want to leave the trades. After I graduated, I took a job with a major university as (yep, you guessed it!) a mechanic in their facilities department. However, within a short time, I was promoted to the supervisor of that department. I now manage a staff of employees. I use sociology everyday in dealing with the different personalities to achieve a mutual goal. Not only did my sociology major give me these sorts of skills but my BA gave me the confidence I didn't have before."

"I moved back to Southern California after I graduated to work as the events planning manager for the Ronald McDonald House Charities. Sociology helped me look at the repercussions of individual action on others (the sociological imagination) and also gave me the foundation for organizational and time management skills."

"While still in college, I interned with a local victim assistance center and continued to work there immediately after I graduated. Following that, I took a position as a probation officer in my county and was subsequently assigned to the domestic violence unit as an intensive supervision officer. Not only has my sociology major helped me greatly in my work but so has my ability to speak a second language."

"As soon as I left college, I began working as a case manager with Para Los Ninos, a non-profit agency in Los Angeles. I was eventually promoted to an in-house counselor working with families that have cases with the Department of Child and Family Services. Now I provide services and support to people afflicted by HIV/AIDS."

"By the time I finished my undergraduate work, I was facing a sizeable student loan debt so the labor market beckoned. I assessed my skills and interests. I'd enjoyed my classes about diverse cultures most of all and, since my mother is part Navajo, I had spent a lot of summers on the reservation with her family. With this to offer, I took a position as a research assistant in a government-funded study that examined the Navajo way of life. This included their attitudes, behaviors, sense of spirituality, and the challenges of living on a reservation in the twenty-first century. What started out as an interim job lasted over 10 years."

"Although I started college as a business major, I transferred to sociology when I realized it gave me a framework and a language to express my own experiences. My parents had emigrated from Belarus when I was a child so I was always sensitive to issues surrounding immigrants and immigration. After I graduated, my university employed

me to help other immigrant students adjust successfully to college. I worked with these students one-on-one and advocated on their behalf for more resources from the university and the state. Later, a professor of education hired me as a consultant for books she wrote to help educators address the problems that immigrant children face."

"After finishing my sociology major, I worked in human relations for a variety of government agencies that focused their work on disability rights, housing discrimination, and civil rights enforcement. It is surprising what I learned about these issues while assisting the employees of these agencies with their own personal concerns. These experiences all helped me get into law school."

"Since the state where I live is in the middle of the rustbelt and the unemployment rate is one of the highest in the nation, I spent the first few years after graduation bouncing from one dead-end job to another. I bartended, waited tables, and drove a cab — anything to pay the bills. Sociology sure did come in handy with the people I met in those situations! Finally, I was admitted to a master's program in architectural design. As I proceeded through my program, I became increasingly grateful for my background in sociology. I realized how buildings need to connect with the human activities that will take place there. I found myself digging through my old textbooks from environmental, organizational, and community sociology. I interviewed people (another skill I learned in my sociology classes) who would be using the spaces I designed and unobtrusively observed their behaviors. Did they gather to talk in busy, narrow corridors, for example? Then I should include alcoves to accommodate their need to socialize. I finally recognized that sociology informs

architectural design at literally every phase of the process."

"Right after I graduated, I took a position as the Director of Support Services in one of San Francisco's most impoverished neighborhoods. We provided voluntary case management and community building activities to homeless individuals and those in supportive housing. Our residents suffered with a variety of issues including mental health, HIV, substance use, and other medical problems. When budget cuts closed that agency, I was hired as the program director for a 90-day residential treatment center where I currently help individuals with chronic mental health concerns. I use my two pet pugs in animal-assisted therapy."

"Sociology gave me the broad parameters to reconnect with my native culture and to 'give back' to the Hawaiian community. Once I returned home, I pursued another degree in Hawaiian Language, studying in Tahiti and Rapanui. I later received a grant to research and craft the traditional implements used in kalo farming and poi making. In addition, I worked as a cultural landscape curator where I managed one of Hawaii's largest native plant landscapes. I developed educational curricula surrounding the many rare and endangered species presently growing in the Islands and propagated native plants. As a participant in an intensive leadership training program, I studied food security and sustainability in Hawaii. I currently work as a cultural resource coordinator at two local high schools. This position allows me to develop strategies that look at the current status of communities; identify their social, cultural, and environmental issues; create awareness among the youth; and furnish solutions through service learning projects. Aside from my work in the

schools, I work as a wetland-kalo farmer and research specialist restoring the land through a cultural place-based education program. There, I teach everyone from children through elders about traditional, sustainable farming practices; water resource management; and native plant restoration. I also conduct research around Hawaiian land tenure, cultural landscapes, and Native Hawaiian water rights, working in collaboration with the Earth Justice Environmental Law Firm and The Office of Hawaiian Affairs. Presently, I am developing a year-round cultural-agricultural program that focuses on producing healthy traditional foods to help sustain the people of the island. All this began with my first sociology class!"

16

SOCIOLOGISTS IN THE PUBLIC EYE

"She (or he) was a sociology major?! I had no idea!" you might exclaim incredulously as you browse the list below. The truth is, however, sociology provides such a diverse foundation of skills that myriad accomplished, well-known individuals began or supplemented their careers with a bachelor, master, or doctoral degree in sociology. As such, sociology majors span the employment spectrum.

POLITICIANS, ACTIVISTS, AND CHANGEMAKERS

Reverend Ralph Abernathy, civil rights leader and co-founder of the Southern Christian Leadership Council (SCLC)

Saul Alinsky, community organizing pioneer

Fernando Henrique Cardoso, president of Brazil

Shirley Chisolm, Congressional Representative

Reverend Jesse Jackson, civil rights leader; founder of People United to Save Humanity (PUSH); National Rainbow Coalition; and Project Wall Street

Dr. Martin Luther King, Jr, leader of the American Civil Rights Movement

Reverend James Lawson, civil rights leader and the chief organizer of the Student Nonviolent Coordinating Committee (SNCC)

Suzanne Malveaux, CNN Whitehouse correspondent

Cardinal Theodore McCarrick, Archbishop of Washington, D.C.

Barbara Mikulski, US Senator

Michelle Obama, lawyer and First Lady

Ronald Reagan, Governor of California and US President

Judy Rothschild, director of research for the National Jury Project

Father Louis Vitale, anti-war and prison reform advocate

Maxine Waters, Congressional Representative

Roy Wilkins, civil rights leader and head of the NAACP

ARTISTS, PERFORMERS, AND ENTERTAINERS

Dan Aykroyd, actor

Saul Bellow, novelist and winner of the Nobel Peace Prize for Literature

James Blunt, singer and songwriter

Kay Liscomb, director of the San Diego Museum of Art and vice president of The Humane Society of the United States

Kent Nagano, music director and conductor for The Berkeley Symphony and Lyon Opera

Regis Philbin, television host

Pepper Schwartz, sex and relationship consultant for television reality show and *AARP Magazine*

Paul Shaffer, bandleader on *The David Letterman Show* and *Saturday Night Live*

Pete Seeger, singer and songwriter

Robin Williams, actor and comedian

Debra Winger, actress

ATHLETES AND SPORTS FIGURES

Eric Bjornson, NFL tight end for the Dallas Cowboys and the New England Patriots

Roderick (Rock) Cartwright, NFL running back for the Washington Redskins and the Oakland Raiders

Brian Jordan, MLB first baseman and sports analyst for the Atlanta Braves

Alonzo Mourning, NBA all-star center and vice president of player development for the Miami Heat

Steve Nash, NBA guard for the Phoenix Suns

Ahmad Rashad, NFL wide receiver and sportscaster for the Minnesota Vikings

Bryant Stith, NBA guard for the Denver Nuggets, Boston Celtics, and the Los Angeles Clippers

Bobby Taylor, NFL defensive back for the Philadelphia Eagles and the Seattle Seahawks

Joe Theismann, NFL quarterback for the Dallas Cowboys and the Washington Redskins

17

EMPLOYERS RESPOND: WHY HIRE SOCIOLOGY MAJORS?

Some of my best staff has been sociology majors. They tend to look at the 'big picture' to understand how an individual's behavior is connected to larger social forces. This is absolutely necessary when dealing with wildlife and environmental issues. In addition, sociology majors seem to have a more compassionate understanding of powerless, disenfranchised beings, both humans and other animals, which are exploited and misunderstood. In my experience, sociology majors are better at their interpersonal relationships and don't let the small things get in the way of acting professionally.

— Steve Karlin, Founder and Director, Wildlife Associates

I've always welcomed sociology majors in social work and community-based internships because they tend to have a broad perspective on social problems and their impact on individuals. In work with diverse populations facing problems of economic hardship, limited education and English language skills, as well as exposure to community

*and family violence both past and present, this apprecia-
tion of the larger issues is especially welcome.*

— Lynn Loar, PhD, LCSW, President, The Pryor Foundation

*My organization works with prisoners and their families,
not the most respected members of our society but nonetheless, deserving of our assistance. As such, I need to hire
people who can look at the causes, effects, and consequences of imprisonment objectively. I need people who,
while teaching personal responsibility, can get past 'blaming the victim' for behaviors that were largely induced by
society. I need individuals who will advocate for changes
in our social institutions. Sociology majors are inclined to
personify these abilities.*

— Director, now deceased, Service League of San Mateo County

*Over the years I've spent building a successful travel
agency, I've found my most valuable resources are those
employees who are knowledgeable and* enthusiastic *about
travel as well as truly* interested *in other cultures. They are
the employees who will jump at the chance to teach a pre-
tour seminar about the wildlife in Botswana, the vineyards
of Italy, or the art of Spain. These same representatives will
eagerly spend extra time with clients quelling their concerns
about upcoming travel and provide suggestions (often from
their own experiences) about acclimation to cultural differences. I need representatives who can put themselves in the
shoes of an anxious tourist, recall their days as novice
travelers, and respond empathetically. These are the touches
that keep our clients coming back year after year and ultimately, build a thriving business. I've found that sociology
majors, far and above others, embody these characteristics.
As a result, I find myself likely to hire majors in this
discipline more often than any other.*

— CEO, now deceased, White Travel Service

Sociology is the birthplace of survey research. As the owner of a marketing research company, I find that marketing and business majors (including MBAs) tend to be strong on marketing skills but weak on research methodology. Sociologists have a broader background in research methods and statistics. I find it much easier to teach marketing to a skilled researcher than research to a skilled marketer.

— Mike Curtis, President, Clarity Research, LLC

In my position, I interview candidates for positions that range from animal control officer to adoption counselor to media relations assistant. I always assume they like animals; why else would they want to work at a humane society! So, I look mostly at whether they can connect with and understand people. I've found that sociology majors are likely to have effective communication skills, work well as team players, care about the larger issues impacting our 'clients' (the animals) as well as our 'business' and to be more compassionate than other majors.

— Scott Delucchi, Executive Director, SPCA of Monterey County

Our organization works with youth in the juvenile justice system, providing them with services while they are incarcerated. In general, sociology majors seem better equipped to understand the challenges faced by our youth. They seem to have a unique ability to help our clientele while not criticizing or stereotyping. These characteristics allow sociology majors to envision opportunities that oftentimes change the lives of these youth.

— Robin Sohnen, Founder and Director, Each One; Reach One

In the field of management consulting, I believe there is no one better trained than a sociologist to work on the wide variety of projects that we tackle. The investigative and

critical analysis foundation gained in the study of sociology is the core skill necessary to work with business, government, municipal, and nonprofit organizations. My consulting practice is only as good as my work which requires me to determine the central problem or issue; identify all available options; and then present findings and solutions that are considerate of cultural, racial, religious, political, economic, and other social norms. I have found that sociologists who work for me continually outperform business school-trained people especially in terms of understanding the larger social implications of any given project.

— Marsha Maloof, Pendergrass Smith Consulting

Sociology majors have the skills and sensitivities that enhance litigation work. My in-house sociologist is excellent for interviewing clients from all social, economic, and cultural backgrounds. She analytically reviews witness testimony and helps in jury selection. The critical thinking skills and ability to identify social constructs that sociology majors bring to the table are particularly valuable for client centered practice.

— Charles Gottlieb, Esq., Gottlieb and Goren, P.C.

When I hire an employee, I look for their ability to build rapport and trust with customers; their capacity to empathize as well as listen for understanding; and to understand the perspectives of our customers. In addition, I appreciate the ability of an employee to comprehend and respect a colleague's point of view and embrace differences as well as similarities. I also want my employees to have the focus, personal effectiveness, and follow-through to solve problems when they arise. Sociology majors generally possess these attributes along with the ability to communicate effectively and function collaboratively as part of a team. Therefore, sociologists tend to work successfully in a customer operation role.

— Ketty Seymour, Project Manager, Independent Contractor

PART III

A person who is broadly educated in [one era] may be widely ignorant [50 years later] unless [s/]he has made a conscious, continuous, and determined effort to keep abreast with development of knowledge and of thought.
— W. E. B. DuBois

18

MAKING THE MOVE

So! You're ready to graduate! You can envision your diploma-in-hand with the word, "Sociology," documenting your major. You can reel off a couple dozen concepts germane to the discipline and theories like symbolic interactionism, structural functionalism, social conflict, and humanism roll easily off your tongue. You can even explain without too much trouble the thoughts of Max Weber, C. Wright Mills, W.E.B. DuBois, and Jane Addams. Now! How are you going to put this new-found, accumulated knowledge to work for you? More specifically, how are you going to get a job, maybe your first *real* job, which puts you on the path to a career?

Let's face it! The world of work has changed dramatically in the past couple of decades. In fact, if you are younger than 25 years old you may have never experienced anything different than what you already know about a job search. You Google; go to Craigslist, LinkedIn, and Facebook. You blog, send out your resume electronically, and use Smart phone apps. If you are much older, however, you might be drawn to more traditional techniques like flooding hundreds of potential employers with your paper resume or checking the classified section of your local newspaper. You might even phone friends and relatives with that awkward question, "Hey, do you know if your company is hiring?"

Changes in the job search are just the beginning of the differences between the twentieth versus the twenty-first century career quest. It might even be fair to say that the entire philosophy of work has changed. Workers in the past were advised to "just find a job, any job that's legal and pays decently." It didn't matter if they found it fulfilling or even liked it. And they often worked at that job for their lifetime. In fact, someone who changed jobs more than a time or two was usually considered unstable and suspect.

Here's another difference: the interview. For generations, job seekers were told to "sell themselves." Today's successful applicant, on the other hand, will have to convince an employer that they can "add value" to the organization with the "gifts they have to offer."

Then, there is the nature of the job itself. Jobs of the twentieth century were often rigidly structured and controlled. A worker usually started their shift at a specific time often with hundreds of other workers that all ended their work day together as well. Typically, the workforce punched a time clock at the beginning and end of their day. The work week consisted of 40 hours; 8 hours a day; 5 days a week. Today, employees find themselves adapting to a "work-as-needed" structure. Perhaps the best example of this new "work-as-needed" model comes from the television industry. For several months, a whole host of people come together to act, film, gaff, edit, mix, cater, dress, and apply cosmetics to produce a successful show for a given season. At the end of that season, the crew takes a hiatus. If the show is renewed for another season, everyone comes back together again and reengages in his or her respective tasks. Should the show be discontinued, the crew is no longer needed. Therefore, they all disperse and look for new jobs elsewhere.

In addition, the work of the past required someone to get educated first whether in college, in high-school woodworking classes, or as a plumber's apprentice. From that point, they were expected to work hard. Whereupon, at around 65 years old, they would retire from the job and a novice 20-something would take their place. If the employee was particularly well-liked, they received, quite literally, a gold watch from the company upon their retirement. Then, in a few years, they died.

With the advent of technology, robotics, and globalization heralded by the twenty-first century, all this changed, at least in the Western world. No longer is an employee's education complete with a baccalaureate or even an advanced degree. Rather, one is expected to engage in lifelong learning, taking classes, updating skills, learning new computer programs, attending conferences, and obtaining certifications. Always, the worker of the twenty-first century must be willing to acquire new knowledge and retool for what might come next.

So, in some ways, the job search process of the two centuries is similar. Self-assessment for a satisfying "fit" is still desirable. Researching and exploring your options, although the methods are different, is still necessary. Yet, some of the changes have been dramatic and even require a different mind-set from the past.

Ready to get started? OK! Let's look first at the "Career Development Process and Decision Making Model," a popular template created by Susan Geifman and adapted for use by *You're Hired! Putting Your Sociology Major to Work.*

Career Development Process and Decision Making Model

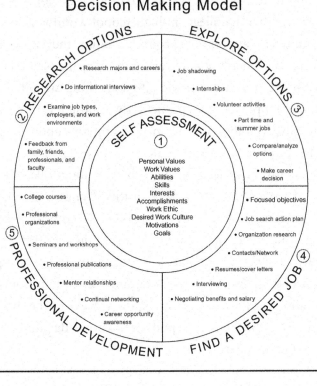

Because Geifman (and the vast majority of contemporary career counselors) believe that the key to finding satisfying work is first discovering yourself, we'll begin with self-assessment. Notice that self-assessment has several components, each of which we'll explore here in greater depth but first let's define "self-assessment" relative to job search and career planning. Self-assessment is a social psychological concept that denotes a process of examining oneself to determine the aspects vital to an individual's identity. These include your talents, interests, personality style, and your values. This self-assessment piece is essential as it will underpin your search for meaningful and fulfilling work. So, work your way through the ensuing list giving serious thought to the questions and the insights provided here. You may even want to write down your responses and reactions someplace where you can return and give them deeper analysis on a continual basis.

SELF-ASSESSMENT

- *Personal values:* These constitute your beliefs about the parts of your life that are most important and valuable to you individually. Ask yourself what aspects in your life are most meaningful to you. What do you "stand for?" What do you want to stand for? What will you have to accomplish to feel that you've led a successful life? It is imperative to self-explore your values and determine what is important to you: Wealth? Power? Respect? Security? Love? Family? Self-satisfaction? Social justice? What? You can use your favorite search engine to find a list of values that will help you explore this piece of the self-assessment process. Googling "Personal Values" produced more than 27,500 hits! A wealth of information is just a click away. Check it out to find the values that resonate with you.

- *Work values:* Does the work you are considering align with your personal values? Are the mission and vision of the organization you are considering congruent with your own principles? For example, if the employees at corporation XYZ regularly work 70 hours a week, you need to determine how this corresponds with your own desire for a healthy family life. If, on the other hand, you are single, enjoy the work, and hope to retire by the time you are 35, this organization might be congruent with your goals. Bill Carlson, the author of *Get Top $$$ in a Job You Love*, found that one's personal values must align with the mission of the organization for both to reach their fullest potential. A Google search of "Work Values" produced over 60,400,000 hits. The number of internet sights dedicated to this topic illustrates its importance.

- *Abilities:* Abilities are those natural and/or acquired talents that make a person unique. What are your own distinctive abilities? Make a list of your top 10. How might you present them in a resume and articulate them in an interview?

- *Skills:* Skills are technical capabilities or the expertise to perform a task. In career development, we talk about "transferable skills" as those you learn in one area and "transfer" to another position. For example, you might learn a complicated computer program as part of one job then continue to utilize it when you get promoted. Are you continuing to develop and fine-tune your current skills with every opportunity you are offered?

- *Interests:* Ask yourself why you chose sociology as your major. What, specifically, interested you about this discipline? What particular area of sociology attracts you most: Different cultures? Deviant behavior? Social class or racial inequality? The Strong-Campbell Interest Inventory is an excellent assessment tool that can help you find your interests relative to various possible work environments. Your college or university career center or a private career counselor can administer this assessment.

- *Accomplishments:* Keep track of any accomplishments that can lend themselves to a professional portfolio on a weekly basis. Save any flyers, thank you notes, news articles in which you are quoted; in essence, anything that will jog your memory about your value to your profession. Note how even seemingly small items can add up to significant statements. By turning these accomplishments into statements on your resume or in an interview, you can easily address your added value.

- *Work ethic:* Work ethic is defined as the belief that work has moral benefit in and of itself as well as the ability to develop and enhance personal character. Ask yourself if you just want to "get by" doing the least amount of work for the most amount of money or if it is important to you that you contribute to the well-being of an organization for which you work. Are you willing to "go beyond" your job description when necessary? Do you normally do the "right thing" even when no one is looking over your shoulder? Are you self-directed?

Do you take the initiative when necessary? Are you generally positive, diligent, and persistent? All of these characteristics speak to a strong work ethic.

- *Desired work culture:* In the same way people like living in different kinds of houses and communities, so too do individuals like to work in diverse environments. Since you will probably spend a minimum of 8 hours a day at work, it is important to know in what setting you are likely to be most productive and comfortable. Will you prefer a large corporate culture where you can maintain anonymity or an intimate setting where you can socialize with your coworkers? Do you want to work in a competitive, for-profit organization or a nonprofit that allows you to pursue social justice? Do you like to make decisions individually or as part of a group? All these are important questions to think about.

- *Motivations:* Think about what drives you to get out of bed and go to class or work every day. When you are feeling uninspired, what makes you put one foot in front of the other? It may be as simple as the negative repercussion of flunking the course if you don't. On the other hand, consider the joys you experience. Do you look forward to engaging with your friends? Solving complex problems? Learning something new? Playing with the animals for which you're responsible? Moreover, how do you keep yourself motivated when the job or the class gets routine and dull? Do you ask questions; take on different tasks; find new activities? It is essential to define that which excites you so you can pursue these incentives in your job search.

- *Goals:* Set goals that are SMART. Be sure they are Specific and Measurable; Attainable; Realistic; and have a Timeline. If you tell yourself you will have the job of your dreams by the end of the month and you haven't even defined that dream job or begun this self-assessment, you are setting yourself up to fail.

On the other hand, if you determine that you will be hired as a community outreach coordinator by August 31 of this year and you meet the necessary requirements, your goals are specific, measurable, attainable, realistic, and have a timeline (SMART, get it?) "But," you shriek, "I can't know when the agency will make their decision or if their budget will be cut!" Of course not. Things happen. In a case like this, you readjust your goals. You establish another timeline or explore a similar position or apply for the same job in a nearby county. The point is: goals keep you on-track. It is imperative, however, that you review your goals regularly (perhaps every 3 months) to check your progress and be certain your goals still align with your needs and values.

RESEARCH OPTIONS

All right! You've completed a thorough self-assessment, gotten clarity on those areas that were vague and perfected your short-comings. Feeling confident? Good! Let's research your options for a thorough job search:

- *Start with the Internet.* This is rich and fertile ground with which to begin your search. At one point, your author simply Googled "careers in sociology" and turned up over 19,500,000 links! Investigate the links in the Appendix at the back of this book. Explore the websites for some of the major professional organizations. For sociologists, this would be the American Sociological Association (www.asanet.org). In addition to listing positions available, they will direct you to the websites for regional and statewide organizations, for instance, the Pacific Sociological Association, the Southwest Sociological Association, or the Illinois Sociological Association. You might examine organizations that are more focused on your own interests as well such as the Society for the Study of Social Problems, Association for Black Sociologists, American Association of University Women, or the American Society of Criminology. Also, be sure to check out: http://unamitoba.ca/student/counselling/media/sociology.pdf and www.salisbury.edu/sociology/careers.html for even more references. Of course, you will need to be judicious in your website review since not everything that is posted is worthwhile or even correct. I do recommend these sites though.

- *Conduct informational interviews.* An informational interview is a meeting between you and a subject matter expert in which you collect information about their job, career field, and/or a specific organization. These interviews give you opportunities to talk with people working at jobs you think you might like. Ask them what they like and dislike about their job. Explore their career path with them. Find out how they obtained their position and what steps they took to do so. Ask them what their typical day might be like. See if you can shadow them or follow them around for a few hours. Use the foundation we established for our respondents in Part I of this book. Here, again, the Internet is a rich resource. In a Google search, I came up with 874,000 hits on informational interviews. One of my favorites is: http://jobsearch.about.com/cs/infointerviews/a/infointerview. htm. Remember that the purpose of an informational interview is to learn about career options; it is a not a job interview and you should not expect a job offer.

- *Examine job types, employers, and work environments.* As you can see from the vignettes in this book, your sociology degree is valuable to a plethora of job types, employers, and work environments. Research the organizations that initially interest you to determine whether the areas you assessed at the beginning of this process are congruent with the organization's mission, vision, and operation. Read their websites, watch the news, and read analyses of these companies. If you know people who are employed at these places, ask them about their experiences. Find out if the company's values are compatible with your own. If, for instance, you just read that an organization you are considering gave "pink slips" to 19,000 workers the day before Christmas and you pride yourself on compassion, you may wish to reconsider. If an organization has publicly announced their opposition to same-sex marriage and you support the rights of gay individuals, think again before you interview with that company.

- *Obtain feedback from family members, friends, faculty, and professionals.* Talk with everyone you know and even people you don't know. This is the time to network. Go to social functions even if you are shy or dismal at making small talk. Start attending alumni events and meetings of professional organizations. Talk to your friends' parents, people in your church group, former teachers, your dentist, or doctor. Strike up conversations with people on elevators, in waiting rooms, on planes. Tell them about yourself and your job pursuit. You might be amazed at what comes your way! A friend of mine was in Morocco when she told a woman she met on a sightseeing tour that she was looking for a job in banking. Turned out the other woman worked at a bank just down the street from my friend — in Tampa, Florida! Guess who was offered a job upon her return home?

EXPLORE YOUR OPTIONS

Actually exploring your options can be either the most exciting part of your job search or the most daunting. While I believe that pounding the pavement is the hardest part of any job pursuit, an acquaintance of mine looks forward to the opportunities it provides. She developed her attitude from Al Levin, one of her mentors and the coauthor of *Luck is No Accident, Making the Most of Happenstance in Your Life and Career*. In this book, Levin actively encourages the job seeker "to prepare for the unexpected, to take advantage of chance events, to make the most of random happenstances." And, since random luck, according to some pundit, is 99% perspiration, let's get started!

- *Job shadowing:* This activity provides an excellent opportunity to spend quality time with an individual who is actually doing a job you think appeals to you. Essentially, you will spend a portion of a day (or sometimes more) alongside this person as he or she perform his or her normal tasks, duties, and responsibilities. This might include sitting in a briefing, preparing a presentation or report, or responding to incoming e-mails and phone calls. At each juncture, ask yourself if you find the activities and communications with the others on the job overwhelming, distasteful, exciting, or interesting. Job shadowing can provide you with information that can begin a fulfilling career or interrupt a major mistake in the pipeline. I had a student who thought she wanted to pursue a career in gerontology until she realized, through shadowing, that work with elderly people could mean emptying bed pans and encounters with angry outbursts. The student had been using her own healthy and energetic grandparents as a yardstick! Job shadowing opportunities can frequently be arranged through your college or university and even through your own contacts. Ask your professors, friends, parents of friends, and community leaders for suggestions and referrals.

- *Internships and volunteer activities:* These options supply such valuable insights into the realities of jobs that many programs now require students to intern or volunteer for a given number of hours before they can graduate. Those in career transition can find an internship or volunteer activities particularly useful ways to test the waters in a new field of interest. Not only do these options provide firsthand insights about a specific job and employer, but also you will be able to develop your network of contacts. The truth is some employers today will only hire from their pool of interns and volunteers. In a way, both options are extended versions of job shadowing. Some internships pay a small stipend but even if your experience is unpaid, you are likely to find it valuable beyond words if you take it seriously. I am constantly dismayed by students who use this potentially life-changing opportunity to simply fulfill a requirement. In a word: don't. The Internet contains a plethora of ideas for internships and volunteer opportunities in a variety of fields no matter where you live or go to school. In particular, I recommend http://college.monster.com/education. Additionally, there is an extensive list of resources in the back of this book.

- *Part-time and summer jobs:* These days, many students work while going to school in order to pay their expenses. If you are going to work anyway, why not find a job that allows you to do so in your area of interest? Do you hope to work with teenagers? Get a job with the local Boys and Girls Club coaching soccer, teaching computer skills, or preparing at-risk adolescents for a community theater production. Does work with animals intrigue you? Walk dogs or pet-sit to earn extra money. Do you enjoy sharing your native language with others? Offer your abilities as a writer, a tutor, or a translator. Be creative and open-minded. I applied for a position as a hospital receptionist when I graduated from high school. Although I didn't get that job, the human resource director at the hospital soon called me to ask if I would tutor his grade school son in writing. It turns out he had read my resume and was impressed with my writing skills. Did I take the job? You bet I did! Not only did it pay well but I had a ready reference from that H.R. Director for years. The job was a great addition to my resume and it beat working at the local pizzeria that summer which was the only other job I could have gotten. Remember, too, that your first job is unlikely to be a lifetime commitment.

- *Compare and analyze options:* After you've assessed yourself, researched your options, and explored them thoroughly through job shadowing, internships, volunteering, and miscellaneous jobs, it is time to compare and analyze your findings. The Career Goals questionnaire below should help you determine the environment in which you want to work, the type of work that most appeals to you, and the manner in which you wish to work.

  1. What is the ideal size of the company in which I'd like to work?

  2. What is the potential for advancement with this company? How important, to me, is the opportunity to advance?

  3. How much responsibility do I want at my job?

  4. How many hours a week do I want to work? Do I want to work full-time, part-time, and/or have a flexible schedule?

  5. Do I want to work with people, data, products, or the environment?

  6. Would I rather work for a public or private company? Government? Nonprofit?

  7. What kind of commute am I willing to tolerate?

  8. Am I willing to relocate?

9. Do I want a job that is routinized or filled with variety?

10. Do I want to work in teams or by myself?

11. Do I want to work with my hands, my mind, my emotions, or a combination?

12. How do I want to dress for work?

13. How much on-the-job stress can I handle?

14. How much business travel do I want to do?

15. Do I want a public contact job or one behind-the-scenes?

16. Do I want an indoor or outdoor job?

17. How important is it for me to work for a company that stresses training?

18. What salary range is important to me?

19. What kinds of benefits are important to me?

20. What kinds of skills do I want to use on a daily basis?

21. How important is job security to me? Could I work on commission or for a start-up where a pay check is seldom guaranteed?

- *Make career decisions:* This step can admittedly be the most paralyzing part of the entire job search process. But what if you make the wrong choice? The truth is: there is no wrong decision. One decision might be better than another but your detour will provide you with tremendous knowledge, skills, and abilities that you will invest at a future time once you get back on track. Besides, those detours are sometimes necessary to give us a different perspective on life. Think of career decisions as a "right decision" and a "left decision," much like the fork in the road that confronts Robert Frost in his poem, *The Road Not Taken.* "Two roads diverged in a wood," he writes, "and I — I took the one less traveled by, [a]nd that has made all the difference."

FIND YOUR DESIRED JOB

While inexperienced job seekers often begin the search process at this point, I firmly believe that the research you've already conducted will prove invaluable and even expedite this next step of finding a fulfilling job that you will enjoy going to each day. As before, it will be useful to follow the plan of action below:

- *Focused objectives:* Students are sometimes tempted to use a shot-gun approach whereby they send out hundreds of resumes in the hope that one will hit the target. In my professional opinion, this is an incredible waste of time and energy. A focused and intentional approach proves far more successful. Start by targeting two or three specific job environments in which you would like to work and then 10 to 15 organizations in those settings. Be ready to put a significant amount of time into this piece. If you are a student or a recent graduate, the folks in your university's career center can be your best resource. They can help you find possible employers and assist you with the tools necessary for this stage of your career development. If you are already a working adult in transition, this can be a time of challenge. Some companies offer workshops and career consulting sessions to those that they dehire. If you are lucky enough to have these services, I strongly suggest you avail yourself of them. The U.S. government also offers classes if you collect unemployment benefits. Community centers and junior colleges sometimes provide classes and services as do churches, libraries, labor unions, and professional organizations. The point is: spread your net far and wide. Although finding a job is a full-time and often difficult endeavor in itself, staying motivated and positive is crucial. Yet, people do it every day. How? Those who are most successful attribute their achievement to their organizational skills. Simply, they establish a plan of action and they stick to it. This leads to the next step.

- *Job search action plan:* A plan of action will be your key to job search success. Write down your plan and keep it handy. Use any method you wish be it a computer program or a three-ring binder; just have a plan. Keep a folder on each organization you target to which you can easily add new tidbits of information. Prepare to devote at least 20 hours per week to your pursuit until you find the job you want. Put yourself on your calendar and commit specific timeframes to continue your research; network; initiate and return phone calls; send and respond to e-mails; fine-tune your resume; and prepare for interviews. Don't allow anything but emergencies to interfere with your plan. Just as you wouldn't let a spontaneous chance to see a movie with a friend prevent you from going to work or class, you shouldn't allow unnecessary activities to keep you from your job search. Keep careful records of your actions and the results. Take notes on the organizations you have already contacted or with which you plan to get in touch. Document the key players and the name(s) of those with whom you've spoken along with the dates on which you did so. Obtain the secretary's name and remember it. A secretary often has more influence in an organization, though informal, than those with impressive-sounding titles. Therefore, be nice to the secretary. Keep a brief description of the interview and other interactions along with your impressions. Ask yourself if your experiences and observations reflected the stated mission of the organization. Did the work environment feel congruent with your personal ethics and values?

   As soon as you've finished an interview, send an e-mail or handwritten thank you note. Write one to each person who interviewed you. Determine which type to send based on the ambience of the organization (is it casual or formal; high-tech or paper-and-pen?) Careers can be made or broken on the basis of this detail. A friend of mine acknowledged he was probably the least qualified of the three candidates who interviewed for a college presidency. Yet, he was hired. He was later told his handwritten thank you card was the deciding factor; the other two neglected this courtesy.

- *Research on the organization:* This is another critical piece in the career search process. In fact, many recruiters will not even consider interviewing an applicant who has not taken the time to review the company website. Fortunately, the Internet has made this step easy. Google will generally produce dozen of sites on any given company. In addition, books, magazines, and newspapers especially on midsize and large organizations proliferate. Step out of your comfort zone and investigate both Internet sites and libraries. Public and university libraries frequently offer free databases on companies that are not generally available without a charge. Moreover, many libraries retain personnel who specialize in the job search arena.

- *Contact your network:* At this point in your life, you should consider everyone you know part of your network. You should have already begun assembling your network when you researched and explored your options. Continue to build it, both formally and informally, through conversations about your job search. Formally, you will want to start informational interviewing. The name itself defines its process: you actually "interview" people but only for "information." Search out "informational interview" on the Internet to find more data on the process and even lists of questions to ask. At the conclusion of any informational interview, ask for three additional referrals with which you might connect using your current interviewee as a conduit. Informally, mention your job search any time you are engaged in a conversation. You never know who might have a lead.

  Having already targeted some of the companies you might wish to work for in the earlier steps, determine whether anyone in your network knows someone who can help you gain entry.

Can anyone in your network provide you with a reference or a referral? Will someone introduce you to an employee who is strategically placed in the company? In addition, continue to attend functions where employers might be; volunteer for projects that will put you in touch with people who can influence your job search success; and go above and beyond in your classes. Make a favorable impression on your professors and instructors as they are going to be the people most likely to write recommendations for your first job.

- *Resumes and cover letters:* Articulating your knowledge, skills, and abilities in print can often be a daunting process. I personally remember being driven to tears (no, sobs) of frustration when I wrote my first academic resume, also called a *vitae*. However, with the many resources available these days, it is possible to write a dazzling resume without entering into the depths of despair. Your college or university might even offer classes even though you may only get elective credit. Many times, students are in such a hurry to graduate that they only take required classes. BIG mistake, I maintain. In addition to taking career development classes, make yourself known at your Career Development Office. It will typically have tons of resources available to you as a student or an alumnus. These will range from books, websites, and workshops to individual sessions with the staff. Of course, you can also find resources on your own. I particularly recommend the resume tutor from University of Minnesota (http://www1.umn.edu/ohr/careerdev/resources/resume/index.html) as well as another website that will help you develop your personal branding statement: www.quintcareers.com/resumebrandingstatements.html. However, another benefit to making the acquaintance of the career development staff is that you will come to mind when they are asked to recommend an individual to an employer — and they are frequently solicited. The cover letter is also a critical part of the job search process. In fact, some employers read no further than the cover letter if it is not well-written and engaging. As such, this document should briefly summarize your accomplishments and the contributions you think you can make to the organization. Moreover, it should reveal a bit about the person behind the words. For this reason, I strongly suggest that you write your own cover letter. Let's face it: no one know better than you know yourself. So, as tempting as it might be to hire a professional to write about you, it will serve you best to resist. Besides, it really isn't that difficult. You don't have to be a prize-winning author; use five-syllable words in every sentence; or write a voluminous to me. You need only introduce yourself, say what you want to say, and do so clearly, accurately, and earnestly. Your cover letter should also include what Joyce Laine Kennedy (*Cover Letters for Dummies*) calls your "professional branding statement" which she defines as "the essence of who you are in the workplace."

Important as the resume and cover letter are to the job search, their entire purpose is to get you the interview. In and of themselves, they seldom procure an actual job. Therefore, it is vital that you target your resume to the specific job in which you are interested whenever possible. If you are attending a job fair, you may need a generic resume but even then you can focus on a particular type of organization or work environment. An effective strategy is to refocus a standard resume by using key words that are industry-recognized. To do this, look at job descriptions for specific positions to see what characteristics are required. These will be your "key words." Then count the number of times a word or term is used in the description. If a term such as "culturally competent" is used more than three times, you can bet you should have it in your resume.

A caveat: the more time and intensity you spend on the foregoing steps of this Career Development Process and Decision Making Model, the easier you will find writing your resume and cover letter. Why? Because you will have more clarity and focus by the time you get to this point. Additionally, career development suggests that you cultivate an ongoing "resume builder mentality" whereby you frequently ask yourself how the tasks, events, and experiences in which you engage will enhance your resume. Then capture these efforts in writing on a regular basis and add them to your generic resume. Conversely, you can use this information to help you focus on a specific position or career.

- *Interviewing:* This is where all your hard work comes to fruition and, on the other hand, "it's only just begun" as a song from the 1970s intones. The key to a successful interview is: preparation, preparation, and more preparation. While there are different types of interviews, the most popular these days focuses on the "behavioral type interview." Its premise and, as research has repeatedly demonstrated, past performance predicts future success. As such, the behavioral type interview will generally start by asking you to "Tell me about a time when ..." or to "Give me an example of an instance when you overcame a challenge and succeeded." With these sorts of questions, the interviewer is looking for specific ways you used your knowledge, skills, and competencies to benefit a previous employer, community, or individual. To ready yourself for this kind of interview, begin by checking out a website provided by the Kansas State Department of Administration: www.da.ks. gov/ps/subject/bei/. In that, you can click on any skill or competency you wish to find a list of questions that might be asked in an interview process. Click again and you will be provided with a template in which to formulate your answers. Spend time with each of the categories: Star/Task/Action/Result (STAR) until you feel comfortable answering myriad possible questions.

Then practice. And practice some more. Have friends, family (or a career counselor) role-play with you, asking you the questions and critiquing you until you feel relaxed and comfortable. Sit in front of a full-length mirror to check your facial expressions, gestures, and body posture. If you generally use your hands when you talk, practice holding them quietly in your lap to avoid distractions. For women wearing a skirt, make certain that whether you cross your legs or plant your feet firmly on the floor, your knees are close together. If you can tape your practice interviews, do so. This will help you curb the high-pitched giggle; too-loud or too-soft voice; the "umms" and the "you knows."

Accept any interview offered whether or not you think you might want to work for a particular employer. The reason: any interview gives you practice. Besides if you are flexible, you may change your mind. In fact, your author got her current job this way! I assumed I wanted to teach at a large, state university. I assured myself I wouldn't fit in at a small, private, liberal arts college. Yet, when I received an offer to interview at just this kind of school I accepted, planning to use it as "practice." One walk around the campus in preparation for the interview and a meeting with strategic faculty, however, convinced me I needed look no further — I had found my perfect job! Who could resist a family of deer on the front lawn of a historic mansion where my office would be located and the warmth of professors committed to the successes of their students? For the record, I've never regretted my decision.

The day of the interview is your chance to shine. From the moment you enter the room, make a connection with the interviewer or the interview panel. Stand tall, feel confident, and project your best smile. An effective handshake, seemingly so simple and yet so powerful, comes next. Be sure your handshake is firm without being a bonebreaker. Connect the web between your thumb and index finger with the web of the other person and make eye contact. One career counselor suggests that you know the color of the person's eyes before you walk away from the handshake. Although the impulse to quickly shake hands, sit down, and get the interview over with is probably quite strong, you want to remember that people hire those they like. By connecting with a handshake and eye contact at the start, you are building rapport and starting a relationship immediately. Of course, you need to do so authentically or your interviewer will see through your deception. Throughout the interview, mentally check your posture, rate of speech, gestures, and any other behaviors that might distract from your words. Keep your eye contact appropriate. In this culture, it is not appropriate to either stare down an individual or avoid eye contact completely. If you are interviewing with someone from another culture, it is best to know ahead of time about the practices in that culture. For example, some cultures do not look kindly at a woman who attempts to make eye contact with a man. If it is not possible to know the norms, try to follow the lead and cues of the interviewer.

Still got butterflies? View those little critters as positive energy that just needs to fly in formation and you are the person who can direct them. Remember, too, that your interviewer is likely to be as nervous as you. While you have the responsibility to present your best self, your interviewer is accountable to his or her organization for hiring the most appropriate person. If they make the wrong decision, the company could waste thousands of dollars on hiring and training. An expensive mistake like this will doubtlessly reflect negatively on the decision-maker. Your job in the interview, therefore, is to make it easy for the interviewer to recognize that you are the right person for the job.

You can do this most effectively with the What's In It For Me (WIIFM) technique. Envision the acronym (WIIFM) emblazoned across the forehead of everyone who interviews you because that is precisely the concern of your interviewer and his or her organization. Once you recognize this fact, you can provide the information they need to recognize you are, indeed, the best candidate for the position. Sit down before the interview and make a list of the "added value" you can bring to the organization. Ask yourself: why should they hire me? Get laser focused clarity on your accomplishments, abilities, and potential as you answer this question. Then get these "gifts" on the table during your interview. Although some people are comfortable "selling themselves" in an interview, most are not. If this is your situation, view the process as "offering your gifts" (or skills, competencies, and added value). Neither way is right or wrong so experiment to find the method that feels most comfortable to you. Always be prepared with questions of your own about the organization, the job, and any logistics that might concern you. This will demonstrate that you conducted thorough research and that you are interested in the position.

Learn from each interview and apply your lessons to the next. If it seems appropriate, ask the interviewers how you might have improved your presentation. Take notes. As soon as you are able, write down anything you want to remember for the future and keep a file for ready reference. Refer back to your resume and the job posting information to self-evaluate your interview successes and remaining challenges. Use every opportunity to consistently improve your skills.

- *Negotiating benefits and salary:* Finally! You have a job offer; perhaps even two or three. Your next step will be an appointment with the Human Resources Department or another member of the organization who will offer you a "Compensation Package." This will include the wage or salary they propose as well as any benefits they wish to include. Be aware that this stage is critical to your career development. Accept an offer that is too low and it can haunt you for the remainder of your work life. Future employers will base their offers on your previous wages possibly cheating you unintentionally out of tens of thousands of dollars over the long run. On the other hand, if you insist on too high a compensation package given your anticipated contributions to the organization you may find their proposal rescinded. So, negotiating your salary and benefits is a delicate yet essential balance to attain. Therefore, before you confer with the company's representative, you will want to be clear about your own needs. Know what dollar amount you will need to meet your daily needs. Start by making a list of all your expenses and plan a budget. This will help you determine the salary you will need to meet your obligations and still enjoy yourself. You should also do some research to determine the going salary range for the position you are pursuing in your region of the country. Find out what other similar-size organizations pay compared with the company you are considering. Know, too, that many companies offer benefits that offset a low salary or enhance one that is agreeable. Some of the most common of these options are:

o *Bonuses* — holiday, performance, or sign-on

o *Cell phone* with fees paid

o *Company car* with gas, mileage, and insurance

o *Company match* in a 401K

o Computer/laptop

o Early performance review for raises and/or consideration for future promotions

o Expense account

o Family/sick/maternity/paternity leave

o Extra vacation days and/or paid holidays

- Flexible work schedule
- *Job description review* to which responsibilities might be added or deleted
- Life insurance options
- Medical/dental coverage
- Relocation expenses
- Parking (free or reduced rate)
- Pension/retirement benefits
- *Professional meetings* — travel, hotel, meals, registration
- Professional organization membership dues
- Starting date
- Stock options
- Training opportunities
- Tuition reimbursement
- Wellness program/paid health club membership

Once you've conducted your research and considered the salary and benefits that are important to you personally, you are ready to negotiate. Following the tips below will assist you immeasurably:

- Wait for the organization's representative to make the first offer
- Be clear about your own needs, budgetary and compensatory
- Be ready to consistently point out the added value you can bring to the company
- Negotiate for the entire compensation package, not just the salary or wages

- ○ Be prepared for a counteroffer from the company representative and with a counteroffer of your own

- ○ Utilize the skills of a career counselor to help you practice negotiation

- ○ Most important, *get the offer in writing before you accept the job*

PROFESSIONAL DEVELOPMENT

In the not-so-distant past, people commonly retired, after 40-some years, from the only job they ever had. In fact, a good-paying job was often passed on from father to son over multiple generations. Moreover, the same expectations demanded by the employees when they started the job, usually in their late teens or early 20s, were still required of them in their 60s. No more. Today's millennial generation can expect to change careers between five to eight times during their lives. This means the need for education, skills upgrade, and personal improvement will remain constant. You will have to continue learning throughout your lifetime if you want to grow and prosper professionally. College is a good place to start.

- *College courses:* Once you recognize that lifelong learning is essential, you will be more inclined to take classes outside your major and your comfort zone. At this point, you have little to lose and much to gain. You may get a grade of "very good" instead of your usual "excellent" should you undertake a technical writing course for example but chances are, it will do little damage to your future. In contrast, being fired from a position because you can't write well enough to meet your responsibilities will leave a decided blemish on your work history. If you've already left college, you may find it desirable to return. Maybe you want to update your technical skills, learn a new language, or develop your public speaking abilities. Explore your *alma mater*, local community colleges, and online classes for opportunities. The point is: develop a love for learning while you are still in school and carry it with you throughout your life.

- *Professional organizations:* Join organizations relevant to your aspirations as early as possible. Personally, I became involved in some sociological associations while I was still an undergraduate and I remain in some of the same groups today. As a student, you are generally offered a reduced membership rate and can often volunteer to staff tables and perform other ancillary activities at their conferences. There you are likely to meet the authors of your textbooks, well-known individuals in your discipline, and even future employers. You might be amazed at how inviting, inclusive, and approachable these individuals will be. In fact, some of the respondents in Parts I and II of this book attribute their career search success to membership in professional organizations. Moreover, some of the vignettes in this book were obtained from individuals I met at these conferences.

- *Seminars and workshops:* At these professional conferences, you will have the opportunity to attend sessions where sociologists and other experts discuss their current research and ideas. These may take place in auditorium-style arrangements or in round-table formats with only four or five interested participants. Most organizations encourage student involvement and even coordinate entire sessions in which students present their findings. Most participants say they almost always leave these events better informed, inspired, and enthused. Aside from the seminars and workshops provided by professional conferences, there are numerous other opportunities to update your skills. Fred Pryor and Career Track present topics on numerous topics that range from communicating with difficult people to managing personnel while an abundance of online seminars proliferate.

- *Professional publications:* Every professional organization maintains at least one journal on a regular basis that contains articles of interest to its readers. Most are available both online and in print. Reading these can be an excellent means by which to stay abreast on new research and ideas in your discipline. As you become more knowledgeable and confident, you may even find yourself writing articles for some of these journals based on your very own research. (Yes. Even though you are probably cringing shyly at the possibility at this very moment!) What better way to catch the attention of other sociologists than by authoring a piece in an academic publication? I've written a number of pieces in my career and confess that I still feel a thrill whenever another sociologist reveals he or she has read my article.

- *Mentor relationships:* A mentor–mentee relationship is a mutually beneficial association in which both parties learn about themselves and contribute to the professional growth of the other. When forming such a connection, it is important for both the mentor and the mentee to establish guidelines and expectations. For example, are there certain skills you want to improve? Do you want to learn more about a particular area of sociology? Do you have the expertise to share? Some jobs and associations have actually formalized mentoring programs. It is wise to take advantage of these opportunities. Otherwise, look for people whom you admire professionally and ask them if they would be willing to mentor you.

- *Continual networking:* I would be remiss if I didn't emphasize, yet again, the value of networking. In this twenty-first century, the opportunities to do so are many and varied. Although we are most familiar with Facebook, LinkedIn, and Twitter, new social networking sites emerge almost weekly. A word of caution, however, that you've probably heard many times already: be careful what you post. Many employers will search you out so give much thought to the potential impact your posting might have. You don't want to lose out on that perfect job because of an all-too-revealing post of you at last Friday night's drunken escapade! On the other hand, having a strong profile is a definite advantage for continual networking. In this regard, many career development experts particularly recommend LinkedIn. Some employers have recently started to use Twitter for job postings primarily because it is free. In addition, they assume that anyone following them on Twitter is already interested in their organization. This results in another avenue of opportunity for you.

- *Career opportunity awareness:* Always keep your eye on the prize; your options open; and explore new opportunities as they arise. In this regard, one expert recommends *Luck is No Accident* as the perfect companion to this Career Development Process and Decision Making Model with which you've just been working. I suggest keeping both the book and the model readily available so you can assess your progress, define new goals, and pursue fresh challenges whenever you feel the desire. Furthermore, open-minded exploration can lead to opportunities you might have never imagined. People are often so afraid of making mistakes that we paralyze ourselves. Think of it this way: FEAR stands for False Evidence Appearing Real. Ask yourself how many worries in your lifetime actually materialized? And, if they did come to pass, you obviously survived. Perhaps you even prospered from the experience. Some of the contributors to this book shared frightening stories of experiences they encountered in their lives. Yet, they overcame them and flourished. So allow yourself to "test drive" your career. When you come to a fork in the road, take either the right road or the left road. Whichever you take, you will undoubtedly gather knowledge and experience that will serve you well as you continue your drive. If it is any encouragement to you, your author has taken the "left road" from time to time. Had I not taken those detours, though, I would have never experienced the heady, exhilarating, and rewarding ride that my journey made possible.

CAREER SELF-RELIANCE

Although Career Self-Reliance is not technically a part of the Career Development Process and Decision Making Model, it a significant piece of professional development. Therefore, no matter how perfect your current job might be, a periodic career "tune-up" is always worthwhile. In much the same manner that regular tune-ups on your car will contribute to a safer vehicle and worry-free driving so, too, will regular tune-ups on your career keep you on the road to career success. As such, the Career Self-Reliance Checklist below is to assist you.

	Agree	Need to Develop
1. I know my strengths and what gives me satisfaction.		
2. I know how and where I do my best work.		
3. I understand and can identify the contributions I make at my work.		
4. I know what values give meaning to my work.		
5. I maintain a written development plan that addresses my short-term and long-term needs and goals.		
6. I pursue a variety of development opportunities to upgrade my skills and keep pace with my field.		
7. I look ahead to assess social needs and business trends.		
8. I reflect those needs and trends in my work and my development plan.		
9. I actively seek feedback and mentoring from others.		
10. I maintain a network of contacts for learning and sharing ideas.		
11. I anticipate changes in the business climate and the social environment.		
12. I adapt quickly to change in my organization.		

Source: Adapted from the Career Action Center, Cupertino, CA

WORK/LIFE BALANCE

I cannot bring this section to a conclusion without mention of living a balanced life. Like the vast majority of sociologists in this book, I love my work and willingly invest far more than the standard 40 hours a week. In fact, I often find it difficult to say "no" to additional responsibilities. Periodically, I need to remind myself that there is more to life than work. This is true of so many contributors to this book. This may be true of you as well. If so, I encourage you to ask yourself from time to time, "What is the best use of my time *right now*?" It may very well be work or career-related. On the other hand, it might be nurturing a relationship or tending to your own health and well-being. You might elect to go to a movie with your spouse or friend; hit the gym; call your mother; or play with your dog. Life is a compilation of little decisions we must make every day. In and of itself, no one choice is likely to make a dramatic difference in your life (though it might) but in totality, your decisions will add up to a life that is either balanced or not. Choose balance. You'll be far happier on your journey through life.

19

CONCLUSION

YOU'VE ONLY JUST BEGUN

So! You've completed this book; read it cover-to-cover, word-for-word. What next? Remember that popular song from the 1970s I mentioned earlier: you've only just begun.

Recognize first that the entire concept of career implies change. If you look back at the vignettes and snippets, you will see vast twists and turns in the career lives of most respondents. Some are intentional and others are serendipitous. With each passing year, the changes in your life are likely to be more frequent and sweeping than those in the past. As a result, for better or for worse, new graduates can expect to live their lives in a consistent state of flux. The good news, however, is that sociology has prepared you to see the big picture and anticipate emerging trends and social changes.

Second, the anticipation of change requires a commitment to ongoing education. Whether it is an additional degree, technology classes at your local community college, workshops provided by your employer, or participation in professional associations, the continuation of learning should be an integral part of your future.

Third, you will need to take advantage of opportunities when they arise — and, if you are passionate about your work they will. Network; ask for business cards and provide your own; write thank you notes; accept and extend invitations to lunch. In short, put yourself out there even when you don't feel like it.

Finally, be persistent and treat the pursuit of a job like it is a job itself. This is, perhaps, the hardest part of any job you will ever have. If a potential employer doesn't respond immediately, e-mail or phone again. And, after a few days — again.

Your career success will hinge on numerous variables like the state of the economy and your own personal circumstances. Do not underestimate, though, the influence of your own choices and actions. Start acting like a sociologist; a professional now. Take the advice of the respondents in the earlier parts of this book. Then use the strategies detailed in Part III. Your career need not be accidental if you are prepared; focused; and seize opportunities when they materialize. In doing so, you can consciously find meaning and relevance in your life. I wish you well.

RESOURCES

20

CAREER WEBSITES

GENERAL INFORMATION

This first section includes a plethora of websites to help you get started on your career search. Some of these resources will allow you to explore job prospects, salary data, and working conditions. Others will provide self-assessment tools and descriptions of specific occupations. Still others will furnish up-to-date job boards for particular geographic locations. For every site listed below, there are dozens of others. I hope not only you will explore those listed here but also you will seek out others and will let me know about those that you find most useful. Go ahead — dive in!

Americas Job Bank: www.ajb.dni.us

Best Jobs USA: www.bestjobsusa.com

Bureau of Labor Statistics: www.bls.gov/oco

Career Builder: www.careerbuilder.com

Career InfoNet: www.careerinfonet.org

Career Matrix: www.careermatrix.com

Career Shop: www.careershop.com

Career Voyages: www.careervoyages.gov

Dice (high tech jobs): www.dice.com

Employment Development Department: www.edd.ca.gov

Employment Guide: www.employmentguide.com

Employment Spot: www.employmentspot.com

EUREKA: www.eureka.org

Federal Jobs: www.usajbs.opm.gov

Flipdog: www.flipdog.com

Green Career Central: www.greencareercentral.com

Green Collar Blog: www.greencollarblog.org

Hot Jobs: www.hotjobs.com

Jim Casio: www.casio.com

Job Bank USA: www.jobbankusa.com

JOBCentral: www.jobcentral.com

KForce: www.kforce.com

Monster: www.monster.com

Net-Temps: www.net-temps.com

NowHiring: www.nowhiring.com

O*Net Online: http://online.onetcenter.org

Quintessential Careers: www.quintcareers.com

Resumes, Cover Letters: www.provenresumes.com

Roadtrip Nation: www.roadtripnation.com

Sloan Career Cornerstone Center: www.careercornerstone.org

Snagajob: www.snagajob.com

The White House: www.whitehouse.gov

Top USA Jobs: www.topusajobs.com

True Careers: www.truecareers.com

U.S.A. Government Jobs: www.usa.gov

Vault Career Intelligence: www.vault.com/wps/portal/usa/companies

WetFeet: www.wetfeet.com

Workforce One: www.workforce3one.org

Worklife: www.worklife.com

Yahoo's Hot Jobs/Green Jobs: http://hotjobs.yahoo.com/jobs-c-green

UNIVERSITY CAREER CENTERS

Career centers at colleges and universities are generally excellent sources for information about careers and jobs in the location of your choice. In addition, they usually provide consulting services, workshops, and suitability assessments for myriad occupations. In most cases, these services are available not only to their students but also to their alumni as well. Some universities offer such outstanding assistance, in person and online, that they deserve mention in this section.

Jacksonville State University: www.jsu.edu/depart/soc/jobs_sociologist

Kansas State University: www.k-state.edu/acic

Mesa State University: www.mesastate.edu/sl/acc/WTDWAD/Sociology.pdf#search

Minnesota State University-Mankato: http:krypton.mnsu.edu/-keating/career

Sonoma State University: www.sonoma.edu/sas/crc

St. Lawrence University: http://web.stlawu.edu/career/soc

University of Kentucky: www.uky.edu/StudentAffairs/Counseling

University of Manitoba (Canada): www.umanitoba.ca/counsel-ling/careers

University of North Carolina-Wilmington: http://uncw.edu/stuaff/career

University of Tennessee: www.uncwil.edu/stuaff/career/Majors/soc

Western Washington University: www.ac.wwu.edu/-socad/careers

SOCIOLOGICAL SITES

While the sections above invite you to investigate careers in general that sociologists often occupy, this section focuses on websites specifically directed to sociology majors.

www.asanet.org.page.ww?section=Careers+and+Jobs&name=Sociology+Major+-++Preparation+for+Careers

www.asanet.org.page.ww?section=Careers+and+Jobs&name=Career+Resources=for=the=Sociology+Major

http://jobbank.asanet.org/jobbank/index.cfm

www.abacon.com/socsite/career

www.niu.edu/careerservices/weblinks/sociology

www.uncwil.edu/stuaff/career/majors/sociology

www.udel.edu/CSC/soc

www.ashland.edu/cardev/cdm-major

www.geneseo.edu/-soc/careers

www.oswego.edu/student/career/careersin/sociology

http://faculty.ncwc.edu/toconnor/jusjobs

www.fbi.gov

www.cia.gov

http://extension.aers.psu.edu

PROFESSIONAL ASSOCIATION LINKS

American Sociological Association: www.asanet.org

Society for Applied Sociology: www.appliedsoc.org

Sociologists for Women in Society: http://newmedia.colorado.edu/-socwomen